59123

Data Communications and Transmission
An Introduction

D0238146

ST
W

1
1

121
RE
A
10.

2

RE
RE.

Other Macmillan titles of related interest

B. Allen, *Analogue Electronics for Higher Studies*
W.A. Atherton, *From Compass to Computer*
M. Beasley, *Reliability for Engineers*
P.V. Brennan, *Phase-Locked Loops – Principles and Practice*
C.W. Davidson, *Transmission Lines for Communications, second edition*
M.E. Goodge, *Analog Electronics*
B.A. Gregory, *An Introduction to Electrical Instrumentation and Measurement Systems, second edition*
Robin Holland, *Microcomputer Fault-finding and Design, second edition*
Paul A. Lynn, *An Introduction to the Analysis and Processing of Signals, third edition*
R.J. Mitchell, *Microprocessor Systems - An Introduction*
Noel M. Morris, *Electrical Circuit Analysis and Design*
M.S. Nixon, *Introductory Digital Design*
R.C. Seals and G.F. Whapshott, *Programmable Logic: PLDs and FPGAs*
P. Silvester, *Electric Circuits*
T.J. Terrell and Lik-Kwan Shark, *Digital Signal Processing*
M.J. Usher and C.G. Guy, *Information and Communication for Engineers*
M.J. Usher and D.A. Keating, *Sensors and Transducers, second edition*
L.A.A. Warnes, *Electronic Materials*
B.W. Williams, *Power Electronics - Devices, Drivers, Applications and Passive Components, second edition*

Macmillan New Electronics Series

G.J. Awcock and R. Thomas, *Applied Image Processing*
Rodney F.W. Coates, *Underwater Acoustic Systems*
M.D. Edwards, *Automatic Logic Synthesis Techniques for Digital Systems*
Peter J. Fish, *Electronic Noise and Low Noise Design*
W. Forsythe and R.M. Goodall, *Digital Control*
C.G. Guy, *Data Communications for Engineers*
Paul A. Lynn, *Digital Signals, Processors and Noise*
Paul A. Lynn, *Radar Systems*
R.C.V. Macario, *Cellular Radio - Principles and Design*
A.F. Murray and H.M. Reekie, *Integrated Circuit Design*
F.J. Owens, *Signal Processing of Speech*
Dennis N. Pim, *Television and Teletext*
M. Richharia, *Satellite Communications Systems - Design Principles*
P. Shepherd, *Integrated Circuit Design, Fabrication and Test*
M.J.N. Sibley, *Optical Communications, second edition*
P.M. Taylor, *Robotic Control*
G.S. Virk, *Digital Computer Control Systems*

Data Communications and Transmission Principles

An Introduction

Andrew Simmonds
School of Engineering
Sheffield Hallam University

MACMILLAN

To my family and friends

First published 1997 by
MACMILLAN PRESS LTD
Houndmills, Basingstoke, Hampshire RG21 6XS
and London
Companies and representatives
throughout the world

ISBN 0–333–64689–4

A catalogue record for this book is available
from the British Library.

This book is printed on paper suitable for recycling and
made from fully managed and sustained forest sources.

10	9	8	7	6	5	4	3	2	1
06	05	04	03	02	01	00	99	98	97

Printed in Great Britain by
Antony Rowe Ltd, Chippenham, Wiltshire

Contents

Preface

Data communications can be a 'dry' subject. To help make it relevant and more interesting this book highlights significant applications of data communications, explains the use of familiar equipment (e.g. the IBM PC), and gives ideas for readers to do some investigating themselves. The theory in this book is explained in terms of the operation of standard communications equipment or protocols. This serves two purposes: firstly to gain an appreciation of the technology; and secondly to develop a necessary degree of familiarity with the standards and jargon. There is an extensive glossary at the back to help with this jargon.

The main aim of communication is to enable people to obtain information, so, although this is a technical subject, it is bound up with how people organize themselves in society, for example, in setting standards or controlling markets. The achievements of individuals and interactions with society are therefore mentioned in passing to set the subject in context.

Each chapter concludes with a number of questions to help readers to test their understanding, with answers provided at the back of the book.

Intended readership

This book is written for students on an undergraduate degree or HND course, studying a unit on data communications, communications engineering, information engineering, or similar. A minimum amount of prior knowledge is needed for the early chapters, whilst later chapters build naturally on the work covered in earlier chapters. The book is based on lectures given over a period of some years to different courses (including short courses for industry); hence much of the material covered has been successfully field tested! However, in producing this book the opportunity was taken to expand on the material covered in the lectures. The aim in doing this is to make the book more useful than a collection of lecture notes, allowing students to gain a deeper understanding of a particular topic where they have the time and interest. The book is suitable for self-study, with an extensive glossary and a set of questions and answers on each chapter.

As anyone involved in the subject knows only too well, data communications is going through a period of rapid change. The fundamentals, however, remain constant and some of the older technologies stubbornly refuse to die. The aim of the book is to enable students to build their own framework of data communication concepts, into which they can fit their own existing (and future) knowledge and experiences.

Although the book is intended primarily for electrical engineering students, it is also suitable for many students of computer studies who need to understand the technological base of the communications industry and how it will determine the future shape of that industry.

Plan of the text

I shall not write at length on this, as a good overview of the material and level can be gained by looking at the contents. Briefly then, the book is divided into three main parts:

- Part I - Basic Data Communications (chapters 1-3). This deals with definitions and basic signal characteristics, as well as covering modem links in detail as a means of introducing ideas on interfaces, protocols, and standards. This enables work to be discussed with reference to practical communications equipment.
- Part II - Transmission Principles (chapters 4-6). This covers transmission lines, free space links and fibre optics. The emphasis here is on how these topics are interrelated, although each is treated separately so that it is possible to cover the topics in isolation.
- Part III - Protocols and Networks (chapters 7-10). Chapter 7 introduces this part by considering synchronous protocols for point-to-point links, especially the bit oriented protocol HDLC. Wide Area Networks (WANs) are then covered, which allows the OSI seven layer reference model to be introduced whilst explaining X.25. TCP/IP is also covered, which leads on to a comparison of open standards. Local Area Networks (LANs) such as Ethernet and Token Ring are then dealt with. Finally, new network protocols and ideas are discussed in the last chapter.

Acknowledgements

Above all I would like to thank the students that I have taught, as I have learned with them and sometimes from them. I am very grateful to those colleagues and friends who reviewed chapters from the book and gave their comments and advice – in particular Bill Barraclough, John Colan, Steve Ferguson, Fary Ghassemlooy, Ian Halliday, Bob Harris, John Holding, John Rowe and Colin Smythe. I would also like to thank and acknowledge the work of my publisher's reviewers, amongst them Steve Bate and Deshinder Singh Gill. Thanks also to my publisher Malcolm Stewart, for his encouragement and advice, and to Nicky Gladwin for her typing.

The impetus for writing this book came from the development of a video-based learning package on Data Communications [MAD]. I worked with Richard Madin and Richard Gibson on that project and would especially like to thank them for their ideas and help; indeed Richard Madin is co-author of chapters 1 and 3. Richard has gone on to produce some Computer Aided Learning packages on data communications [CAL]. Although this book has been written as a stand-alone text-book, it is divided into much the same topic areas as the CAL material and can be used as a back-up text.

Finally, my grateful thanks to my wife Roma, for her help and encouragement.

Andrew Simmonds
August 1996

School of Engineering
Sheffield Hallam University
Pond Street
Sheffield S1 1WB
UK

E-mail: A.Simmonds@SHU.AC.UK

1 Basic Concepts

Communication technology changes rapidly. To cope with this it is important to understand the basic principles of the subject; the purpose of this book is to help the reader achieve that aim. However, it is not just change that makes the subject difficult but also the extensive use of jargon, e.g. the liberal use of TLAs – or Three Letter Acronyms! Jargon helps an expert to be precise and avoid misunderstanding, but it also enables fellow practitioners to recognize each other and exclude other people; after all, large salaries can be obtained by people working in the communications industry. Some people take a strange delight in inventing acronyms: an acronym which puzzled me was POTS, see the glossary at the back of the book for help with terms such as this.

In this first chapter the concept of information is investigated. A working idea of what is meant by the term 'information' is first developed, and then this somewhat loose idea is tightened up in the section on information theory.

1.1 Communications and information

Data communication is the process of transferring information between two places in a form which can be handled by data communication equipment. Data communication is also often referred to as computer communication, because computers, or computer peripheral devices such as printers, are usually involved.

Information in data communication terms loosely refers to the symbols or signals used to make up a message. In data communications the meaning or facts (an alternative definition of information) conveyed by the message is usually irrelevant. This is reassuring as it means that it is not a function of the communication equipment to consider the sense or importance of the messages sent.

Messages can be sent in many ways, using various transmission media from the information source to its destination. Speech, for example, enables people to communicate over short distances using sounds carried by air, which is the transmission medium in this case. An electrical communication channel that we are all familiar with is the telephone line, which allows us to hold voice conversations over long distances. A standard telephone line uses a pair of copper wires as the transmission medium to carry the electrical signals produced by the telephone equipment. These signals, generated by the microphone of the handset when the caller speaks, are an electrical analogue of the pressure waves in the air. The receiving telephone converts the electrical signals back to sound vibrations to deliver the messages.

The telephone line may also be used to carry data. Interface devices are needed to convert the electrical signals used by data communication equipment to a form suitable for transmission over a telephone line. Figure 1.1 shows a communication channel between two computers. The two computers are examples of DTEs (Data Terminal Equipment) and the interface devices are called DCEs, which stands for Data Circuit-terminating Equipment. A common example of a DCE is a modem (modems are covered in chapter 3) which can be used to establish a link across the Public Switched Telephone Network (PSTN – the network to which the telephone of a member of the public is connected).

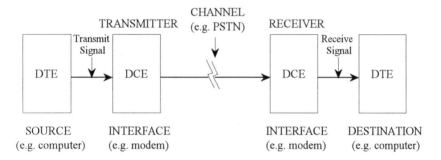

Figure 1.1 Communication channel

In general, a point-to-point data communication system comprises a DTE, which is the source of information, another DTE, which is the destination of the information, and two DCEs, which are needed to interface to the data communication channel itself. The interface device at the source end is often referred to as the transmitter or modulator, with the information from the source referred to as the transmit signal or data. At the destination the signal from the DCE to the DTE is often referred to as the receive signal or data, with the DCE itself referred to as the receiver or demodulator. Thus a modem combines the functions of a MOdulator and a DEModulator.

The signal will have been affected in various ways by being sent over the communication channel, as explained in chapter 2 when we look in more detail at the communication channel. Two major aims of this book are to explain the different ways in which an interface device can match information from a source to a particular communication channel and how the interface device at the receiver can recover that information.

Considering the information source, familiar forms of information carried as data are: text, numerical data, and graphical data.

• **Text** refers to alphabetic characters that are used, for example, to send business messages using telex systems or by more up-to-date electronic mail (E-mail) services.

- **Numerical data** is information in the form of numbers, possibly relating to a bank account, which might be accessed by means of a data communication device such as the ATM (Automatic Teller Machine) at a local branch.
- **Graphical data** is in the form of pictures or diagrams which can be sent, for example, by fax (facsimile) machines.
- Other kinds of information can also be carried by data communications systems. The modern telephone system sends **voice** signals over long distances between exchanges using data signals (for reasons that we shall see later on) and television pictures (i.e. **video**) can be sent in a similar way.

These divisions are somewhat arbitrary; for example, the predominant use of fax machines is not to send diagrams but to send text messages. This illustrates the point that a data network is not concerned with the type of data being transmitted. A data network establishes a link between two DTEs, e.g. two computers. It is up to the users to decide how they wish to exploit that link.

Part of the reason why fax machines are so common today is the difficulty of providing an electronic text-based system for the Japanese alphabet, which is partly ideographic (the ideographs are known as kanji) and partly syllabic. There are approximately 1800 kanji symbols for official and daily use, which a keyboard would need to generate for a text-based system. The fax, being a graphical system, allows people to write messages by hand and then send them electronically. This provided an excellent solution to the problem facing Japanese businesses of how to send hard copy electronically. But it was not only Japanese business that found the fax so useful: for a fee, prayers can be said at Shinto shrines for good luck in exams or other important events; normally a middleman takes care of the arrangements but one enterprising shrine cut out the middleman by allowing prayers to be faxed in.

A more important distinction between types of data for us is not its source but how the destination expects it to arrive. Computers can handle data arriving in bursts and at irregular times; people cannot. Hence for voice or video the data needs to be available at regular intervals, e.g. regularly enough to update a video picture so that the illusion of continuous movement is maintained. Such data is called isochronous from *isos*, the Greek for equal, and *khronos*, the Greek for time (non-isochronous data is called anisochronous).

To summarize, all kinds of information can be transported by data communication systems, over distances ranging from a metre in the case of a computer talking to a printer next to it, to millions of kilometres when a space probe sends data back to Earth. But in all these systems the basic principles are the same: the information is converted to a suitable form and then transferred over a communication channel.

1.1.1 Bits, bytes and nibbles

To understand more about the way data is transmitted in data communication systems we need to look at the nature of signals. The electrical signals used in normal telephone conversations have already been identified as analogue signals. This means that they have the same shape as the sound vibrations that produce them but, instead of a variation in pressure, an electrical voltage or current changes, as shown in figure 1.2.

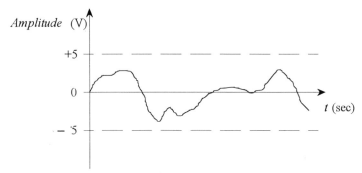

Figure 1.2 Analogue speech waveform

In this waveform diagram the variation in voltage against time is shown. The voltage is regarded as a continuous signal because it can take any amplitude value within a specified range; this is the definition of an analogue signal for transmission purposes.

Data communication devices, on the other hand, operate on digital signals where the signalling event is selected from a discrete set of possible events. Consider figure 1.3 where the set of signalling events is either the voltage +5 V or 0 V. This waveform is much simpler than the analogue one since it has only two discrete levels, corresponding to either a high or a low voltage.

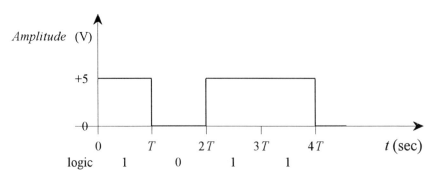

Figure 1.3 Digital data signal

Figure 1.3 actually shows a binary signal, so called because there are only two possible states (voltage levels in this case). The signal is made up of binary digits, called bits, each lasting for T seconds where T is the bit period. Thus if positive logic is used, with +5 V taken as logic 1 and 0 V as logic 0, the waveform of figure 1.3 represents the logic pattern 1011. The choice of logic levels is conventional but arbitrary, as negative or inverse logic levels could equally well have been chosen with +5 V representing logic 0 and 0 V for logic 1. The rate at which data is transferred, i.e. the data rate or throughput, is measured in bits per second (bps) and is simply the inverse of the bit period T.

The particular type of binary signal shown in figure 1.3 is known as Non Return to Zero (NRZ) because the voltage level is constant for the entire bit period T. Other types of binary signals will be met later on. If nothing is said to the contrary it is normal to assume that a binary signal is of the NRZ type and uses positive logic. But note one important point: 'digital' and 'binary' do not mean the same thing; although a binary signal is an example of a digital signal the converse is not true and, later on, we shall meet examples of digital signals where there are more than two possible states.

A single bit has $2^1 = 2$ states and cannot convey more meaning than on/off, open/closed, true/false, etc. So it is usual to use groups of eight bits, called bytes, which can be coded to represent more useful information. With eight bits a byte has $2^8 = 256$ possible combinations, or patterns, of 0s and 1s. By allocating symbols to each pattern we can use the bytes to transfer useful data. The process of allocating symbols to unique patterns of bits is called coding; for example, 256 combinations is more than enough to code all the keys on a computer keyboard. This is the basis for the character codes of the next section.

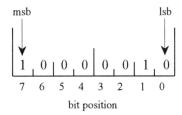

Figure 1.4 A byte

As in decimal notation the position of bits in a binary number is important, but in binary the number two is used as the base for calculation rather than ten as in decimal. For example, consider a byte as in figure 1.4 with bits numbered 7..0 (N.B. this is just one possible way of numbering a byte, others are 8..1, 1..8 or 0..7!). The bit in position 0 gives the number of weights of power $2^0 = 1$ (i.e. units), the bit in position 1 gives the number of weights of power $2^1 = 2$, whilst the bit in position 7 gives the number of weights of power $2^7 = 128$. Hence, adding the weights together, the binary number shown in figure 1.4 (10000010_2) corresponds to the decimal number 128 + 2 = 130. The bit in *position 7 is referred to as the most significant bit (msb) and the bit in position 0 as the least significant bit (lsb).*

Sometimes groups of four bits are used, especially in the hexadecimal number system, usually shortened to hex, which uses the base 16. Considering again the byte of figure 1.4, bits 4..7 would be referred to as the high nibble and bits 0..3 as the low nibble (byte..nibble..☺). Hence in hex the number in figure 1.4 is 82_{16}. Computers generally operate on many bits in parallel. The width of the registers used for operations in the computer determines the standard operand length, i.e. the word length of the computer. For example, the word length for an Intel 486 processor as used in an IBM PC is 32 bits, for a Pentium it is 64 bits. The word length is usually, but not always, an integral number of bytes.

1.1.2 Character codes

These are used to encode a set of symbols or characters, e.g. the characters on a computer keyboard. Of course, for successful communication both communicating devices must interpret the codes in the same way. Standard codes have been introduced to ensure this, the most widely accepted being ASCII.

'ASCII' is an acronym for American Standard Code for Information Interchange. It was originally put forward by ANSI (the American National Standards Institute) and has become the international standard character set. ASCII is an 'open' standard because anyone can make use of it. The International Alphabet No. 5, which is defined by the ITU-T (International Telecommunications Union - Telecommunications), is the same as ASCII with only minor variations. The ITU-T is the United Nations standards body responsible for many communication standards. It has replaced the CCITT, whose acronym still appears in many books on communications.

ASCII uses 7-bit codes to represent the following characters:
upper case letters	A B C D . . . . Z
lower case letters	a b c d . . . . z
numbers	0 1 2 3 9
punctuation symbols	, . ! : ; ?
special control characters	ESC CTRL STX ETX XON XOFF etc.

A full list of ASCII codes is given in appendix D.

The format of the bits is arranged so that lower case letters can be changed to upper case by altering only one bit of the code: thus A = 1000001 and a = 1100001. This is for ease of implementation of the code on a keyboard and users simply press the shift key to obtain upper case letters.

Only seven bits are defined for ASCII, but often ASCII is taken as referring to eight bit codes, as in the eight bit code used in the IBM PC, with the extra 128 codes being used for graphic and foreign language characters. Alternatively, escape sequences can be used to increase the number of characters. For example, in an IBM PC the ANSI.SYS device driver can be loaded with the DEVICE command in the CONFIG.SYS file. This enables the PC to support ANSI X3.64 terminal emulation of escape sequences to control the PC's screen and keyboard. The escape sequences start with the ASCII characters ESC (Escape) and '[' (left square bracket), followed by a particular command (e.g. move the cursor to a particular position on the screen). This enables the PC to emulate a forms-mode terminal, for example for standard data entry applications as in filling in a name in a particular data field of a form.

The other widely used standard character code is EBCDIC (Extended Binary Coded Decimal Interchange Code), which is used in IBM mainframes. The EBCDIC (pronounced Ebb-Sea-Dick) code uses all eight bits to define the characters (allowing $2^8 = 256$ possible characters). Unlike ASCII, EBCDIC originated as a proprietary standard. Since they use different standards, an ASCII terminal cannot communicate with an IBM mainframe computer unless some form of code conversion takes place.

The difference between open and proprietary standards is important. If a standard is open then any company can make equipment to that standard. Customers prefer open standards because they have confidence in the future of the product and competition keeps prices down (even though a customer may buy everything from a single supplier). On the other hand, producers try to lock customers into their product range. One way of doing this is by proprietary (i.e. closed) standards, where the only source for a customer to buy new equipment to work with their existing equipment is from the original supplier. It is generally only large companies that can set standards designed to shut out competition whilst keeping customer confidence in their product. Sometimes, though, a proprietary standard becomes a *de facto* open standard, in that the company allows other manufacturers to use it, or it can become (as EBCDIC now is) an official open standard if it is taken up by a standards body.

1.1.3 Coding for efficient transmission

The function of the transmitter is to change the source information into a form suitable for transmission over the communication channel. Various ways of doing this will be discussed later, but for now let us consider how the information itself (i.e. the symbols or signals of the message) can be best arranged to maximize the rate of information transfer across the channel. In effect the aim is to maximize the data rate, although strictly speaking this is not always the same as the information transfer rate – see next section. It is essentially the subject matter of data compression.

If the source information contains redundant information, then data compression can shorten the message by removing redundancy. A simple example would be sending a text file over a link between two modems where the source modem strips out unnecessary bytes of data before transmission. Assume that the file contains the sequence ACCOUNT-------AMOUNT where a dash represents a space on a form. The modem would compress it to ACCOUNT$7AMOUNT and send this to the destination modem which would detect the space compression character $ and re-insert the spaces before passing the text on to the destination terminal (see figure 1.5). This process is called run length coding.

ACCOUNT ------- AMOUNT

Figure 1.5 Run length coding

More powerful algorithms are available, but they all work by identifying redundancy in the message and removing it. Note that the actual information content of the message is not altered by these processes; strictly this is data compaction, whilst the term data compression is reserved for processes that compress the data at the expense of losing some information (e.g. losing the fine detail in a picture). However, data compression is loosely used for both these cases.

Another example of coding source information is the Morse code. The code in use today (not quite the same as Morse's original code) is given below in figure 1.6, together with the expected percentage occurrence of letters in an English text [CHE].

Morse code was developed in the 1830s by Samuel F. B. Morse (1791-1872), an American painter noted for portraits who was also a founder and first president of the National Academy for Design in New York City. In 1844 Morse demonstrated his system by sending the now famous message 'what hath God wrought' via an experimental telegraph from Washington DC to Baltimore. Morse announced his invention of the Telegraph in 1837, the same year as Charles Wheatstone and William F. Cooke in Great Britain announced their development of an electrical telegraph, an example of the simultaneous development of new ideas when circumstances are right. (Wheatstone also invented the concertina; and the Wheatstone bridge, as used for the accurate measurement of a resistance, was named after him.)

	Morse character	Length	% Occurrence	Character	Morse character
A	. —	8	8.25	.	. — . — . —
B	— . . .	12	1.78	;	— . — . — .
C	— . — .	14	3.14	, (comma)	— — . . — —
D	— . .	10	3.38	:	— — — . . .
E	.	4	12.77	?	. . — — . .
F	. . — .	12	2.38	' (apostrophe)	. — — — — .
G	— — .	12	2.04	-	— . . . . —
H	. . . .	10	5.06	/	. . . .
I	. .	6	7.03	Ä	. .
J	. — — —	16	0.19	Á or Å	. — — . —
K	— . —	12	0.58	É	. . — . .
L	. — . .	12	4.30	CH	— — — —
M	— —	10	2.29	Ñ	— — . — —
N	— .	8	7.02	Ö	— — — .
O	— — —	14	7.13	Ü	. . — —
P	. — . —	14	2.03	(or)	— . — — . —
Q	— — . —	16	0.14	"	. — . . — .
R	. — .	10	6.30	—	. . — — . —
S	. . .	8	7.06	=	— . . . —
T	—	6	9.17	SOS	. . . — — — . . .
U	. . —	10	2.83	Attention	— . — . —
V	. . . —	12	1.20	CQ	— . — . — — . —
W	. — —	12	1.80	Go ahead	— . —
X	— . . —	14	0.28	Wait	. — . . .
Y	— . — —	16	1.76	Break	— . . . — . —
Z	— — . .	14	0.09	Understand	. . . — .
				Error	. . . .
				OK	. — .
				End of message	. — . — .
				End of work	. . . — . —

Figure 1.6 Morse code

The dot length is the basic timing element. A dash is equivalent to three dots. A space between the dots and dashes in a character is equivalent to one dot and the space between characters is three dots long. Words are separated by seven dot lengths. The character length in the table shows the length, including the space between characters, in terms of the dot length. It can be seen that the more frequently occurring letters (A, E and T) are given the shorter Morse characters whilst J, Q and Y are the longest characters.

From table 1.6 the average length of a Morse character is 11.2 dots. However, if the letters are weighted by their percentage occurrences, as given above, the weighted average character length is 9.04 dots, thus achieving a real saving. Morse matched the information source (an English text) to the telegraph channel, eliminating some redundancy in the message by efficiently coding the letters of the alphabet.

1.1.4 Parity

Parity is a way of detecting some of the errors which may occur in a message between a transmitter and receiver. To correct the error, the message (e.g. 7 bits of an ASCII character plus the parity bit) must be sent again. Parity is a very simple scheme and a single parity bit is generally only adequate for detecting errors for message lengths of a dozen or so bits. For longer messages each byte needs its own parity bit. However, there are more powerful error detection schemes that we will consider later which are more appropriate for long messages. In all of these schemes, redundancy is added to the message to enable faulty received messages to be distinguished from correct messages. If there is no redundancy, then every message is valid, so there can be no way of distinguishing between correct and incorrect messages. For example, consider the sentence 'Thf cat sat'. You probably read that as 'The cat sat' or, even if you spotted the error, you could make a guess as to the correct message. There is considerable redundancy in the English language which enables mistakes to be detected and even corrected. However, if 'Thf cat sat' is not a sentence but a sequence of random combinations of any three letters (i.e. we have removed the redundancy), there is no way of saying whether the combinations are correct or not.

In a parity error detection scheme, the parity bit is used to ensure that the transmitted message (which includes the parity bit) has either an odd or even number of ones, depending on whether odd or even parity has been selected. The receiver must obviously be set to the same parity scheme as the transmitter. For example, consider sending the ASCII character 'J' over a channel using odd parity. Character 'J' is 1001010 in binary (see appendix D), so the parity bit is set to 0 to make the overall number of 1s an odd number. Setting the parity bit in the msb position gives the 8-bit message

```
P7  ...   0
| |       |
01001010
```

Parity can detect any odd number of errors (i.e. including any single bit error). For example, assume bit position 2 is corrupted by noise and received in error. The received message is therefore

```
P7 ... 2  0
| |    | |
01001110
```

The number of bits is now an even number so an error must have occurred. Which particular bit is wrong is not known by the receiver, so the character must be sent again to correct the error. This is true even if the character code is correct but the parity bit is received in error. Note that any even numbers of errors will not be detected, since an even number of errors will not affect whether there is an even or odd number of 1s in the message (try it with, say, bit positions 2 and 3 in error). On the other hand, all odd numbers of errors will be detected by the single parity bit error check. Considering single bit errors, two bit errors, etc., as different types of errors, parity will detect half of all these types of errors. Note however that in considering numbers of errors rather than types, a parity check will detect virtually all random, independently occurring errors, since in practice the probability of a single error, although very small, is generally much greater than the probability of two errors. For example, if the probability of any bit being in error (p) is 1 in 10^6 then for $n = 1000$ bits the probability of just one error is approximately 1 in 10^3, whilst the probability of any two bits being in error is approximately 1 in 10^6; since for low error rates the probability of there being just m errors $\cong (np)^m$.

Unfortunately, there is a different class of error, called a burst error, in which the occurrence of errors is not independent. The burst starts with the first bit which is an error and ends with the last bit in error; obvious enough, but note that between the start and finish the bits will be random, so it can be expected that half of them will be correct. The number of errors in the burst is equally likely to be odd or even, hence parity will only detect half of all such errors. So, for long messages parity is efficient but not very effective. An improved error detection scheme for long messages is the Cyclic Redundancy Check (CRC, considered in chapter 8); this is mentioned here because parity is actually a CRC for the limiting case of a single check bit.

There are 128 possible combinations with 7 bits; adding a parity bit gives 8 bits. Hence there are actually 256 possible combinations but only 128 valid codes, i.e. the parity bit has added redundancy in the form of 128 invalid codes. If an invalid code word is received, the receiver recognizes that an error has occurred; but if a valid code word is received, the receiver must assume that it is correct (even if it is not the same code word as was sent). Hence one cannot be absolutely certain that a received message is correct (on the other hand, if there is an error the message is definitely incorrect). This is true of any possible error detection scheme, so in this sense communications is an uncertain business. However, with a parity check for a few characters, or more powerful error detection schemes for longer messages, the chance of an error not being detected is small.

1.2 Information theory

The ideas in this section (on information theory and Huffman coding) can be difficult to grasp. It may be better for the reader to whom the ideas and concepts so far in this chapter are new to skip these sections for now and continue with the next chapter. The justification for putting the material here is that information theory answers a fundamental question of communication engineering: i.e. what is information? Huffman coding is one application of the theory which aims to improve the efficiency of information transfer by eliminating redundancy from a message. It is commonly confused with Hamming coding, which has a totally different aim in that it is used to correct errors which occur in transmission (see chapter 7).

The first thing to note in information theory is that it is not concerned with the importance that we attach to messages; it treats equally messages such as 'aliens have landed' and 'you've burnt the toast'. The second thing to note is the link between information and surprise. A surprising message gives us a lot of information, a message that we are already expecting provides little information. In information theory information (I) is always taken as positive, i.e. $I \geq 0$. In the real world, of course, we are exposed to misinformation, which could be considered as negative information.

In terms of probability, a message we are expecting has a high probability of arrival (i.e. it is probable), whilst a message we are not expecting has a low probability of arrival (i.e. it is improbable). The probability (P) of an event occurring is defined mathematically as being in the range $0 \leq P \leq 1$, where if $P = 0$ the event is impossible, if $P = 1$ the event is certain, and if $P = 0.5$ there is a 50:50 chance of it happening.

It is intuitively reasonable that if an event is certain then a message about its occurrence tells us nothing new, hence if $P = 1$ then $I = 0$. On the other hand if an event is impossible a message telling us about its occurrence conveys an infinite amount of information, i.e. if $P = 0$ then $I = \infty$. Information is measured in bits, with the relationship between the information (I) contained in a message and the probability (P) of that message being sent given by

$$I = \log_2 \frac{1}{P} \quad \text{bits} \tag{1.1}$$

N.B.
$$\log_2 x = \frac{\log_{10} x}{\log_{10} 2} \tag{1.2}$$

Substituting $P = 1$ in equation (1.1) gives $I = 0$ bits whilst substituting $P = 0$ gives $I = \log_2 \infty$, i.e. an infinite number of bits, as expected from the previous discussion.

Consider now an event with two possible outcomes, A and B, which occur with equal probabilities P_A and P_B. The sum of the probabilities of all possible events must be 1, as it is certain that some event must occur, i.e.

$$P_A + P_B = 1 \tag{1.3}$$

Since $P_A = P_B$ it follows that the probability of either A or B occurring is $P_A = P_B = 0.5$. Hence the information contained in a message giving the outcome of the event (i.e. whether event A or B has occurred) is $I = \log_2(1/0.5) = 1$ bit, i.e. the message can be transmitted by a single binary digit. (Obvious really, as by definition a single binary digit can signal A/B, on/off, etc.)

As shown above, the information contained in the state of the binary digit is one bit if the events A and B are equiprobable. However, we will show later that if A and B are not equiprobable the average information contained in the state of the binary digit is less than one bit. There is obvious scope for confusion here in the choice of bit for the unit of information and its other meaning of a two-state signal (which we have carefully called a binary digit in the preceding sentences). It is generally clear from the context whether it is really the inform-ation content or the number of two state signals that are being considered. The two definitions coincide if messages are equiprobable.

The average information contained in a message is known as the entropy *(H)*, a term borrowed from statistical mechanics. Again consider an event with two outcomes A and B but now with the probabilities P_A and P_B. no longer necessarily equal,

$$H = P_A \log_2 \frac{1}{P_A} + P_B \log_2 \frac{1}{P_B} \tag{1.4}$$

but, from equation 1.3, $P_B = 1 - P_A$. Hence

$$H = P_A \log_2 \frac{1}{P_A} + (1 - P_A) \log_2 \frac{1}{(1 - P_A)} \tag{1.5}$$

The average information *(H)* contained in a single digit from a binary source is plotted in figure 1.7 against P_A, assuming that the source is memoryless so that successive digits are statistically independent [SHA]. One message (binary 1) occurs with probability P_A and the other (i.e. binary 0) occurs with probability

$(1-P_A)$. Note that the average information reaches a maximum of one bit when $P_A = 0.5$, i.e. when both events are equiprobable.

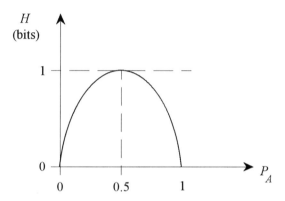

Figure 1.7 Average information (H) of a binary source

This analysis can be extended to more than two messages. If there are n *equiprobable* messages then the probability of occurrence of each one is

$$P = 1/n \tag{1.6}$$

and the information associated with each message is (from equation 1.1)

$$I = \log_2 n \text{ bits} \tag{1.7}$$

If the messages are not equiprobable, then the information associated with each message is

$$I_i = \log_2 \frac{1}{P_i} \tag{1.8}$$

and the expected information gained from any message (i.e. the average information of the set of messages) is

$$H = \sum_{i=1}^{n} P_i I_i$$
$$= \sum_{i=1}^{n} P_i \log_2 \frac{1}{P_i} \text{ bits} \tag{1.9}$$

(with a maximum value for equiprobable messages of $H = \log_2 n$ bits).

Note that the number of bits needed to send a message from a set of equiprobable messages can be found from equation 1.7. For example, if there are eight equiprobable messages then the information gained by the arrival of any message is $\log_2 8 = 3$ bits, which is also the minimum number of bits needed to code eight messages (with the same code length for each message). This is because the definitions of a 'bit' of information and a two state signal 'bit' coincide for equiprobable messages. As an example, a possible coding scheme for the eight messages is

message	code (bits)
A	000
B	001
C	010
D	011
E	100
F	101
G	110
H	111

1.2.1 Huffman coding

The purpose of this coding process is to produce a compact code with average code length ($\overline{L}$ bits) close to the average information contained in a message (H, called the entropy of the source, also measured in bits). If the received data is to be unambiguously decoded, no code can be designed with an average code length less than the source entropy. This is known as the source coding theorem, mathematically

$$\overline{L} \geq H \tag{1.10}$$

So far we have assumed a one-to-one correspondence between a message and a symbol (e.g. eight messages coded by the symbols *A..H*). This is too restrictive, so we define a message as information composed of one or more consecutive source symbols (e.g. a sentence is a text message made up from alphabetical symbols).

In Huffman coding [HUF] we are concerned with increasing the efficiency of message transfer by coding the source symbols only. Given symbols with known probabilities of occurrence, Huffman coding produces optimum solutions. The process is best illustrated by an example shown in figure 1.8. Suppose we have six symbols (labelled *A..F*) with the (unequal) probabilities arranged in descending order in the first column to the right of the symbol. At each stage we reduce the number of symbols remaining by one, by combining the two symbols with the lowest probabilities (e.g. in the first stage the symbols E and F are combined to make a composite symbol 'E or F' with a probability of occurrence of 0.2). It is best if the composite symbol is placed at the highest possible place in the rankings (hence it displaces the symbols B and C which also have probability 0.2). This reduces the difference in bit length between the shortest and longest code words, which makes the code slightly simpler to implement. The process continues automatically until only two choices remain. Each choice is then arbitrarily labelled 1 or 0. It makes no difference to the length of the code word whether 1 or 0 is chosen, but for neatness sake the upper choice of each pair has been labelled the same (0 in this case).

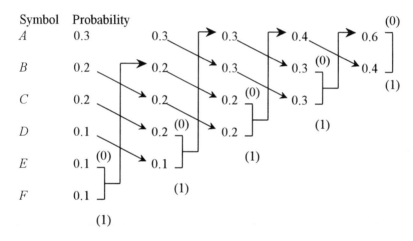

Figure 1.8 Huffman coding process

Finally, the code for each symbol is read out, e.g. for the symbol A the choice of bits gives the codeword 01. It is important that the code is read out from right to left, as this follows the binary tree structure implicit in figure 1.8 and generates codewords which are not a prefix for another codeword. For example, as soon as 01 is received it can be translated as A without waiting until the end of the message. Hence the result from the Huffman coding process is

symbol	probability	codeword
A	0.3	01
B	0.2	11
C	0.2	000
D	0.1	001
E	0.1	100
F	0.1	101

The average length per symbol for this set of symbols is

$$\overline{L} = \sum_{i=1}^{n} P_i L_i \tag{1.11}$$

$$= 0.3 \times 2 + 0.2 \times 2 + 0.2 \times 3 + 3 \times (0.1 \times 3)$$

$$= 2.5 \text{ bits (two state signals)}$$

The average information per symbol (i.e. the source entropy) is

$$H = \sum_{i=1}^{n} P_i \log_2 \left(\frac{1}{P_i} \right)$$

$$= 2.45 \text{ bits (units of information)}$$

Note that $\overline{L} > H$, consistent with equation 1.10. Longer symbol sequences could be coded to reduce the average code length but the improvement is often only marginal, e.g. in this case the code efficiency η is

$$\eta = \frac{H}{\overline{L}} \tag{1.12}$$

$$= 0.98$$

i.e. the efficiency is 98% and the remaining redundancy is

$$r = 1 - \eta \tag{1.13}$$

$$= 0.02$$

Chasing an improvement of only 2% is in most cases not worth the extra complexity of coding needed to achieve an average code length closer to the source entropy. A modified Huffman code is used in fax machines, see below.

There is a drawback to Huffman coding, which is the need to know the symbol probabilities before sending them. An alternative scheme for generating compact code is the Lempel-Ziv algorithm [HAY] as specified in the ITU standard V.42 *bis*. This is adaptive, i.e. it learns about the source characteristics whilst it is coding the message. One of several alternative coding schemes used by the software package PKZIP for compressing files is a modified Lempel-Ziv algorithm (PKUNZIP is used to decompress these files).

1.2.2 Fax machines

We have talked about fax in this chapter, so here is an appropriate place to note details of fax standards. Loosely, faxing a message can be thought of as long distance photocopying. Fax machines scan the original document or image in lines, in a similar way to how a TV picture is composed of lines. Groups I and II are obsolete now; they are analogue standards in that, like standard TV, the line signal is analogue, so their resolution is only given in one dimension (by definition, ignoring noise, it is infinite in the other). Group III or IV fax machines are digital fax standards because they convert the analogue line signal into a stream of bits. A group III or IV scanned line is a series of black or white dots or picture elements (Pixels or Pels). Each pixel can be represented by either a '1' or a '0' (or, in the case of grey scale images, each pixel is represented by a word corresponding to a particular grey level). For group III fax the digitized line message is changed into a series of code words, each representing a particular run length of either black or white pixels, using modified Huffman coding (group IV fax uses MMR – Modified Modified Read – to code the pixels) [PUG].

Fax groups

Group	Max resolution (dots per inch) vert × hor	Transmission time, standard A4 page (ITU R1)
I	100	6 min
II	100	3 min
III	200 × 200	30 s at 9,600 bps
IV	200 × 400	3 s at 64 kbps

For group III fax, modem speed is stepped down in stages to 2,400 bps if the telephone circuit will not support 9,600 bps. Group IV fax machines can only be used on an end-to-end digital network (e.g. ISDN, the Integrated Services Digital Network).

Exercises

(1)   What does MODEM stand for and what is the function of a MODEM?

(2)   What do the terms DTE and DCE stand for?

(3)   Categorize data into different forms.

(4)   Define (i) an analogue signal; (ii) a digital signal.

(5) Compare and contrast a digital and a binary signal.

(6) State two common character codes.

(7) Code the word 'Hello' in Morse code.

(8) How many dot lengths in Morse code is the message 'Hello world'?

(9) Plot on linear v. linear graph paper the Morse code character length versus percentage frequency of occurrence of the character. Comment on your graph.

(10) Can a parity check detect that a message is wrong if three bits are in error?

(11) State the types of errors which parity can and cannot detect and whether using odd or even parity makes any difference to this.

(12) Code the character 'X' using the ASCII character code and even parity, using the format: parity bit, msb ... lsb.

(13) Given that the same format as in question (12) is being used, decode the following messages: (i) 11101000; (ii) 01010100.

(14) The hex word 6A is received. What was the ASCII character sent, assuming the same data format as question (12) and (i) even parity; (ii) odd parity is being used.?

N.B. to answer the following question on parity you need to understand probability and permutations, see e.g. [HAY], [KRE].
(15) (a) If the probability of any bit being in error is p, state the expression for the probability that an n bit message will be received with no errors. Hence calculate the probability of there being no errors in 1000 bits, given $p = 1$ in 10^6.

  (b) (i) Derive the accurate expression to give the probability of m errors in n bits, given that the probability of any bit being in error is p. The approximate expression was given in this chapter as $(np)^m$. Check that your answer gives the same expression as for part (a) for $m = 0$.

  (ii) Calculate the accurate probability of there being just one error in 1000 bits, given $p = 1$ in 10^6.

  (iii) Determine the percentage of errors which are single bit errors for the given conditions.

(16) How much information does a single decimal digit convey?

(17) Determine the information gained when one of 26 equiprobable messages is received.

(18) Determine the expected information content of a single letter of the alphabet in English (refer to figure 1.6 on the Morse code for the percentage occurrence of letters). Hence determine the percentage redundancy of the letters of the English language.

(19) For fixed length messages, what is the condition for the redundancy to be a minimum and the information to be a maximum?

(20) State two coding schemes to minimize redundancy in a set of symbols.

(21) A communication system uses a set of eight symbols. The list of symbols and their probabilities of occurrence, as averaged over a large number of messages, are given below. Construct a code such that individual symbols can be transmitted with the fewest number of bits. Calculate the theoretical minimum average number of bits per symbol and the average number of bits per symbol for your code.

A	B	C	D	E	F	G	H
0.04	0.08	0.05	0.11	0.06	0.5	0.07	0.09

(22) A fax image consists of 2000 lines, each of 1500 pixels. Determine the amount of data (in bits and ignoring redundancy) for: (i) a black and white image, black or white being equally probable; (ii) a grey scale image, there being 16 equiprobable shades of grey (ranging from white to black).

(23) Compile a list of the more important equations used in this chapter.

(24) Write your own summary of what you have learnt in this chapter.

2 Signal Characteristics

Compare the analogue speech telephone signal, which is restricted in its frequency range to between 300 Hz and 3,400 Hz, with the frequency range required for hi-fi, see figure 2.1.

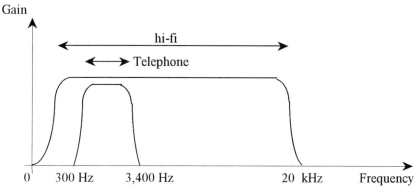

Figure 2.1 Frequency ranges of hi-fi and telephone channels

The difference between the upper and lower limits of the frequency range is the bandwidth of the signal: for the analogue speech channel it is 3,100 Hz. It is kept low in telephony because the wider the bandwidth, the more noise is picked up, and the higher the cost. The telephone channel bandwidth is adequate for understanding speech and, in most cases, recognising the speaker. A wider bandwidth would waste money.

For listening to music a wider frequency range is needed, say from 10 Hz to 20 kHz; although above the age of 20 it would be unusual to be able to hear the higher frequencies (there is a general loss of hearing with age but the effect is greater at higher frequencies).

Filters are used to select the required frequency range and reject other frequencies.

In this chapter the concepts covered in section 2.1 on summing sine waves and section 2.3 on filters are important to the understanding of the commun-ication channel and should not be missed. Section 2.2 investigates the Fourier transform, which provides the mathematical basis for section 2.1; it may be appropriate to pass over this section at a first reading. The unifying theme of this chapter is the consideration of signals in both time and frequency. Fundamental to this is the study of the sine wave. In the time domain a sine wave $v(t) = A\sin(2\pi f_0 t)$ is represented as a waveform. In the frequency domain the same sine wave is considered as a frequency spectrum, i.e. as a signal which varies with frequency f. To show this explicitly, the sine wave equation becomes:

$V(f) = A\sin(2\pi f_0 t)$ (N.B. conventionally capital letters are used for spectra) with the spectrum as shown in figure 2.2.

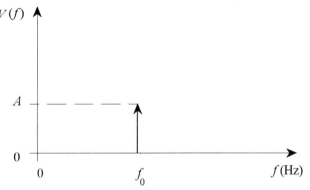

Figure 2.2 Sine wave spectrum

The instantaneous sine wave voltage will clearly vary between $+A$ and $-A$, though to show this change a third axis (of time) is needed. Figure 2.3 shows the relationship between the spectrum and waveform representations of two sine waves of equal amplitude, but where the frequency of one sine wave is twice the other.

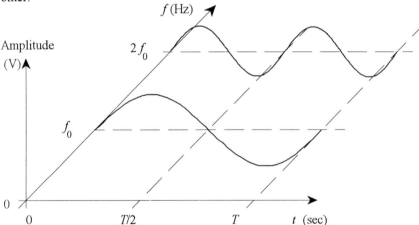

Figure 2.3 Spectra and waveforms of two sine waves

To return to the frequency spectrum as in figure 2.2, this is essentially the same display as would be shown on a spectrum analyser or an FFT (Fast Fourier Transform) analyser, two different types of instrument for displaying spectra.

Perhaps one way to help grasp the concept of a frequency spectrum is to consider a piano. One of the white keys in the middle is 'middle A'; its musical pitch or frequency is 440 Hz, i.e. when struck by the hammer linked to the key the string vibrates 440 times per second. The keys are arranged in ascending order of frequency. A repetitive pattern or grouping of seven white and five black keys can be identified, the frequency of each key in a group being an octave above the corresponding key in the group to the left. An octave corresponds to a doubling or halving of frequency. Thus, counting seven white notes to the right of middle A is another A, which is an octave above middle A with a frequency of 880 Hz, whilst counting seven notes to the left is an A with a frequency of 220 Hz. The piano keyboard shows a logarithmic frequency scale, with a note of a certain pitch being generated each time a key is struck. Indeed, there is a rumour that in the Second World War a military research establishment managed to acquire a piano for its mess by asking for an 'acoustic frequency generator capable of generating multiple frequencies simultaneously'!

2.1 Square wave as sum of sinusoids

The spectrum of a signal can give us important information about the channel needed to transmit the signal. As an illustration consider a square wave, as shown in the waveform diagram of figure 2.4. This is a pulse waveform with an equal mark to space ratio and a pulse repetition frequency (p.r.f. – loosely termed frequency) of $f_0 = 1$ kHz, which corresponds to a period of 1 ms.

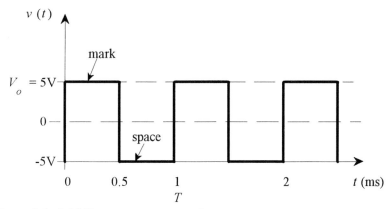

Figure 2.4 A 1 kHz square wave waveform

The spectrum corresponding to this waveform is shown in figure 2.5, i.e. the spectrum of a square wave consists of the fundamental frequency f_0 and all odd harmonics at frequencies nf_0 (n odd number ≥ 3) with amplitudes of $1/n$ compared to the amplitude of the fundamental.

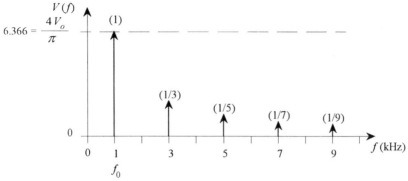

Figure 2.5 A 1 kHz square wave – spectrum

This, by no means obvious, result can be shown to be reasonable by adding sine waveforms together with the amplitudes and frequencies as given by the spectrum of figure 2.5. Thus, adding the third and fifth harmonics with appropriate amplitudes to the fundamental, as in figure 2.6, results in a signal which approximates to a square wave. Note that the magnitude spectrum of figure 2.5 gives no information about the phase; all the sine waves have been given zero phase shift to generate the result of figure 2.6 (in general, both magnitude and phase spectra are required to recover a waveform). The maximum ripple amplitude tends to a constant value as the number (n) of harmonics added is increased; this is called Gibb's phenomenon. However, the ripple width, and hence the ripple energy, decreases as n increases, so in the limit as n approaches infinity the ripple energy is zero and the result is a true square wave.

Figure 2.6 (and other figures in this style) were generated using the software simulation package MATLAB running on an IBM PC. Although the visual design leaves much to be desired [TUF] they have been left as they are to show the actual program output.

Looking at figure 2.4 tells us little about the channel requirements, whereas figure 2.5 gives us far more information. The harmonics go on to infinity but their amplitude decreases with frequency. We can limit the upper frequency to an arbitrary value by considering the signal power. Clearly, from figure 2.4, the power of this square wave delivered into a resistance R is $P_o = V_o^2 / R = 25 / R$. The power delivered by a sine wave of peak amplitude A into a resistance R is $A^2 / (2R)$. Hence, from figure 2.5, the power contained in the first four sine wave terms (at 1 kHz, 3 kHz, 5 kHz and 7 kHz) is

$$P = \frac{1}{2R} \left(\frac{4V_o}{\pi} \right)^2 \left\{ 1 + \frac{1}{3^2} + \frac{1}{5^2} + \frac{1}{7^2} \right\}$$

(2.1)

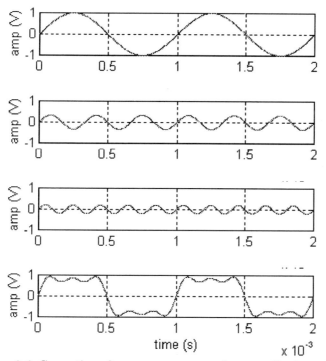

Figure 2.6 Generation of a square wave, waveform amplitude against time

$$= \frac{0.950}{R}V_o^2$$

$$= 95.0\% \, P_o$$

Thus the fundamental and first three odd harmonics contain 95% of the signal power for a square wave (ignoring any d.c. component).

Incidentally, since the sum to infinity of all harmonics by definition contains 100% of the power, this enables us to derive the result:

$$\sum_{n=0}^{\infty} \frac{1}{(2n+1)^2} = 1 + \frac{1}{3^2} + \frac{1}{5^2} + \frac{1}{7^2} + ... = \frac{\pi^2}{8} \tag{2.2}$$

Note from figure 2.6 how at time $T/4$ the fundamental and 5th harmonic are at a maximum, but the 3rd harmonic is a minimum. The amplitude of the square wave can thus be found by summing to infinity the series

$$x = \frac{4V_o}{\pi}\left(1 - \frac{1}{3} + \frac{1}{5} - \frac{1}{7} + \frac{1}{9} - ...\right) \qquad (2.3)$$

Summing to the 7th harmonic gives $x_7 = 0.9216\, V_o$, whilst summing to the 9th harmonic gives $x_9 = 1.063\, V_o$. Clearly, the required answer is $x = V_o$ (which lies between the two results), i.e.

$$1 - \frac{1}{3} + \frac{1}{5} - \frac{1}{7} + \frac{1}{9} - ... = \frac{\pi}{4} \qquad (2.4)$$

2.2 Fourier series

In section 2.1 we derived a waveform, given the spectrum. To do the reverse operation, i.e. derive the spectrum given the waveform, is more difficult; it requires the use of the Fourier series, named after Baron Jean Baptiste Joseph Fourier (1768-1830), French mathematician.

Fourier took part (1798-1802) in the first modern, comprehensive survey of any nation – done by the French in Egypt – and was also governor of lower Egypt. He subsequently published important material on Egyptian antiquities but he is referred to in this book because of his work on thermodynamics.

Fourier showed that *any* signal can be expressed as the sum of an infinite series of sines and or cosines. The key to this technique is that sine waves form an *orthogonal* set of functions. Conventionally, orthogonal refers to one line being at right angles to another but here the concept is extended to cover functions [KRE]. Two functions

$$\text{e.g. } \sin\left(n\frac{2\pi}{T}t\right) \text{ and } \sin\left(m\frac{2\pi}{T}t\right)$$

are orthogonal if the integral of their product (in some interval) is zero unless $n = m$.

$$\text{e.g. } \int_{-T/2}^{T/2} \sin\left(n\frac{2\pi}{T}t\right)\sin\left(m\frac{2\pi}{T}t\right)dt = \begin{cases} 0 & n \neq m \\ T/2 & n = m \end{cases}$$

hence $\sin\left(n\frac{2\pi}{T}t\right)$ is orthogonal to $\sin\left(m\frac{2\pi}{T}t\right)$ in the interval $-\frac{T}{2} \leq t \leq \frac{T}{2}$.

Similarly

$$\cos\left(n\frac{2\pi}{T}t\right) \text{ and } \cos\left(m\frac{2\pi}{T}t\right)$$

are orthogonal and

$$\int_{-T/2}^{T/2} \sin\left(n\frac{2\pi}{T}t\right)\cos\left(m\frac{2\pi}{T}t\right)dt = 0 \text{ for all } n, m$$

hence sines and cosines form an orthogonal set.

An even function, i.e. a function for which $x(t) = x(-t)$, can be represented solely by cosine waves; an odd function, i.e. a function for which $x(t) = -x(-t)$, solely by sine waves; whilst any other signal requires both sine and cosine waves. In the Fourier series the period T of the waveform determines the fundamental frequency f_0 and the signal is composed of sine (and / or cosine) waves at all harmonics of this frequency (nf_0, n integer ≥ 0, i.e. including the d.c. case for $n = 0$). Put mathematically, any periodic signal $v(t)$ can be represented by the Fourier series as

$$v(t) = a_0 + \sum_{n=1}^{\infty} a_n \cos(2\pi n f_0 t) + \sum_{n=1}^{\infty} b_n \sin(2\pi n f_0 t) \tag{2.5}$$

where a_0 is the d.c. term given by the average value of $v(t)$ over a period, i.e.

$$a_0 = \frac{1}{T} \int_{-T/2}^{T/2} v(t) dt \tag{2.6}$$

and a_n and b_n are the amplitudes of the cosine and sine waves respectively, given by:

$$a_n = \frac{2}{T} \int_{-T/2}^{T/2} v(t) \cos(2\pi n f_0 t) dt \tag{2.7}$$

$$b_n = \frac{2}{T} \int_{-T/2}^{T/2} v(t) \sin(2\pi n f_0 t) dt \tag{2.8}$$

To derive b_n start from equation 2.5 and use the property of orthogonal functions, i.e. multiply both sides by $\sin(2\pi n f_0 t)$ and integrate in the interval $-\frac{T}{2} \leq t \leq \frac{T}{2}$. Most terms vanish, leaving

$$\int_{-T/2}^{T/2} v(t) \sin(2\pi n f_0 t) dt = \int_{-T/2}^{T/2} b_n \sin^2(2\pi n f_0 t) dt$$

$$= b_n \int_{-T/2}^{T/2} \frac{(1 - \cos(4\pi n f_0 t) dt)}{2}$$

$$= b_n \frac{T}{2}$$

i.e.
$$b_n = \frac{2}{T} \int_{-T/2}^{T/2} v(t) \sin(2\pi n f_0 t) dt$$

as required (and similarly for a_n).

To express $v(t)$ as a sum of sine waves clearly involves considerable effort; however, the task can often be reduced by making intelligent choices. For example, expressing the waveform of figure 2.4 by the Fourier series we note that:

(i)   There are equal areas of positive and negative voltages over one period, i.e. the average or d.c. voltage a_0 is zero;

(ii) The waveform is odd, so only sine wave terms are present, i.e. all the cosine terms a_n are zero.

Hence, for this waveform,

$$v(t) = \sum_{n=1}^{\infty} b_n \sin(2\pi n f_0 t) \quad \text{where} \quad b_n = \frac{2}{T} \int_{-T/2}^{T/2} v(t) \sin(2\pi n f_0 t) dt$$

Evaluating b_n,

$$b_n = \frac{2}{T} \int_{-T/2}^{0} (-5) \sin(2\pi n f_0 t) dt + \frac{2}{T} \int_{0}^{T/2} 5 \sin(2\pi n f_0 t) dt$$

$$= \frac{2}{T} \left[\frac{5 \times \cos(2\pi n f_0 t)}{2\pi n f_0} \right]_{-T/2}^{0} + \frac{2}{T} \left[\frac{(-5) \times \cos(2\pi n f_0 t)}{2\pi n f_0} \right]_{0}^{T/2}$$

$$= \frac{5}{n\pi} - \frac{5}{n\pi} \times \cos(-n\pi) - \frac{5}{n\pi} \times \cos(n\pi) + \frac{5}{n\pi} = \frac{10}{n\pi} (1 - \cos(n\pi))$$

hence $b_1 = \dfrac{20}{\pi}$, $b_2 = 0$, $b_3 = \dfrac{20}{3\pi}$, $b_4 = 0$, $b_5 = \dfrac{20}{5\pi}$, etc. and

$$v(t) = \frac{20}{\pi} \sin(2\pi f_0 t) + \frac{20}{3\pi} \sin(6\pi f_0 t) + \frac{20}{5\pi} \sin(10\pi f_0 t) + \dots$$

The even harmonics are zero, the amplitude of the fundamental is $4V_0/\pi$, and the amplitude of the odd harmonics are $1/n$ compared to the amplitude of the fundamental. So, in this section we started with the waveform of figure 2.4 and derived the spectrum of figure 2.5, whilst in the previous section we started with the spectrum and derived the waveform.

In general, the Fourier series will have cosine waves with amplitude a_n and sine waves with amplitude b_n. This enables both the magnitude and phase of the sinusoid of frequency nf_0 to be found. The magnitude is given by

$$c_n = \sqrt{a_n^2 + b_n^2} \tag{2.9}$$

and the phase by

$$\theta = \tan^{-1}\left(\frac{a_n}{b_n}\right) \tag{2.10}$$

i.e.

$$v(t) = \sum_{n=0}^{\infty} c_n \sin\left(2\pi n f_0 t + \theta\right) \tag{2.11}$$

2.2.1 Related transforms

The Fourier series is applicable to periodic signals, whilst the Fourier transform is used for aperiodic (single event) signals. Nowadays, for signals up to say 100 kHz, the transformation can be done by computers using the Fast Fourier Transform (FFT) and the resulting frequency spectrum is then displayed. Instruments dedicated to this task are called FFT analysers. For higher frequency signals a completely different hardware based technique is required (using amplitude modulation, as used in AM radio), such test gear being known as spectrum analysers.

The FFT is generally a more efficient implementation of the Discrete Fourier Transform (DFT). They are both based on the Fourier series and hence assume that the signal is periodic (if being used to analyse a non-repetitive event the FFT and DFT simply assume that the event is repetitive). But whilst the Fourier series deals with continuous signals (analogue or digital, but continuous in time) the FFT and DFT operate on sampled data (where a 'sample' of the waveform of a continuous signal is taken at repetitive sampling times). These relationships are summarized in figure 2.7:

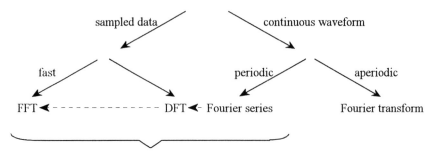

n.b. all these consider the signal as periodic

Figure 2.7 Relationship between various transforms

The Fourier transform, DFT and FFT are beyond the scope of this book. The interested reader is referred to [CON], [IFE] and [STR].

2.3 Introduction to filters

One example use of a filter is as a radio receiver's tuning circuit. Commonly, turning the dial changes the value of a capacitor. The capacitor and the aerial inductance form a filter which is used to select a radio station signal (i.e. changing the capacitance changes the frequency selected). This example demonstrates that we generally consider filters as having an effect on the spectra of signals, although a filter will obviously affect the waveform as well. We will come back to considering the effect on a waveform in section 2.3.6 but for now we will concentrate on a filter's effect on the spectrum of a signal.

Although there are other specialised types of filters, commonly filters can be classified as one of four types: low pass, high pass, band pass or band stop. These types, with their associated block diagram description and ideal gain frequency characteristic, are shown in figure 2.8.

For example, the ideal low pass filter passes all frequencies with no loss up to its cut-off frequency of f_0 and blocks all frequencies $> f_0$. This frequency characteristic is sometimes referred to as a 'brick wall' characteristic. Clearly, the high pass filter has the opposite characteristic. Also, it should be obvious that band pass and band stop filters can be constructed by combining ideal low pass and high pass filters in series or parallel (see the exercises at the end of this chapter).

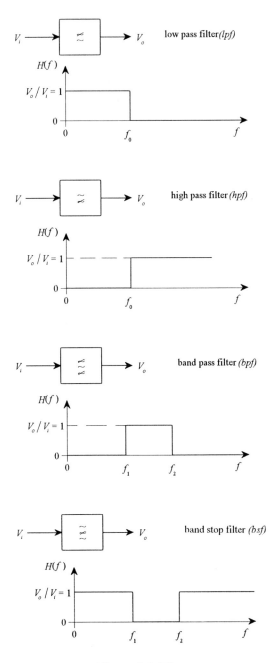

Figure 2.8 Filter types

The filtering process is simply multiplication of the signal's spectrum by the filter's frequency characteristic. For example, consider the signal and ideal band pass filter of figure 2.9 (N.B. the signal's magnitude spectrum is purely arbitrary here, chosen to highlight the effect of the filter). Where the filter characteristic is zero, the output is zero; where it is one, the output is the same as the input, i.e.

$$V_o(f) = V_i(f) \times H(f) \tag{2.12}$$

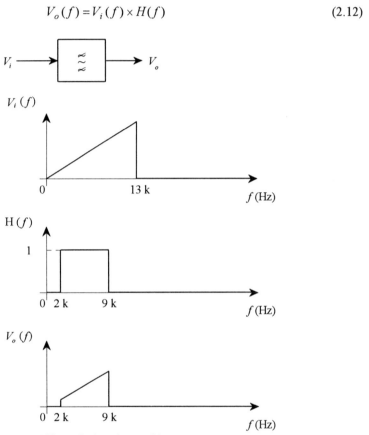

Figure 2.9 Effect of a band pass filter.

2.3.1 The communication channel

A filter can be thought of as a system building block whose effect is to alter the amplitude or phase spectrum of a signal. A communication channel affects the transmitted signal by delaying the signal and by dissipating signal power, thus attenuating the signal (i.e. making it 'weaker'). If the delay and attenuation introduced by the channel vary with frequency then the communication channel itself acts as a filter (conversely, the effects of a real communication channel can be simulated by a filter).

The other change which happens to a signal when sent over a communication channel is that it is corrupted by 'noise'. For an electrical signal the source of this unwanted interference may be cross-talk from telephone calls going along other wires in the same cable, noise due to electrical machines or circuits being switched on and off, lightning, unsuppressed car ignitions, etc., or indeed noise from the components in the electronic circuits of the link (see e.g. [HOR]).

A communication channel can be modelled as in figure 2.10. Here, the channel is considered as a filter and noise is generated by a 'white noise' source (i.e. it generates noise at the same average power level at all frequencies). Strangely, the name for band limited noise (i.e. white noise after being passed through a lpf) is 'pink' noise!

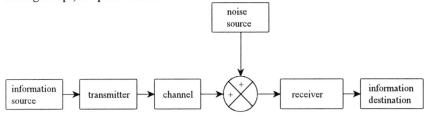

Figure 2.10 Communication channel

The function of the transmitter is to match information from the source to the channel and the function of the receiver is to recover this information. The transmitter may be a modulator, i.e. it uses the information signal to modulate a carrier waveform (types of modulation are considered in chapter 3), or the transmitter may be a coder, coding the signal in such a way that it can be recovered at the receiver (see e.g. the asynchronous protocol in chapter 3 or line-codes in chapters 7 and 9). Coding done by the transmitter is called *channel coding*, as it is needed in order to transmit the information over the channel. In chapter 1 we considered *source coding*, where information transfer was made more efficient by eliminating some redundancy from the message (e.g. by Huffman coding) before passing it to the transmitter. In a certain way, channel coding is the opposite to source coding, as redundant information is added to the signal to ensure the receiver recovers the information correctly.

2.3.2 First order low pass filter

The simplest way to implement this filter is with just a single resistor and capacitor, as shown below in figure 2.11. However, since the effect of this filter will change depending on input and output circuit impedances, it may be necessary to buffer it by using op-amps configured as unity gain amplifiers (with low output impedance to drive the following circuit and high input impedance to avoid loading the previous circuit, see e.g. [HOR]), as shown also in figure 2.11.

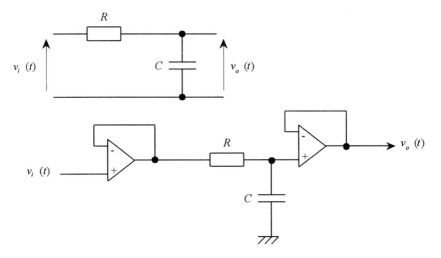

Figure 2.11 First order low pass filter

The impedance of the capacitor C is $Z_c = \dfrac{1}{j\omega C}\ \Omega$.

At high frequencies the impedance will be low and hence v_o will be low. The circuit stops (or rather attenuates) high frequencies whilst passing low frequencies; it is therefore a low pass filter.

By voltage divider theory

$$\frac{V_o}{V_i} = \frac{\dfrac{1}{j\omega C}}{R + \dfrac{1}{j\omega C}} = \frac{1}{1 + j\omega CR} \tag{2.13}$$

hence the filter's magnitude frequency characteristic is

$$\left|\frac{V_o}{V_i}\right| = \sqrt{\frac{1}{1 + (\omega CR)^2}} \tag{2.14}$$

and its phase characteristic is

$$\angle\left(\frac{V_o}{V_i}\right) = -\tan^{-1}(\omega CR) \tag{2.15}$$

CR is called the time constant (τ) of the circuit and $\omega_0 = 1/(CR)$ is the cut-off frequency of the filter. Substituting for ω_o in equations 2.14 and 2.15 gives

$$\left|\frac{V_o}{V_i}\right| = \frac{1}{\sqrt{2}} \cong -3 \text{ dB} \quad \text{and} \quad \angle\left(\frac{V_o}{V_i}\right) = -45^\circ$$

Hence ω_0 is also called the -3 dB (or half power) frequency. Alternatively, in Hz,

$$f_0 = \frac{\omega_0}{2\pi} = \frac{1}{2\pi CR} \quad \text{Hz} \tag{2.16}$$

Any frequency up to f_0 is in the pass band of this filter. The stop band is defined arbitrarily. In this example let us specify the stop band as the frequency band where the attenuation is greater than 20 dB. The frequency range between the pass and stop bands is called either the transition or the guard band. Therefore, for our example, the stop band starts when

$$\left|\frac{V_o}{V_i}\right| = \frac{1}{10}$$

i.e. $1 + (\omega CR)^2 = 100$ hence $\omega = \dfrac{\sqrt{99}}{CR} \cong 10\omega_0$

Note that for frequencies $\omega \gg \omega_0$ then $\left|\dfrac{V_o}{V_i}\right| \cong \dfrac{1}{\omega CR}$

that is, the attenuation is proportional to frequency. Hence a $10 \times$ increase in frequency (a decade) will cause a $10 \times$ decrease (-20 dB) in gain; or a $2 \times$ increase in frequency (an octave) will cause a $2 \times$ decrease (-6 dB) in gain. Well above the cut-off frequency the filter characteristic is therefore -20 dB/decade or -6 dB/octave. This filter characteristic will be shown as a straight line if plotted as dB against a logarithmic frequency axis. Such a plot, shown below in figure 2.12, is known as a Bode plot. A linear gain against linear frequency axis is also shown for comparison.

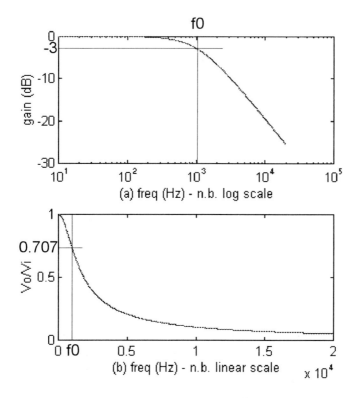

First order low pass filter $R = 1.5$ kΩ, $C = 100 \times 10^{-9}$ F, $f_0 = 1.061$ kHz
Figure 2.12 (a) Bode plot (b) linear spectrum

2.3.3 First order high pass filter

A high pass filter can be made by simply swapping the positions of the resistor and capacitor of the low pass filter, as in figure 2.13.

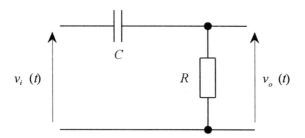

Figure 2.13 First order high pass filter

At high frequencies, since the impedance of the capacitor is low, the output will be approximately the same as the input. This is therefore a high pass filter. Doing the same analysis as for the low pass filter:

$$\frac{V_o}{V_i} = \frac{j\omega CR}{1 + j\omega CR} \tag{2.17}$$

$$\frac{V_o}{V_i} = \frac{\omega CR}{\sqrt{1 + (\omega CR)^2}} \tag{2.18}$$

$$\angle\left(\frac{V_o}{V_i}\right) = \tan^{-1}\left(\frac{1}{\omega CR}\right) \tag{2.19}$$

Note that the angle $\angle\left(\dfrac{V_o}{V_i}\right)$ is positive.

This is a phase lead circuit, whereas the first order filter is a phase lag circuit.

The concept of swapping filter elements around to turn a low pass filter into a high pass filter is generally true. Hence, to design a high pass filter with -3 dB frequency f_0, the first step is usually to design a low pass filter with this -3 dB frequency and then swap the components.

2.3.4 Higher order filters

The order of a filter is determined by the number of reactive elements used, e.g. the first order filters considered before only have one capacitor. A filter with two capacitors, or one capacitor and one inductor, would be a second order filter, etc.

With second or higher order filters there comes the flexibility of different filter design choices; common types of filter being the Butterworth, Chebyshev and Bessel [HOR]; the Butterworth having no ripples in its frequency characteristic, the Chebyshev having ripples but also having the greatest stop band attenuation of the three types, and the Bessel having the most linear phase response. These filter designs can be implemented as active filters using op-amps (e.g. as Sallen-Key or its derivative: voltage-controlled, voltage-source filters [HOR]). Component tolerance variation, temperature changes and ageing all affect the filter characteristic and this limits the maximum achievable order of a filter using such techniques to, say, the eighth order. Higher order filters can be obtained with crystal filters or by using sampled data filters, e.g. Surface Acoustic Wave (SAW) filters, or digital filters.

Considering low pass filters, around the -3 dB frequency the filter characteristic depends on the filter design; however, well beyond the -3 dB frequency the characteristic is simple to predict. As seen in section 2.3.2, the first order low pass filter's gain characteristic decreases by 6 dB per octave. For a low pass filter of order n, the attenuation figure is $n \times 6$ dB per octave.

2.3.5 Delay and phase characteristics

The phase characteristic of a first order low pass filter, with the same values for R and C as for the magnitude plots of figure 2.12, is given in figure 2.14.

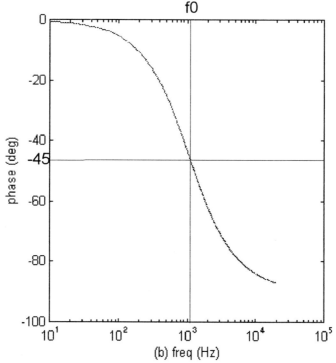

First order low pass filter $R = 1.5$ kΩ, $C = 100 \times 10^{-9}$ F, $f_0 = 1.061$ kHz

Figure 2.14 Phase spectrum

From this it can be seen that at higher frequencies the output will lag behind the input, as seen in the waveform of figure 2.15 which shows the effect of the filter on a 1 kHz sine wave. This shows the output from an oscilloscope: the top trace is the input to the filter and the lower trace is the output. Note that the measured phase delay is approximately 45°, as expected for a filter with a nominal −3 dB frequency of 1.061 kHz.

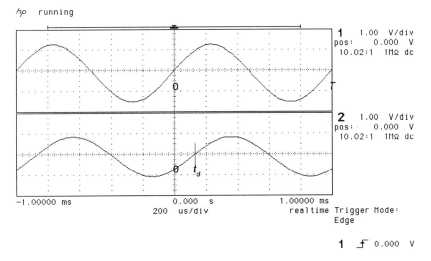

First order low pass filter $R = 1.5$ kΩ, $C = 100 \times 10^{-9}$ F, $f_0 = 1.061$ kHz
Figure 2.15 Effect of a filter on a 1 kHz sine wave

An important point to note is the relationship between phase and delay. Consider a circuit which introduces a constant delay at all frequencies of, say, t_d = 1 ms. A 100 Hz sine wave has a period of 10 ms, so the delay corresponds to 1/10 of this. The period of a 200 Hz sine wave is 5 ms, so the same delay corresponds to 1/5 of the period. That is, the phase delay is proportional to the frequency or, mathematically,

phase: $$\theta = \frac{t_d}{T} \times 2\pi \quad \text{rad}$$

i.e. $$\theta = \omega t_d \tag{2.20}$$

This is a linear phase characteristic as seen in figure 2.16, i.e. a linear phase characteristic implies a constant delay.

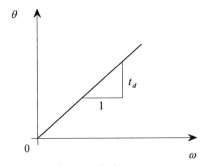

Figure 2.16 Linear phase characteristic

2.3.6 Rise-time bandwidth product

In this chapter we have concentrated on looking at signals in the frequency domain. In this final section we consider the response of a filter in the time domain. Not surprisingly, there is a link between a filter's frequency character-istic and its effect on a waveform. This link can be expressed by the 'rise-time bandwidth product' for a step voltage input waveform.

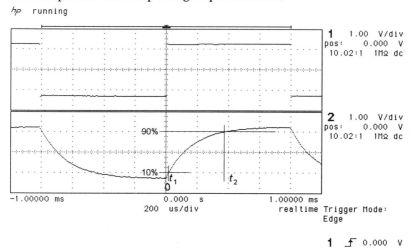

First order low pass filter $R = 1.5\ \text{k}\Omega$, $C = 100 \times 10^{-9}\ \text{F}$

Figure 2.17 Step response of first order low pass filter

The rise-time is conventionally defined as the time that a signal takes to rise from 10% to 90% of its final value.

For a voltage step $V_i(t) = \begin{cases} A & t \geq 0 \\ 0 & t < 0 \end{cases}$ (see figure 2.17)

passed through a low pass filter the output signal will be

$$v_o(t) = A\left(1 - e^{-\frac{t}{CR}}\right) \quad t \geq 0$$

The rise-time t_r is found from $t_r = t_2 - t_1$, where t_1 is defined by $0.1 = 1 - e^{\frac{-t_1}{CR}}$ and t_2 by $0.9 = 1 - e^{\frac{-t_2}{CR}}$; hence $t_r = -CR(\ln 0.1 - \ln 0.9)$. The bandwidth B of the filter is simply its -3 dB frequency

$$B = f_0 = \frac{1}{2\pi CR}$$

Hence the rise-time bandwidth product is

$$t_r B = \left(-CR(\ln 0.1 - \ln 0.9)\right)\frac{1}{2\pi CR} = 0.350 \tag{2.21}$$

The −3 dB frequency of a first order low pass filter can thus be found by simply measuring the rise-time. For example, in figure 2.17 the rise-time is 355 μs, hence the −3 dB frequency is 986 Hz; this compares with the value of 1.061 kHz as calculated from the values of R and C (7% error due to component tolerances and measurement errors).

For filters of 2nd or greater order (including ideal filters, i.e. filters of order ∞) the rise-time bandwidth product is

$$t_r B = 0.5 \tag{2.22}$$

Exercises on section 2.1

(1) What is the bandwidth of an analogue telephone channel?

(2) Why is the bandwidth for an analogue telephone channel appreciably less than the bandwidth needed for hi-fi?

(3) Write down the equation for the square wave shown below, up to and including the term for the 5th harmonic.

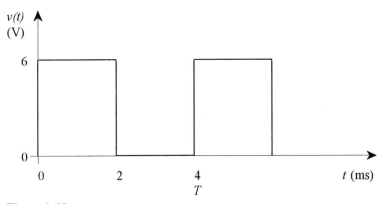

Figure 2.18

(4) What percentage of the total power of a square wave (ignoring any d.c. power) is present in the terms up to and including the 9th harmonic?

(5) What is the name of the effect that predicts ripples in a waveform reconstructed from a truncated series of harmonics?

Exercises on section 2.2

(6) Determine the d.c terms for the following waveforms:

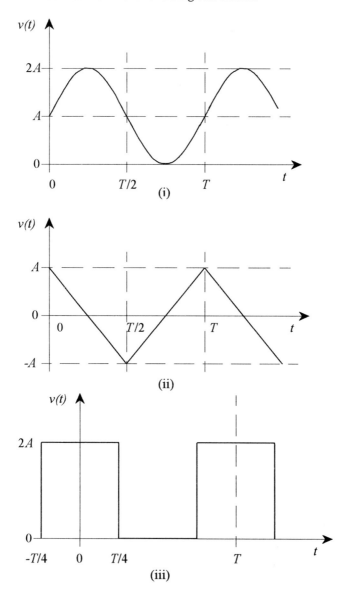

(i)

(ii)

(iii)

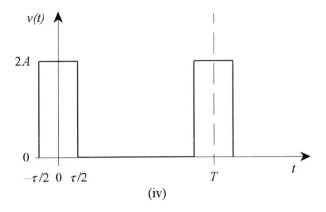

(iv)

Figure 2.19

(7)   State which of the waveforms of question (6) are even and which are odd, ignoring any d.c. terms.

(8)   After checking that your answers to questions (6) and (7) are correct, determine the Fourier Series representation for the waveforms of question (6). *(NB. the solution to part (ii) requires integration by parts.)*

(9)   Determine the amplitude spectrum for the waveform below.

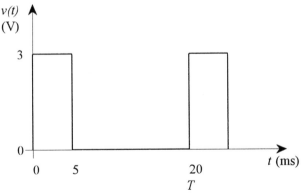

Figure 2.20

(10) Which transforms (out of the Fourier Transform, Fourier Series, DFT and FFT) deal with:
    (i) sampled signals;
    (ii) aperiodic signals?

(11) Prove that $\sin\left(\dfrac{n2\pi t}{T}\right)$ is orthogonal to $\sin\left(\dfrac{m2\pi t}{T}\right)$

(12) Investigate the computational savings which can be made by using the FFT rather than the DFT; state any extra conditions required for the FFT algorithm.

(13) It is not just sine waves which form an orthogonal set. For example, another set of orthogonal waveforms is given by Walsh functions. Investigate these functions, their properties and their uses.

Exercises on section 2.3

(14) Given an unlimited supply of ideal low and high pass filters with cut-off frequencies of 10 kHz and 20 kHz, show how band pass and band stop filters for the frequency range 10 kHz to 20 kHz can be constructed. You may also use any other non-filter circuits (e.g. adders, multipliers, etc.).

(15) The circuit below is made from an ideal lpf with a cut-off frequency of 5 kHz. State what this circuit does. (N.B. this technique is not usually a practical option due to non-ideal phase characteristics.)

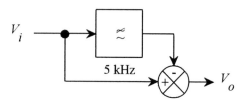

Figure 2.21

(16) What happens if you pass a 1 kHz square wave over a communication channel characterized by an ideal bpf with a pass band from 2 kHz to 6 kHz?

(17) For a first order low pass filter, with $R = 10$ kΩ and $C = 0.1$ μF, determine:
   (i)   the time constant;
   (ii) the -3 dB frequency (f_0);
   (iii) the rise-time.

(18) Determine the attenuation in dB of a first order lpf at a frequency one octave above its -3 dB frequency.

(19) Determine the attenuation in dB and phase shift in degrees of the filter of question (17) at a frequency of $3 f_0$.

(20) State what type of circuit results when the resistor and capacitor of question (17) are swapped around. Determine the attenuation in dB and phase shift in degrees of this new circuit at a frequency of $3 f_0$. Compare your results with the answers to question (19).

(21) If two first order lpfs, with -3 dB frequencies of 10 kHz, are connected in series, determine:
  (i)   the attenuation at 10 kHz;
  (ii) the -3 dB frequency of the overall circuit.

(22) For a third order lpf with a -3 dB frequency of 10 kHz, determine:
  (i)   the attenuation at a frequency two decades above its -3 dB frequency;
  (ii) the rise-time.

(23) State the type of phase characteristic necessary for a circuit not to distort the time relationship between different frequency components of a signal.

(24) Explain why, for the same bandwidth, the rise-time for a first order low pass filter is faster than for higher orders of filter.

(25) Compile a list of the more important equations used in this chapter.

(26) Write your own summary of what you have learnt in this chapter.

3 Data Communication over an Analogue Telephone Channel

This chapter considers a data communication channel, using the example of a modem link across the telephone network to connect two computers. The channel can be considered in two parts: from the computers to the modems, and between the modems. In both cases we need a transmission path and some means of coding the data to ensure that it can be transmitted over the link.

A standard interface for connecting a computer to a modem is RS-232. It is the basis of many serial interface standards and is covered in detail in section 3.1, enabling other serial interfaces to be related to it in section 3.1.4. One way of coding the data to enable it to be transmitted over an RS-232 link is to use the asynchronous protocol, which is covered in section 3.2. The telephone network between the modems is considered in terms of its limitations for data transmission, which leads on to a discussion of modem modulation techniques in section 3.3.

An example use of modems is in shops for checking credit cards. Modems can also be used to access the Internet by establishing a connection to the network of an ISP (Internet Service Provider). Generally, telephone calls to these companies are charged at local rates, the money going to the telephone company, whilst the ISP charges separately for access to the Internet. The Internet and its protocols TCP/IP are covered in chapter 8.

3.1 Serial interfaces

Serial transmission is the method adopted by almost all data communication systems for long distance links. Serial data transfer involves sending each bit of data along a single circuit (signal wire and ground) in sequence, bit by bit.

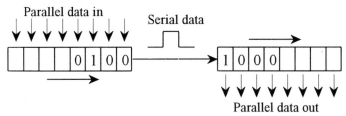

Figure 3.1 Serial interface

The parallel data used by the source terminal equipment must be converted to serial form by a shift register. Another shift register, at the other end of the line,

converts the serial data back into parallel form for use by the des
The time required to transmit a byte serially is obviously longer t.
transmission, but only a two wire (2W) connection is needed, wh
a byte over a parallel link a minimum of nine wires are needed (e ... uata lines
and one ground). For long-distance communication the advantage of the 2W
connection far outweighs the disadvantages of slower speed and the extra
complexity of the interface circuits.

One way for a return signal to be sent is to use another 2W circuit, making a
4W (4 wire) circuit. However, dial-up links over the Plain Old Telephone
System (POTS) are only 2W; in section 3.3 on modems we see how they can
send data in both directions over the same 2W circuit.

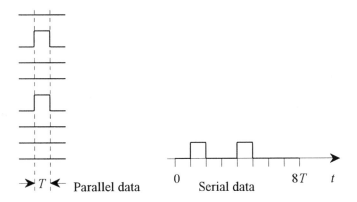

Figure 3.2 Parallel and serial transmission compared, sending data 01001000

3.1.1 The RS-232 standard

The most widely known standard for a serial interface is probably RS-232-C, as
defined by the US trade group Electrical Industries Association (EIA). This
standard is essentially the same as the ITU V.24/28 recommendations (often
simply called V.24), V.24 defining the signals, pins, etc. and V.28 covering the
electrical characteristics of the interface. These standards define how to connect
a DTE (e.g. a terminal) to a modem (a DCE), which provides the interface to a
telephone line, see figure 3.3. In the case of the PSTN the line will be a two
wire (2W) link, whilst for a leased line it may be a four wire (4W) link.

Leased lines are permanently set up and reserved solely for use by the
organization leasing them. There is no extra charge for sending data over such
a line, hence it makes sense to use such a line as much as possible (as a rule of
thumb for an average of at least two hours per day). Apart from the economic
advantage, the advantages of a leased line are a shorter call set up time, as there
are no switches to set up, and consistent and guaranteed line quality since the

same path is always followed. Clearly a 4W circuit allows at least twice the data rate of a 2W circuit, since each 2W link can be optimized to carry data one way.

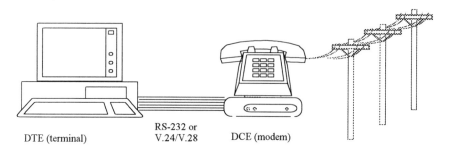

DTE (terminal)   RS-232 or
                         V.24/V.28   DCE (modem)

Figure 3.3 RS-232 interface

Being a serial interface, it is reasonable to suppose that only one circuit is needed to carry the data, but in fact there are over 20 circuits specified in the standard. Most of these are control signals to set up and control the link for the duration of the data interchange, see section 3.1.2. The RS-232-C standard specifies the use of a multiway cable, of up to 25 wires and up to 15 m in length, and supports a maximum data rate of 20 kbps. The maximum distance of 15 m is often exceeded by RS-232 users without causing difficulties. Referring to figure 3.4, because the link over the telephone network is serial the RS-232 link between the terminal and modem is serial; but because the RS-232-C link is a maximum of 15 m long the extra cost of multiway cable is small (this should explain the seeming paradox of a serial link having a multiway cable).

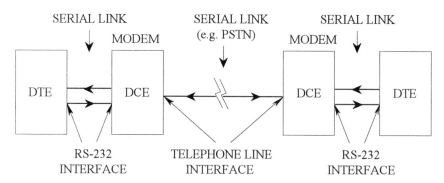

Figure 3.4 RS-232 end to end link

The standard specifies the use of inverse logic with voltage levels at the receiver in the range +3 to +15 V for binary 0 and −3 to −15V for binary 1, see figure 3.5. For the control circuits a positive voltage means that the signal is active or ON.

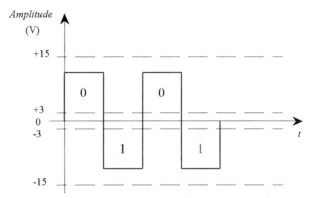

Binary 1: between −3 and −15 volts. Binary 0: between +3 and +15 volts.

Figure 3.5 RS-232 voltage levels

RS-232 transmitters are actually specified to output a voltage more negative than −5 V for binary 1 and more positive than +5 V for binary 0. This allows a noise margin of 2 V, i.e. if the amplitude of the noise picked up by the circuit is less than 2 V the receiver will still identify a valid RS-232 level, even for the minimum output voltage. The actual output voltage depends on the power supply voltage at the transmitter, typically ±10 V or ±12 V is used, whilst the voltage at any pin must not exceed ±25 V. A useful feature of RS-232 electrical connections is that they permit an indefinite short-circuit between pins without damaging line driver or receiver circuits. This means that it is 'forgiving' to the type of person who invariably connects things incorrectly at the first attempt.

RS-232-C does not specify the type of connector to be used, only that the DCE should have female connection pins and the DTE have male pins (female connection pins are also known as sockets). Usually a 25-pin D-type connector, conforming to the ISO 2110 standard, is adopted.

EIA-232-D and later revisions
The majority of equipment in use today conforms to the RS-232-C standard. The C refers to the third revision which was published by the EIA in 1969; unless stated otherwise RS-232 refers to this standard. In 1986 EIA-232-D was introduced. This is compatible with RS-232-C but has some amendments, notably the 25-pin D-type connector is specified as standard and the line length is determined by the maximum allowed capacitive load of 2500 pF, which gives a typical line length of 15 to 20 m. Also, three new circuits were included for

test purposes: pin 21 - remote loopback, pin 18 - local loopback, pin 25 - test mode.

The standard was changed again in 1990 to become EIA/TIA-232-E (TIA stands for Telecommunications Industry Association). The major change was to remove the 5 μs minimum limit for the pulse transition time between −3 and +3 V introduced by the D revision. The standard now states that the transition time must be more than 4% of the nominal period of the data, similar to but not identical with the V.28 standard which specifies 3% [TEX].

3.1.2 RS-232 data interchange

The circuits are identified by letter codes in RS-232 terminology or circuit numbers in the V.24 specification. For example, the transmit data line is pin number 2 on the connector and is identified as circuit BA in RS-232 terminology or as circuit 103 in the ITU V.24 specification (see figure 3.6). Fortunately, common abbreviations, such as TXD (transmit data), are usually adopted as they have obvious meaning in terms of the function of each pin (see figure 3.7).

V.24	RS-232				V.24	RS-232
				1	101	AA
118	SBA	14		2	103	BA
114	DB	15		3	104	BB
119	SBB	16		4	105	CA
115	DD	17		5	106	CB
141		18		6	107	CC
120	SCA	19		7	102	AB
108/2	CD	20		8	109	CF
110	CG	21		9		
125	CE	22		10		
111/112	CH/CI	23		11	126	
113	DA	24		12	122	SCF
142		25		13	121	SCB

Figure 3.6 RS-232-C / V.24 interchange circuits (viewed at DTE connector)

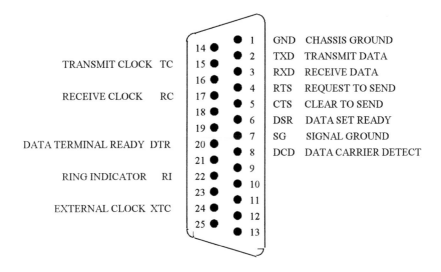

Figure 3.7 Common abbreviations for RS-232 circuits

These circuits can be grouped into four categories: timing, data, ground and control. *Timing* is needed to provide a common clock signal for synchronous applications:

XTC   eXTernal Clock signal
RC   Receive Clock signal
TC   Transmit Clock signal

However, in this chapter we are concentrating on asynchronous operation (see section 3.2 on the asynchronous protocol), so we will not consider these timing signals further. Hence for many standard applications only the ten pins in the remaining three categories need to be considered.

The *data lines* are used to carry the serial data:

TXD   Transmit Data from DTE to modem
RXD   Receive Data from modem to DTE

RS-232 was designed specifically to interconnect a DTE to a modem. Hence, for example, the transmit data is output on pin 2 of the DTE and received on the same pin at the modem. This means that the interface is different at the DTE and at the modem.

There are two *ground connections*:

SG   Signal Ground
GND   protective ground

SG is required to complete the electrical circuits. GND is not necessary for data transmission but can be used to minimize errors caused by electrical interference; one end *only* is connected to the braid of a shielded cable.

The most common *control* signals are:

DTR   Data Terminal Ready
DSR   Data Set Ready
RTS   Request To Send
CTS   Clear To Send
DCD   Data Carrier Detect
RI   Ring Indicator

(N.B. Data Set is an obsolete US term for a modem.) The main function of these signals is to establish a connection and to turn a half duplex link around, as discussed below.

Links can be classified as Full Duplex (FDX), Half Duplex (HDX) or Simplex (SX). A duplex link allows two-way communication, whilst a simplex link does not have a return channel from the receiver back to the transmitter. For example, with a deep space probe beyond Jupiter it takes hours for a signal from Earth to reach the probe; hence the link is effectively a simplex link. Whether a link is duplex or simplex has important consequences in the type of error correction scheme used. Generally a duplex link uses some form of automatic repeat request (ARQ), i.e. automatic retransmission of data once an error has been detected (see chapter 7), whilst a simplex link must use Forward Error Control (FEC), i.e. add sufficient redundancy to the transmitted message to enable errors to be corrected from the received message alone. ARQ is generally more efficient, but it relies on the receiver signalling back to the transmitter to ask for the message to be repeated. A FDX link allows simultaneous two-way communication, whilst a HDX link only allows traffic to go one way at a time (similar to how traffic lights are used to regulate traffic going over a narrow bridge). With a HDX link, two-way communication is achieved by the modems switching the direction of data transfer around; with a FDX link, the modem modulation scheme must allow two channels to be carried over the same 2W circuit for dial-up connections.

The sequencing of the control signals for a HDX link is best illustrated with an example. Consider a terminal attempting to connect to a host computer using asynchronous, dial-up modems, as in figure 3.8.

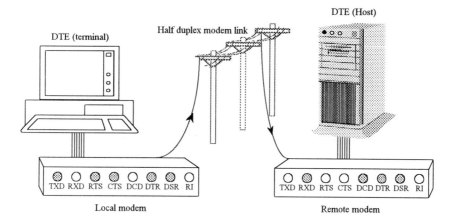

Figure 3.8 Half duplex modem link

- The local terminal indicates to the local modem that it is ready to make a call by turning on DTR (Data Terminal Ready). A connection through the PSTN is established by dialling the number associated with the remote computer. The remote modem detects the ringing tone on the phone line and sets its ring indicator (RI) to tell the remote computer that a call has arrived. The remote computer responds by activating its DTR to accept the call.

- The remote modem then turns RI off and replies by sending an answer tone over the telephone line. Both modems activate DSR (Data Set Ready) to tell their DTEs that the link is established and they can now send data.

- The local terminal now makes a request to send by turning RTS (Request To Send) on. The local modem responds with CTS (Clear To Send) and turns its carrier tone on. When the remote modem detects this tone it activates DCD (Data Carrier Detect) to stop the remote computer sending at the same time.

- The local terminal can now transmit data over its TXD circuit to the local modem which modulates a carrier to send the data across the telephone line. The remote modem receives the modulated signal, demodulates it to recover the data, and passes the data to the remote computer over its RXD circuit.

- When the local terminal has finished sending data it turns RTS off and the local modem replies by setting CTS to off and drops the carrier. The remote modem then turns DCD off, allowing the remote computer to send in the opposite direction by going through a similar process (i.e. starting with turning RTS on).

- Finally, to terminate the connection, either end deactivates DTR and then both DSRs are deactivated.

In summary, in HDX mode all modems are initially in receive mode and need to be 'turned round' to transmit. DTR and DSR must be on whilst transmitting or receiving data. RTS and CTS are involved in handshaking for transmitting data, whilst DCD is raised to signal that data is arriving on the RXD line (see the modem displays in figure 3.8). The process is simplified considerably for a full duplex link since two channels, one for each direction, are established during the connection phase. DCD, RTS and CTS are on all the time, as they are not required to turn the link around.

3.1.3 Null modems

Having described the standard use of RS-232, a non-standard use that is both common and troublesome should be mentioned. This is the interconnection of two local DTEs without using modems. The cable used is often called a null modem, or modem eliminator, for obvious reasons.

Cross-over interconnections are needed to simulate the connection of a DTE to a modem, see figure 3.9. Why the connections are set up in this way should be clear if the preceding example of RS-232 interface operation over a half duplex modem link has been understood. As a hint, remember that RS-232 is a standard designed to interconnect a DTE to a modem and that the null-modem must simulate a modem to both DTEs simultaneously.

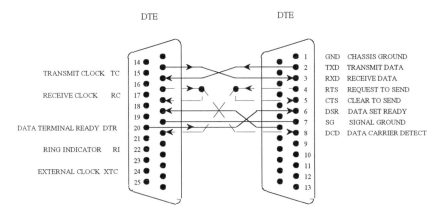

Figure 3.9 Null modem

Problems can arise with null modems when DTEs do not support all the control signals, or when some form of flow control is needed, for instance in the case of a serial printer. Careful study of the manufacturer's literature will then be needed to make the interconnection work.

3.1.4 Other standard interfaces

The 9 pin serial port as fitted to IBM PCs is often referred to as RS-232, although it is actually standardized as EIA-574, see section 3.2.3. But although RS-232 is the most common serial interface for data communications, it is not the only one in use today; indeed it has many limitations for modern systems in respect to speed, distance and complexity of the interchange circuits.

A later EIA standard, RS-449/RS-422-A, provides much better performance by using a balanced mode of transmission (balanced mode means that the signal is sent over two wires with one wire carrying the inverse voltage to the other – see chapter 4). However, this also means more interconnections, since each balanced circuit has two wires which makes it more expensive to implement. RS-449 specifies a 37 pin connector; mainly due to this reason it was not a success and EIA-530 was introduced instead, using the 25 pin ISO 2110 connector but sacrificing some circuits. Note that the interface specification has been split, with RS-449 or EIA-530 defining the signals, pins, handshaking, etc. and RS-422-A defining the electrical characteristics (data rate, balanced or unbalanced transmission, etc.) – following the same split as the ITU used for its V.24/28 interface.

The most widely used balanced line standard now is RS-485, which is an improvement on RS-422-A in that it supports half duplex transmission, allowing bi-directional multipoint communication [TEX]. A further EIA electrical standard which does not use balanced mode, RS-423-A, can be used instead, saving on interconnections if high data rates are not required. Important characteristics of these interfaces are summarized in the table below; note the much greater data rate possible using balanced mode transmission:

Electrical interface	Max. distance*	Max. data rate
V.28, RS-232-C, EIA-574	15 m	20 kbps (unbalanced)
RS-422-A	1200 m @ or 12 m @	100 kbps 10 Mbps (balanced)
RS-423-A	1200 m @ or 12 m @	1 kbps 100 kbps (unbalanced)
RS-485	1200 m @ or 12 m @	100 kbps 10 Mbps (balanced)

Mechanical interface	Number of pins
EIA-574	9
V.24, RS-232-C (with ISO 2110), EIA-530	25
RS-449	37

* apart from RS-232-C, line lengths are estimated from the maximum electrical load allowed.

However, the trend now is towards interfaces with fewer interchange circuits, with control signals passed by coded information over the data lines. This approach is exemplified by ITU X.21, the current standard interface for digital data services. Because no modem is involved, the interface is much simpler than V.24. The connections are (see figure 3.10):

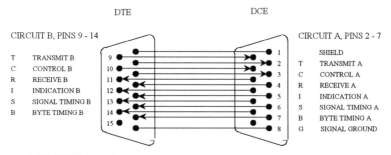

Figure 3.10 X.21 interface

X.21

Control (C) and Indication (I) are both control signals, whose level provides information on the state of the call to the DCE and DTE respectively. Transmit

(T) and Receive (R) are used both for data and for passing control signals, depending on the state of the C and I signals. A 15 pin D-type plug is specified in the standard.

The reader may also come across X.20 *bis* and X.21 *bis*, which are alternative standards (*bis* is Latin for second) to support access to data networks by existing V.24 terminals. X.20 *bis* is essentially the same as the V.24 full duplex asynchronous mode, whilst X.21 *bis* is for synchronous mode operation. The ITU V-series is a set of standards for the transmission of data over the analogue telephone network whilst the ITU X-series covers data transmission over a digital public data network. To keep this scheme consistent, the ITU decided that the adapted V.24 interfaces should have 'X.' references. Note, however that there are differences between X.20 *bis*/X.21 *bis* and V.24, e.g. X.20 *bis*/X.21 *bis* must be capable of supporting a data rate of 64 kbps. A third choice to a standard is indicated by *ter*, again from the Latin.

3.2 Asynchronous protocol

The simplest protocol in common use today is an asynchronous protocol that developed from the early telex systems. These formed the backbone of non-voice business communications for over half a century. The terminal devices used in these early systems evolved long before electronics and were based on relatively slow, electromechanical teletypewriters (TTYs) which combined a keyboard for input and a printer for output.

The protocol used by early teletypes is called asynchronous because no common synchronization signal is used to govern the time at which data arrives at the receiving end of a link. In asynchronous transmission each device has its own clock to time the transmission and reception of data. The clocks are set to the same nominal data rate but may run slow or fast with respect to each other, so causing errors. For example, if the receive clock is slightly slow, before long the data will be sampled at the wrong instant and an error caused, see figure 3.11.

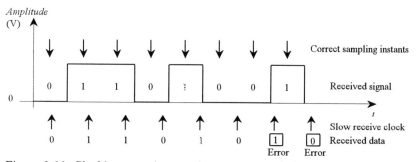

Figure 3.11 Clocking error in asynchronous transmission

The alternative to asynchronous operation is synchronous operation, where the receive clock is locked in step with the transmit clock. This can be achieved by sending the transmit clock over a separate circuit, as in RS-232, or by recovering timing information from transitions in the received signal. Clock drift errors are avoided with synchronous operation since the receive clock is locked to the transmit clock.

The asynchronous protocol gets around the clock drift problem by only permitting data to be transmitted in very short bursts (a few bits, usually a character, at a time), each burst preceded with a transition on the line to re-establish bit synchronization. In TTYs this transition corresponded to the press of a key on the keyboard. This engaged a clutch mechanism causing an armature to rotate and send the bits corresponding to the switch settings of the keyboard. After the data bits were sent the armature always returned to a stop position for at least two clock periods, to allow time for the mechanism to reset before the next character could be sent.

This technique worked quite well for low data rates (typically 50 or 110 bps), but the motor clocks were not accurate enough to achieve higher data rates. Today we still use the same protocol for ASCII-encoded terminals, but accurate electronic timing permits higher data rates.

A modern terminal generally uses transmitter/receiver devices called UARTs (Universal Asynchronous Receiver Transmitters) which sample the received signal at 16 times the data rate to ensure that the start transition is detected soon after it occurs. The received data is then sampled in the approximate middle of each bit period. The asynchronous protocol can be transmitted across an RS-232 interface, in which case the data will be an inverse logic bipolar signal as shown in figure 3.12.

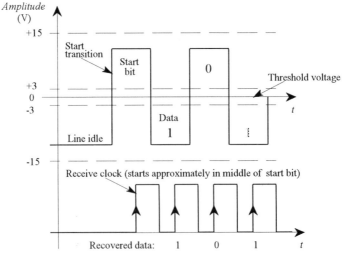

Figure 3.12 RS-232 data recovery

3.2.1 Asynchronous data format

Initially, the line is in an idle state (a negative voltage in RS-232). A key press causes the line voltage to change state (a positive transition) to generate a start bit. This signals to the receiver that a character will follow together with any parity bit. The data and parity is then sent using negative logic. The line is then returned to the idle state for one or two bit periods (called 'stop' bits) so that the line is prepared for the next character, which may occur at any time after the last stop bit.

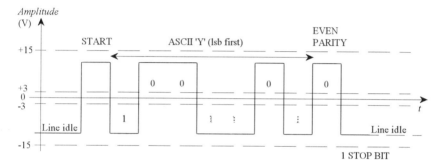

Figure 3.13 Asynchronous waveform

Figure 3.13 shows the waveform as it might be seen on an oscilloscope. Here, ten bits are transmitted for each character (with the least significant bit of the character sent first). The data format in this example is:
    1 start bit
    a 7 bit ASCII character (lsb transmitted first)
    1 even parity bit
    1 stop bit

However, there is no standard format, so care must be taken to ensure that both ends of the link are set up in exactly the same way (using either physical switches or commands given from the keyboard to set the parity, number of data bits, number of stop bits, and the data rate), otherwise data may be lost. This underlines the importance of standards in communications.

As another example, consider sending the letter 'J' as an ASCII character over an RS-232 interface using the asynchronous protocol, with odd parity and two stop bits.

'J' = 1001010. Using the asynchronous protocol with odd parity, this becomes:

	start bit	lsb		msb		parity bit	stop bits
	0	0101001				0	11

which is transmitted as the RS-232 waveform of figure 3.14.

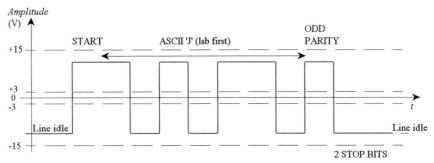

Figure 3.14 Asynchronous waveform for 'J'

In this example three bits are used for synchronization purposes (the start bit with its positive going transition to signal the start of transmission and the two stop bits to return the line to its idle state) and one parity bit is used for error detection. Hence four bits out of eleven are not information bits but are required to ensure successful transmission of the information; as far as the message is concerned they are redundant. The redundancy in this example is 4/11 or 36.4%. This is a high figure; synchronous protocols have a far lower overhead which explains why they are the preferred choice for many high throughput data communication applications.

Since not all the bits of the asynchronous protocol are data bits the true data rate will be less than the line rate. To try to avoid confusion the true data rate should be measured in bits per second (bps), whilst the line rate is measured in baud (the number of signalling events per second). Using the protocol as specified above, the data rate is 7/11 of the baud rate, i.e. for a 1200 baud link the maximum data rate is 764 bps.

3.2.2 Error correction using echoplexing

Characters may still be corrupted by line noise but, with the receiver set to the same parity convention as the transmitter, it is possible to detect parity errors. Unfortunately, the asynchronous protocol does not allow for correction of these errors! At best the receiver terminal can only flag the errors by printing a special character in place of the incorrectly received ones.

Extra protection against transmission errors in data typed at a terminal is possible using a technique called echoplexing. This is not really part of the protocol because the terminal operator must check for errors and correct them manually.

Echoplexing involves setting up the link to remote-echo, which means that characters are not immediately printed or displayed but are first transmitted to the remote (host) computer which then sends (echoes) them back. The operator can then see any mistakes and correct them by sending delete characters (DEL-an ASCII control character).

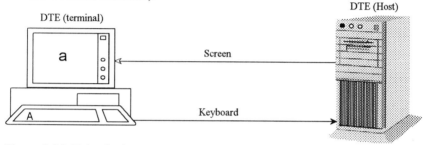

Figure 3.15 Echoplexing

3.2.3 IBM-PC serial interface

An IBM-PC generally has at least two serial ports (referred to as COM 1 and COM 2) to which a serial mouse, serial printer, modem, etc., may be connected. The PC ports are normally nine pin male sub-miniature 'D' type connectors (DB9S). The interface standard is RS-232, although it is now formalised under the EIA-574 standard with the pin connections shown below.

pin	Description
1	Carrier Detect, DCD
2	Receive data RXD
3	Transmit data TXD
4	Data Terminal Ready DTR
5	Signal Ground
6	Data Set Ready DSR
7	Request To Send RTS
8	Clear To Send CTS
9	Ring Indicator RI

The asynchronous protocol can be set using the MODE command in MS-DOS, e.g. the baud rate can typically be set as 110, 150, 300, 600, 1200, 2400, 4800, 9600 or 19,200 baud. Using this command loads the control register in the Universal Asynchronous Receiver Transmitter (UART) chip in the PC. Errors may occur if higher data rates than 19.2 kbaud are attempted, although some UARTS will support 116 kbaud. At these higher rates the line length should be limited to 3 m. A common default setting for a PC is COM1, even parity and seven data bits, with one stop bit normally or two stop bits if the baud rate is 110 baud. To check which type of UART is fitted in a PC, type MSD at the DOS prompt and choose COM Ports.

3.3 Modems

The telephone bandwidth is too narrow to carry digital signals in binary form at the data rates required today. A voice-grade line is limited by international agreement to a bandwidth of only 3100 Hz, covering the frequencies from 300 to 3400 Hz. This does not go down to d.c. and is much narrower than the normal hi-fi bandwidth of 20-20,000 Hz, see figure 2.1. If you listen to speech through a telephone it sounds 'colourless'; it is not high-fidelity because most of the high frequencies (treble) and some of the low frequencies (bass) have been filtered out.

Telephone lines were optimised for analogue speech transmission, originally being loaded with extra inductance (by inserting electrical coils between the wires every mile or so) to make voice signals travel the maximum distance with minimum distortion. Noise is more of a nuisance than a serious problem so far as voice communication is concerned, but it can introduce errors in data communications. The result of this optimisation was a system capable of transporting intelligible speech over long distances for minimal line equipment costs, but wholly inadequate so far as high speed digital data transmission was concerned. The limited bandwidth and the line noise were serious obstacles to be overcome before data could be transported effectively across the analogue PSTN.

One solution to the problem is to modify the digital signals before transmission to a form that can be carried by the telephone system. In other words to change them into a quasi-analogue form, like the speech signals that the system was intended to carry; this is the topic of this section. Another solution of course is to change the telephone system itself – replacing the analogue equipment and extending the bandwidth so that the PSTN will transport digital data directly (see chapter 8 on circuit switching).

3.3.1 Modulation techniques

To transport data signals via the analogue telephone system, without changing the system itself, we need an interface device capable of converting the binary signals used by terminal equipment to a form that can be carried within the limited bandwidth of the telephone system. Note that the signals remain digital, although they will be in a form suitable for transmission over a network designed for analogue signals.

The conversion process at the transmitter is called modulation and the device needed to do it is called a modulator. If you want to hear what modulated signals sound like try dialling up a fax number. At the other end of the telephone line the reverse operation (demodulation) is performed by a demodulator, restoring the signals to their original form for use by the destination terminal equipment. Most data communications involve two-way transmission, so a modulator and demodulator are often combined in one unit, called a modem. The name MODEM is simply a shortened form of MODulator - DEModulator. The line may switched between the two, according to the required direction of data flow for HDX operation, or a channel may be kept open in both directions for FDX operation.

There are various methods of modulation used by modems, all of which involve altering in some way the basic characteristics of a sine wave to carry the data. The characteristics of a sine wave are its amplitude, its frequency and its phase. These are changed, either singly or in combination, to modulate the data on to the carrier sine wave.

ASK

Amplitude modulation, or ASK (Amplitude Shift Keying), involves altering the amplitude (loudness) of the carrier tone according to whether a binary 0 or 1 is being transmitted. An ASK version of a data signal, which uses a high amplitude carrier for binary 1 and a lower amplitude for 0, is shown in figure 3.16.

FSK

Frequency modulation, or FSK (Frequency Shift Keying), uses a constant amplitude carrier but two separate frequencies – e.g. a high frequency is used to carry 1s and a lower frequency for 0s. An FSK modulator effectively alters the pitch of the signal. This produces a characteristic warbling sound if the signal is heard through a loudspeaker as the data is transmitted. An FSK waveform is also shown in figure 3.16.

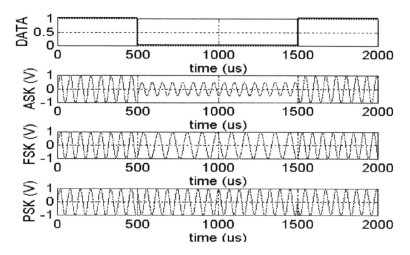

Figure 3.16 ASK, FSK and PSK compared

PSK

The third possibility is to have a carrier signal of fixed amplitude and frequency but alter its phase. This is called phase modulation or PSK (Phase Shift Keying). The phase of a signal refers to where it starts with respect to a reference of 0 degrees. A sine wave with no phase shift is regarded as an in-phase signal, whereas a signal that starts half a cycle later is 180 degrees out of phase and is called an anti-phase signal. A PSK modulated version of a data signal, which uses 180 degree phase shifts to represent the data bits, is shown in figure 3.16. The in-phase signal represents 1 and the anti-phase signal represents 0. There is clearly a problem here as to which signal is in-phase and which is anti-phase; we will come back to this below in DPSK.

This particular modulation scheme can be plotted on an amplitude/phase diagram, as in figure 3.17 (also called a constellation diagram for reasons that will be apparent later). Since there are only two signal states, this is called Binary PSK (BPSK). A constant amplitude of 1 V is shown by a circle of radius 1 centred on the origin. The transmitted signal can be either in-phase (phase = 0°) or anti-phase (phase = 180°); hence the two points marked *A* and *B* correspond to the two possible states of the modulator, with *A* used to signal binary 1 and *B* used to signal binary 0.

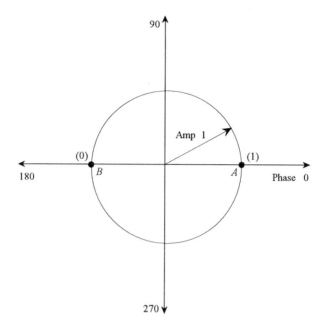

Figure 3.17 Constellation diagram for BPSK

DPSK

Simple PSK relies on comparing the phase of the received signal with a reference signal. This requires a complex circuit at the demodulator, but the need for this can be avoided by using a modulation technique called Differential PSK (DPSK). In such a scheme it is the change in phase between the *current* signalling event and the *previous* signal which carries the information. A possible scheme would be for a phase shift of +90° to signal a binary 0 and a phase change of −90° (i.e. +270°) to signal on binary 1. Every bit is therefore indicated by a change of phase, the amount of phase change indicating whether a binary 0 or 1 is being sent. For example consider the data 10001; if the initial phase is 0° then the subsequent phases will be:

Data		1	0	0	0	1
Phase	0°	270°	0°	90°	180°	90°
Phase change		−90°	+90°	+90°	+90°	−90°

3.3.2 *Modulation techniques compared*

An ASK modem is simple to implement but, like AM radio broadcasting, the signals are prone to outside interference (or noise) caused by, for example, lightning strikes or the switching of inductive loads such as electric motors. This kind of noise is a common problem on switched telephone lines and, if it is of sufficient amplitude and duration, could cause transmission errors. For example, a little noise added to a low amplitude carrier can turn it into a high amplitude carrier that the demodulator will interpret as a 1 instead of a 0.

FSK, like FM radio, does not suffer from noise as much as ASK, since noise tends to affect the amplitude rather than the frequency of signals. However, because FSK uses two carrier frequencies, it occupies more bandwidth than ASK and is therefore only suitable for use in low speed modems. The better performance of FM in the presence of noise can be heard by bringing an electrically noisy, battery operated toy close to an AM/FM radio and comparing the effect on different wave bands.

PSK is also tolerant of noise and, since it only uses one carrier frequency, makes better use of the telephone bandwidth than FSK. It is therefore the technique adopted for most high speed modems.

Speed and data rate
It is useful at this stage to consider in more detail what we mean by speed with respect to modems since there are two ways to specify it: either as a data rate in bits per second (bps) or as a baud rate. We have already come across the baud rate when we looked at the asynchronous protocol in section 3.2.1, where the data rate was less than the baud rate due to the redundancy in the protocol. In the following section we look at how a data rate higher than the baud rate can be achieved. This is necessary for high speed modems because, as we shall see, the channel bandwidth limits the baud rate but not the data rate.

In the modulation techniques considered so far each binary digit has been coded as one of two different amplitudes, frequencies or phases. This is known as two-state signalling for obvious reasons. With such signalling, the number of signalling events per second is equal to the number of bits transmitted per second. The number of these signalling events (phase, frequency or amplitude) per second is called the signalling rate, or baud rate, of the modem. Clearly, in the case of two-state modems, and ignoring any redundancy due to the protocol, the baud rate is the same as the data rate. For example, a two-state PSK modem with a specified baud rate of 300 baud can deliver 300 bits in one second.

The maximum signalling rate (C) for a two-state signalling system is given by

$$C = 2B \quad \text{bps} \qquad (3.1)$$

Where B is the channel bandwidth and an ideal noiseless channel is assumed. For example, if the channel bandwidth is 3400 Hz then C is 6800 bps. As the bit period is half the period of the 3400 Hz carrier wave, this implies a half cycle per bit is the minimum requirement, as shown in figure 3.18 for PSK.

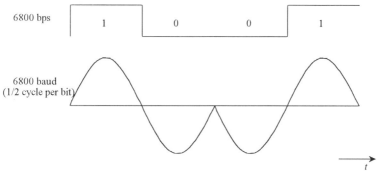

Figure 3.18 PSK maximum data rate

In practice, for reliable communication over noisy dial-up telephone circuits, modems are restricted to a baud rate of, say, 1200 to 2400 baud. With two-state signalling this would mean that 2400 bps is the practical limit, so how is it that some modems specify data rates much higher than this? For example 9.6, 14.4 and 28.8 kbps are common nowadays, whilst the fastest current data rate is 33.6 kbps. The answer is the use of multi-state signalling techniques.

3.3.3 Multi-state signalling

High-speed modems use multi-state signalling techniques to achieve high data throughput at low baud rates (i.e. within the limits imposed by the PSTN). If a modem can output, for example, four signal frequencies instead of two, then two bits can be sent per frequency. Let us say that the two bit data combination 00 is carried by a 500 Hz tone, 01 by a 1000 Hz tone, 10 by a 1500 Hz tone, and 11 by a 2000 Hz tone. Then the eight bit data stream 00011011 can be transmitted by the modem changing its signalling frequency only four times. This means that the baud rate is half the data rate, so a 2400 baud modem could deliver 4800 bps; i.e.

data rate = baud rate × number of bits per signalling event

Using two bits per baud like this is called dibit coding. Since the channel capacity depends on the baud rate this technique doubles the maximum data rate, i.e. with dibit coding

$$C = 4B \qquad \text{bps} \tag{3.2}$$

Dibit coding is commonly done with four phases instead of four different frequencies and is then called Quadrature Phase Shift Keying (QPSK). A QPSK constellation diagram is shown in figure 3.19; note that this is an example of differential PSK and, moreover, a Gray code is used to order the four states – this ensures that a single phase in error results in only a single bit in error.

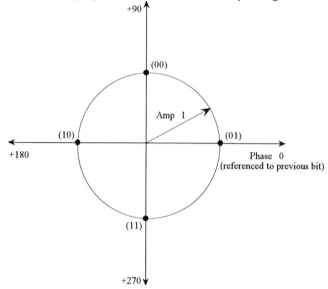

Figure 3.19 Constellation diagram for V.22 QPSK

Tribit PSK coding, which uses eight 45° phases to give a threefold increase in throughput, and even quadbit coding, which uses sixteen phases to give a fourfold increase, are possible but require more complicated electronics.

Still higher data rates can be achieved by using hybrid modulation tech-niques. For example, many standard modems use QAM (Quadrature Amplitude Modulation) which combines both phase and amplitude modulation techniques. An example QAM modem, to the ITU V.29 modem standard, can achieve a reliable 9.6 kbps using 8 phases (selected by three bits of the data) and 2 amplitude levels (selected by a fourth data bit) with a 1700 Hz carrier. The constellation diagram for a V.29 modem is shown in figure 3.20 with 16 signal points as expected for a compound four bit coding scheme. Actually, four amplitude levels are used: $\sqrt{2}$, 3, $3\sqrt{2}$ and 5 V; but only two levels are associated with any one phase. The utility of this type of diagram and why it is called a constellation diagram is now obvious.

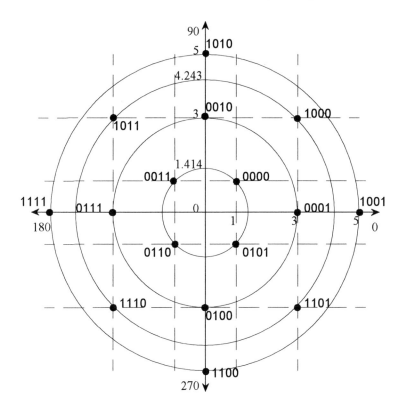

Figure 3.20 Constellation diagram for a V.29 modem

The baud rate for this example can be found from

$$\text{baud rate} = \frac{\text{bit rate}}{\text{data bits per signalling event}} \tag{3.3}$$

Here four data bits are transmitted as one of the 16 possible points in the constellation diagram; hence for a 9.6 kbps data rate the baud rate is 2400 baud.

The following formulae can be used to determine the *theoretical* maximum data rate (C) for a transmission medium as a function of its bandwidth (B) in Hz and the number of signal states (M).

$$C = 2B \log_2 M \text{ bits per second} \tag{3.4}$$

For example, for a two-state system $M = 2$ and the formula reduces to equation (3.1). As another example, for a QAM modem with eight phases and two amplitude levels:

the number of signal states M = 16
$\log_2 16$ = 4
B = 3100 Hz for a telephone channel
therefore C = 2×3100×4 = 24.8 kbps

However, the practical limit for QAM on its own is about 9.6 kbps. Above this rate errors become too frequent and Trellis Coded Modulation (TCM) is used by higher speed modems over the PSTN. TCM is covered in section 3.3.6. As an example application, in a V.32 modem there are 32 points in the constellation diagram, but only four data bits are recovered from each point. A baud rate of 2400 baud results in a data rate of 9.6 kbps, as for V.29 which uses QAM without TCM. However, the advantage of TCM is that V.32 can achieve 9.6 kbps FDX over dial-up lines, whilst V.29 needs a 4 wire leased-line circuit to achieve FDX working.

Noise
The maximum attainable data rate is limited by noise. Note that equation (3.4) predicts an infinite channel capacity for an analogue signal and noiseless channel since, by definition, such a signal has an infinite number of levels. However, in the presence of noise, information theory shows that the maximum channel capacity obeys the Shannon-Hartley law [SHA], partly named after Claude Elwood Shannon (born 1916), an American mathematician who did much of his work for Bell Telephone Labs:

$$C = B \log_2 \left(1 + \frac{S}{N} \right) \text{ bits per second} \qquad (3.5)$$

where S/N is the signal to noise ratio (expressed as a power ratio, not in dB). For example, the theoretical minimum signal to noise ratio for the new V.34 standard at 28.8 kbps over a standard telephone channel is given by

$$1 + \frac{S}{N} = 2^{C/B} \text{ , i.e. } S/N = 625 \equiv 28.0 \text{ dB}$$

N.B. $\log_2(x) = \dfrac{\log_{10}(x)}{\log_{10}(2)}$

Proof of equation (3.5) [CON]: for signal power S and noise power N, the maximum signal amplitude is $\sqrt{(N + S)}$ and the minimum signal amplitude which can be distinguished between two adjacent signal levels is $\sqrt{N}$. Thus there are $\sqrt{(N+S)/N}$ distinguishable levels and the channel capacity (from equation 3.4) is

$$C = 2B \log_2 \sqrt{\frac{N+S}{N}} = B \log_2\left(1+\frac{S}{N}\right) \text{ bits per second.}$$

3.3.4 Modem standards

The main problem of such a wide choice of modems is compatibility. Modems of identical type and from the same manufacturer are likely to be compatible but other modems will be incompatible, unless they have the same specification of speed, modulation technique, carrier frequencies, etc. To ensure compatibility, standards were introduced so that different manufacturers could produce modems that would interface with each other.

The ITU introduced a range of standards for modems that is recognised internationally (except in the USA and some far-eastern countries where Bell standards apply). All the ITU standards for data transmission over the analogue telephone network begin with V. and are collectively referred to as the V series.

The earliest common standard was V.21. The modems that conform to this standard operate at 300 bps in both directions in full duplex mode, using FSK modulation with frequencies for originate mode (i.e. for the modem initiating the call) of

Transmitting: 1180 Hz for logic 0
980 Hz for logic 1

Receiving: 1850 Hz for logic 0
1650 Hz for logic 1

(and vice versa for the answering modem). Hence two channels have been set up over the same physical 2W circuit. The similar 300 baud Bell 113 modem uses different carrier frequencies and therefore is incompatible. The later Bell standards for 1200 baud modems and above do conform to the ITU recommendation, so there is movement towards true world-wide standards. Some ITU and Bell standards are summarised in the following table:

Standard	Data rate (bps) Transmit/receive	Modulation	Method of Working
V.21	300/300	FSK*	FDX
V.22	1200/1200	QPSK**	FDX
V.22 *bis*	2400/2400	QAM	FDX
V.23 (75 bps channel is termed the 'back' channel)	1200/1200 or 1200/75 or 75/1200	FSK FSK FSK	HDX
V.29 (leased lines)	9600/9600	QAM	FDX
V.32	9600/9600	TCM	FDX
V.32 *bis*	14,400/14,400	TCM	FDX
V.34 (V.Fast)	28,800/28,800	TCM	FDX
Bell 103	300/300	FSK*	FDX
Bell 202	1200/1200	FSK	HDX
Bell 212A	1200/1200	QPSK**	FDX

Notes: (i) All used on 2-wire circuits unless stated otherwise; (ii) * Different frequencies! (iii) ** Compatible at 1200 bps; (iv) Group III fax can use V.21, V.27 *ter*, V.29, V.32 and V.33.

Non-standard modems
Having discussed standard modems, there are still many modems in use today that do not conform to a standard. Non-standard dial-up modems are not common but for dedicated, point-to-point, private or leased-line applications, non-standard modems can offer a high-speed solution. Short-haul modems, for example, are used for high-speed, short-distance, leased-line work.

DOVE (Data Over Voice Equipment) modems do a similar job, carrying data over wide bandwidth PABX (private branch exchange) lines using modulation frequencies well above the telephone bandwidth, so that voice signals can share the same connections.

Baseband modems (or line drivers) also provide economical, short distance links over wider bandwidth lines. These are not really modems at all since they do not modulate digital signals but provide a suitable line driver/receiver to interface to a digital link.

3.3.5 *Modem options and facilities*

If a modem is to have the potential to communicate with the majority of other modems connected to the PSTN then, besides needing to be a 2W modem, it must also adhere to a V. series standard. Usually the later V. series modems can also support earlier standards. A leased line is generally a four wire (4W) connection and, since it is a fixed link permanently set up between two modems, the modems need not be standard.

First generation modems had limited features but were easy to operate. The user dialled up the destination computer, listened for a ringing tone followed by a carrier tone and then pressed the data button on the modem to connect it to the line. Only a few other switches, to set speed, originate/answer mode, etc., were needed.

Later modems were more sophisticated and, with the arrival of micro-processor control, automatic dialling and many other useful features were included to produce what are now called intelligent or smart modems.

Intelligent modems

Instead of setting switches or pushing buttons, commands are given to this type of modem from the terminal keyboard. The Hayes company were among the first modem manufacturers to include an autodial facility and a control language (similar to a computer operating system) based on commands issued from the terminal. For example, if '**ATD** *number*' is typed at the terminal it gets the attention (AT) of the modem and asks it to dial (D) the number.

Hayes included further commands to control other modem functions from the terminal keyboard. For instance

ATH is the command to hang up or drop the line
ATZ is the modem reset command
ATO puts the modem on line
ATC turns the carrier signal off
ATA answers a call.

These AT commands soon became a *de facto* standard used by almost every other manufacturer of intelligent modems, but they are not accepted by the ITU as a true international standard. The ITU V.25 recommendation deals with autodial/answer, with which some modem manufacturers also comply.

Synchronous modems

As shown in figure 3.4 the interface between the DTE and modem is RS-232. For lower speed modems the asynchronous protocol is used to transmit Hayes commands or data. Higher speed modems assemble asynchronous data into synchronous data packets to increase data throughput, e.g. using the Microcom Networking Protocol MNP-3. Synchronous protocols such as HDLC are the subject of chapter 7.

Error correcting modems

To transmit at high data rates over telephone lines modem manufacturers had to solve the problems caused by high error rates. To improve reliability they designed modems with built-in error-detection and correction capabilities.

Basically, when a receiving modem detects a data error it corrects it by asking the transmitter to send the data again.

There are various ways of doing this and standards are required to ensure compatibility. The modem manufacturer Microcom was among the first to introduce error correction using their proprietary scheme called MNP-4 (Microcom Networking Protocol), which soon became a *de facto* standard and has since become part of the ITU V.42 recommendation for error-correcting modems. The main V.42 standard uses the synchronous protocol LAP-M (Link Access Procedure - Modems, similar to HDLC) but MNP-4 is supported as a secondary standard; in MNP-4 data passed to the originator modem from the local terminal is assembled into blocks before transmission and a checksum is appended to each block. The combined packet is then sent using synchronous transmission. The answering modem, on receiving the packet, performs its own checksum on the data and compares it with the appended checksum from the source modem. If they match, the data is assumed to be error-free and is passed to the destination terminal. If the checksums do not match, an error has occurred and the modem calls for a retransmission. All this activity is invisible to the terminal-user who sees only an error-free connection.

For those users without an error-correcting modem, terminal software is available to perform error correction using similar techniques. Xmodem, Ymodem, Zmodem and Kermit are a few of the many protocols designed to promote error-free file transfer between data terminal equipment using asynchronous communication. Error control is considered in more detail in chapter 7.

Data compression
Data compression is a technique used in modems to improve data throughput. Run length coding and Huffman data compression (strictly data compaction) methods are covered in chapter 1.

The Lempel-Ziv algorithm is used to perform data compression in ITU V.42 *bis* (N.B. this is a different standard to V.42 which covers error correction). The MNP level 5 data compression standard is also popular, but is not compatible with V.42 *bis*. Typically, data compression techniques can double the data rate compared to uncompressed data. However, if applied to data which has already been compressed the amount of data to send may actually increase.

Finally, to put these advanced options in a framework, the effectiveness of a data communication system is determined by its ability to transport information quickly and without error. Modems today use error-correction techniques to improve link reliability. To improve data throughput they use advanced modulation techniques, such as QAM and TCM (see below), together with data compression and synchronous operation. This has ensured that modems have remained an important part of data communications.

3.3.6 Trellis Coded Modulation

TCM was mentioned in section 3.3.3, as a way of increasing the data rate for high speed modems. The data is first coded, using convolutional coding [HAL, HAY], then, for high speed modems, the output from the convolutional coder is modulated using QAM. The combination of convolutional coding and modulation is called Trellis Coded Modulation. TCM is not an easy topic, so it may be appropriate for readers working through this chapter for the first time to come back to it at a later stage. The topic shares some common ground with chapter 7, but it is appropriate to consider it in this chapter because TCM is the modulation scheme for high speed modems.

The convolutional coding results in a Forward Error Control (FEC) code, i.e. one where some errors can be corrected at the receiver without the message having to be sent again. A simple convolutional coder, see figure 3.21, typically consists of an m-bit shift register connected to n modulo-2 adders. In modulo-2 arithmetic, carries into bit position 1 are ignored (N.B. bit position 0 is the lsb).

The XOR (exclusive OR) logic operation is modulo-2 addition, as $0 + 0 = 0$, $0 + 1 = 1$, $1 + 0 = 1$ and $1 + 1 = 0$. Incidentally, the AND logic operation is modulo-2 multiplication and note the relationship between even parity and modulo-2 addition.

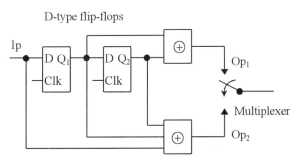

Figure 3.21 Convolutional coder, with $m = 2$ and $n = 2$

The adder outputs are multiplexed together, so that each message bit results in n code bits being output, i.e. the code rate $r = 1/n$. More complex coders have k shift registers in parallel. Such coders code k message bits at a time, but still output n code bits, i.e. the code rate $r = k/n$. Convolutional coders in general have a memory level, or depth, of m. Thus, the output depends on the previous m bits plus the latest bit input (for all k inputs), i.e. on $m + 1$ bits, which is the constraint length. The next n bits output will, in turn, depend on the state of the m-bit shift registers after being clocked, plus the next input bits.

This is in contrast to block codes, such as the Hamming single bit code considered in chapter 7, where the message is divided into k bit blocks. Each of which is taken independently of the others to generate the output. Block codes are thus memoryless.

Note that in TCM not all the message bits need to be coded by the convolutional coder, e.g. for every 6 bits of data, only two bits might be encoded in a rate 2/3 coder. The three coded bits would be used to select a subset of the QAM constellation diagram, whilst the remaining four bits would indicate a point in that subset. This would be for a 128 point constellation diagram. Essentially, the selection of the subsets would follow the same scheme as outlined below for selecting bits, but with differences (see e.g. [HAY]).

Figure 3.21 shows a convolutional coder with $m = 2$, $n = 2$ and $k = 1$. Hence, the constraint length is 3, the memory level is 2, and the code rate $r = 1/2$. Taking this coder as an example, since the constraint length is 3 there are 8 unique input combinations for this coder:

node	Ip	Q_1	Q_2	Op_1	Op_2	next node
A	0	0	0	0	0	A
C	0	0	1	1	1	A
B	0	1	0	1	1	C
D	0	1	1	0	0	C
A	1	0	0	0	1	B
C	1	0	1	1	0	B
B	1	1	0	1	0	D
D	1	1	1	0	1	D

Starting with $Q_1 = Q_2 = 0$, an Ip $= 0$ results in $Op_1 = Op_2 = 0$, whilst an Ip $= 1$ results in $Op_1 = 0$ and $Op_2 = 1$. This is shown diagrammatically in the first level of figure 3.22, starting from node A with a dotted line for a 1 input and a solid line for a 0. The nodes are determined by the state of the D-type flip-flop outputs Q_1 and Q_2. In the second level, if the previous input was a 1 we start from node B, with $Q_1 = 1$ and $Q_2 = 0$; whilst, if the previous input was a 0, we again start from node A. By the time the third level has been completed, the diagram begins to repeat, since the constraint length is 3. The resulting diagram is called a 'trellis diagram', hence Trellis Coded Modulation. In mathematical terms, a trellis is a tree with remergent branches, which also describes a trellis in the garden. Note that only certain code sequences are allowed.

N.B. nodes are sometimes referred to as states. A state diagram, with 2^m nodes, can also be constructed for the convolutional coder. This is a more conventional way of deriving the trellis diagram, but it has not been employed here to avoid making state diagrams a pre-requisite for understanding TCM. Readers who already know about state diagrams should draw one for figure 3.21, as an exercise.

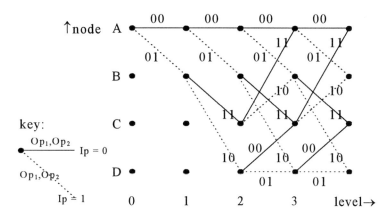

Figure 3.22 Trellis Diagram for the coder of figure 3.21

At the receiver the Viterbi algorithm [VIT] is used to select the most likely transmitted sequence of nodes, i.e. it considers more than just the most immediately received node in deciding what was transmitted. As an example of its operation, assume the original data is 0 1 0 0. From figure 3.22, the transmitted data will be 00 01 11 11, but let 1 bit be corrupted so that the received sequence is 01 01 11 11. The cumulative number of bits in error for each path (i.e. the path Hamming distance, see chapter 7) is plotted in figure 3.23.

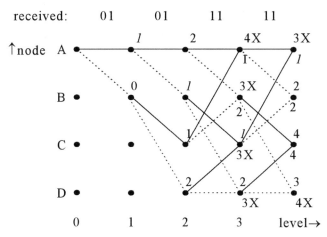

Figure 3.23 Operation of the Viterbi algorithm

Where two paths converge, the path with the lowest path difference is kept (the other path is marked by an X in figure 3.23) or, if the path differences are the same, a random choice is made as to which to keep. From figure 3.23, it can be seen that the path which results in the lowest cumulative error is 00 01 11 11. This path is marked by the path differences being in italic type. Tracing this path generates the data 0 1 0 0, hence the single bit error has been corrected.

The Viterbi algorithm results in an optimum decoder (for a white noise channel where the noise power can be represented by a Gaussian probability density function). The signal to noise ratio is effectively increased by this process, enabling the data rate to be increased despite the added redundancy.

Exercises

(1)   What voltage levels are acceptable at the receiver for control and data signals in RS-232-C; and what levels are used to signal data 1 and control signal ON?

(2)   In RS-232-C interfacing, state the purpose of the signal ground, the RTS/CTS control signals, and the DCD control signal.

(3)   What is the function of a null modem?

(4)   Describe the handshaking required at both the near and far end to transmit data via a modem over a half duplex PSTN link, using the DTR, DSR, RTS, CTS, DCD, and RI control lines.

(5)   What is the purpose of the stop bits in the asynchronous protocol?

(6)   Determine the redundancy and efficiency for the asynchronous protocol when transmitting 8 bit characters with no parity, a start bit and two stop bits.

(7)   Code ASCII 'C' using the asynchronous protocol of question 5. Finally show the waveform as it would be seen on an oscilloscope when transmitted across a V.24 interface with ± 12 V logic levels.

(8)   Explain why the analogue PSTN is unable to carry digital data directly.

(9)   Explain how ASK, FSK and PSK modulators transmit 0s and 1s. Compare and contrast these techniques, with particular reference to bandwidth and noise.

(10) Design a logic circuit to generate a DPSK signal, giving a change of phase of 180° for a data 1 and no change for a 0, using the BPSK modulator as specified in figure 3.17.

(11) Why are 300 baud Bell standard modems incompatible with V.21 modems?

(12) Explain how full duplex operation is possible using a 2-wire, dial-up circuit.

(13) What is the general function of the Hayes command set. In particular, what does ATD 207958 do?

(14) Why are error correction and data compression useful to a dial-up modem user?

(15) Compare and contrast each of the following pairs of terms, as used in communications:
   (i)   HDX and FDX;
   (ii) duplex and simplex;
   (iii) leased and dial-up;
   (iv) synchronous and asynchronous;
   (v) serial and parallel;
   (vi) 2W and 4W;

(16) A V.32 modem uses QAM over the PSTN, with a carrier frequency of 1800 Hz and twelve phases, four of which have two amplitudes. Calculate the theoretical maximum data rate.

(17) For a telephone speech channel with a signal to noise ratio of 30 dB calculate the maximum channel capacity in bps.

(18) A QAM modem is used to send data at 9.6 kbps without data compression. Given that the QAM scheme uses two amplitude levels and eight phases, determine the baud rate on the line.

(19) Ignoring noise, calculate the channel capacity for a QAM modem with 4 phases and 8 amplitude levels when used to transmit data over a channel of bandwidth 2000 Hz.

(20) Explain the importance of the baud rate being less than the data rate for multi-state signalling.

(21) Determine the output code for the data 1 1 0 1, when using the convolutional coder of figure 3.21.

(22) Using the convolutional coder of figure 3.21, determine the most likely original data, if the received signal is 01 00 00 10.

(23) Determine the trellis diagram for the convolutional coder in figure 3.24. The diagram should be drawn as in figure 3.22, as for any coder with $m = 2$ the diagram can be made to follow figure 3.22, apart from the state of the outputs Op_1 and Op_2.

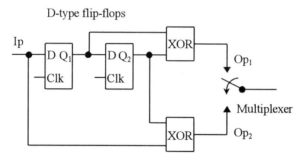

Figure 3.24 Convolutional coder

(24) Compile a list of the more important equations used in this chapter.

(25) Write your own summary of what you have learnt in this chapter.

4 Transmission Lines

The communication channel makes the link between transmitter and receiver. At the physical level this channel is provided by a particular transmission medium. Three different classes of media are covered in this and the following two chapters: copper cables, free space (or wireless) links, and fibre optic cables. Although treated as three different cases it is important to grasp the similarity between them: in all cases signals are being sent as electromagnetic signals (or light signals in the broadest sense). The speed of light in free space (i.e. a vacuum) is approximately 3×10^8 m/s, and our atmosphere is sufficiently like a vacuum that the same value applies here too. Coincidentally, the speed at which an electromagnetic signal propagates in typical examples of both coaxial and fibre optic cables is approximately 2×10^8 m/s. The most basic equation in all three cases is the relationship between the wavelength of the signal (usually given the symbol λ – Greek *lambda*; the Greek alphabet is given in appendix A), the frequency (f), and the speed of light or velocity of propagation (V_p)

$$\lambda = \frac{V_p}{f}$$

This chapter develops the theory of transmission lines to explain the electrical behaviour of cables. The cable provides a copper link as the communication channel. The two most common types of cable used for communications are the twisted pair cable and the coaxial cable, and we start by considering the physical aspects of these cables and the different ways in which they can be used.

4.1 Copper links

4.1.1 Twisted pair

A twisted pair is simply a pair of copper wires, in their insulating sleeves, which are twisted together. It can be used in a single ended mode, where one wire carries the signal and the other is the earth (or ground) connection, or in a balanced mode (also called differential mode) with equal but opposite voltages on the two wires (since the voltages are equal and opposite they balance and there is no need for an earth return).

Baseband (i.e. unmodulated) binary normally uses either unipolar or bipolar signalling. Unipolar is where one logic level is signalled by 0 V, as in the Non Return to Zero waveform met in chapter 1, and bipolar is where the logic levels are signalled by equal but opposite voltages, as in the RS-232-C waveform met in chapter 3. Either method can be used for single-ended transmission, but a balanced link implies the use of bipolar signalling.

Although simple, a twisted pair is a good communication channel when used in a balanced mode. Being balanced means that zero volts is not used as a signal, so the effect of earth-borne noise is eliminated. Being twisted ensures that both wires pick up virtually the same noise; which is all to the good since common mode noise, i.e. noise which is the same on both wires, can be eliminated at the receiver with a differential line receiver. Figure 4.1 shows a differential line driver and receiver connected by a twisted pair. To show how the common mode noise can be rejected assume a binary 1 is signalled by +5 volts on one wire and −5 volts on the other, which is a difference of 10 volts. A binary 0 would be signalled by reversing both polarities. Now let both wires pick up noise of, say, +1 volt. Ignoring attenuation, the signal amplitudes at the receiver will be +6 volts on one wire and −4 volts on the other. However, the signal, which is the difference between the voltages on the two wires, is still 10 volts. Despite the interference a good signal is received with the common mode noise rejected.

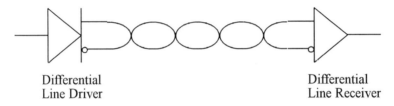

Differential   Differential
Line Driver   Line Receiver

Figure 4.1 Balanced mode twisted pair channel

A single twisted pair is a two wire (2W) circuit and can carry a two-way analogue telephone channel. In the old analogue Public Switched Telephone Network (PSTN) the action of the telephone exchanges was essentially to set up a continuous copper link between two telephones. To carry the many telephone calls between exchanges many hundreds of twisted pairs would be put together to form one large cable. The noise picked up between adjacent twisted pairs, called cross-talk, could be severe in such a cable. To minimize cross-talk the twisted pairs were combined in such a way that no twisted pair ran continuously alongside another twisted pair. This was achieved by twisting each twisted pair around the cable, the amount of twist varying for each twisted pair. These cables were expensive in terms of both materials and construction and have been superseded by coaxial cable or fibre optic cable. However, individually, the twisted pair is still an important medium for a communication channel. As well as providing a two wire link from the local telephone exchange to private houses, two twisted pairs are used in telecommunications to provide a four wire (4W) circuit for 30 digital telephone channels (30 channel PCM at 2 Mbps, see chapter 8) and it is also used in Local Area Networks (for example in Token Ring at 16 Mbps and 10BaseT Ethernet at 10 Mbps, see chapter 9).

Twisted pairs, either singly or combined, may be covered by a thin metal braid or foil, acting as a shield, with an outer insulating sheath. In this case the cable is called Shielded Twisted Pair (STP); conversely, without a shield it is called Unshielded Twisted Pair (UTP). STP provides better protection against noise, either impulsive noise or cross-talk, but costs more.

Twisted pair is also classified as either voice grade or data grade depending on the application, the difference being in the amount of twist in the cable. For data over a 100 m length of cable, category 3 cable can work at 10 Mbps, category 4 at 16 Mbps, whilst category 5 cable (UTP and STP) should be capable of working at 100 Mbps, assuming that it has been properly installed and connected. This, however, is no easy task, as at such high data rates the installation procedures must be precisely adhered to in order to avoid electromagnetic interference (EMI). Common problems are:

(i)   excessive untwisting of the wires to terminate them (13 mm is the maximum amount of untwisting permitted);
(ii) tight bends (bend radius to be more than four times the cable diameter);
(iii) over tightening of cable ties.

4.1.2 Coaxial cable

In comparison with a twisted pair, a coaxial cable permits higher data rates and has the added advantage in being less susceptible to high frequency electrical interference because of the outer cylindrical conductor (braid) which acts as a shield or screen. Coaxial cable is only used in the single ended mode of transmission where the central copper conductor carries the signal and the copper braid is earthed.

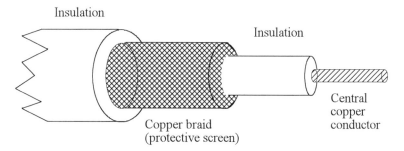

Figure 4.2 Coaxial cable construction

Such a cable is characterized by its characteristic impedance, common values being 50 Ω or 75 Ω. This is not a measure of the resistance of the cable but is derived from the ratio of the cable's inductance to its capacitance (resistance and conductance also play a part, as we shall see in the next section on transmission line theory). Being a ratio, the characteristic impedance is independent of the length of any piece of cable and can therefore be used to characterize types of cable. TV aerial cable is 75 Ω whilst 50 Ω cable is used in both the 10Base5 and 10Base2 Ethernet local area networks.

A common type of connector used with coaxial cable is a BNC connector, with a characteristic impedance of either 50 Ω or 75 Ω. Even at relatively low data rates (say 1 Mbps) it is very important that all connectors and cables in a system have the same characteristic impedance. A mismatch will give rise to signal reflections which may interfere with correct operation of the channel.

4.2 Basic transmission line theory

A transmission line is a cable considered as an electrical circuit or indeed the other way round: electric circuit components considered as a communication channel. The suitability of a cable for a communication channel depends primarily on its characteristic impedance.

The equation for the characteristic impedance of a cable is derived from a model of a transmission line. For many analogue applications it is important that the characteristic impedance does not vary over the frequency range of the signal, as if it did the received signal would be distorted. Distortion is caused because components of the signal at different frequencies are attenuated and delayed by different amounts (e.g. see figure 4.3 where, clearly, the signal at the receiver does not resemble the transmitted signal). On the other hand, if the characteristic impedance is constant then all the signal components will be attenuated and delayed by the same amount and the signal at the receiver will have the same shape as the transmitted signal. Both a 'lossless line' and a 'distortionless line' are special cases where the characteristic impedance is constant over the frequency range of the signal and hence they are suitable transmission lines for analogue signals. It is less important with digital signals to have a communication channel with a flat attenuation versus frequency characteristic since the digital signal will be regenerated at the receiver. However, it is still important to understand the theory for high speed digital circuits, as is shown in section 4.3.1 on the layout of a Printed Circuit Board (PCB) for analogue and high speed digital signals.

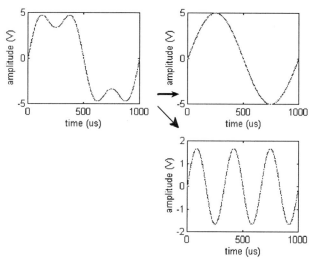

(a) Transmitted signal decomposed into 1 kHz fundamental and third harmonic, starting in-phase

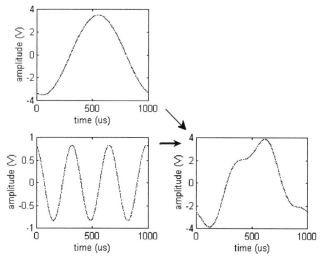

(b) Received signal composed of 1 kHz fundamental and third harmonic, no longer in-phase and with different attenuation factors

Figure 4.3 Distortion caused by attenuation and delay varying with frequency

In the following sections we will be concerned first with transmitting analogue signals and so we will investigate the conditions under which a cable has a constant characteristic impedance, considering first the 'lossless line' and then a 'distortionless line'. But we need to recognize that there are other ways to set up a link to provide a suitable channel for an analogue signal. One way is to use an equaliser; this is a filter at the receiver with the inverse characteristic to that of the cable over the frequency range of interest, see figure 4.4, where the equaliser compensates for the effect of the cable. Figure 4.4 illustrates the effect on gain characteristics, but it is also necessary to make the delay the same for all signal components by ensuring that the overall phase characteristic is linear, as discussed in chapter 2. Alternatively, even if the characteristic impedance is not constant it can be considered constant over a narrow frequency range, as in narrowband communication (see chapter 5).

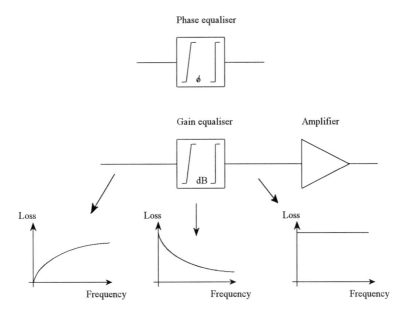

Figure 4.4 Gain equalization of a line

Another method to achieve an overall flat attenuation versus frequency characteristic is to convert the analogue signal to a digital bit stream, transmit the data, regenerate the digital signal, and then convert it back to an analogue signal. This can have considerable benefits: for example, with the twisted pairs used for telephone speech channels typically a digital line can carry 15 times as many calls as an analogue line. When the analogue links between telephone exchanges became congested, converting them to digital links relieved the congestion without the expense of digging up streets to lay new cables.

One twisted pair can provide an analogue transmission path for a two-way telephone channel over the frequency range 300 Hz to 3,400 Hz (using a distortionless line, as explained in section 4.2.3). Alternatively, a one-way digital link can be set-up over the same cable, supporting a data rate of 2.048 Mbps – sufficient to carry 30 digitized telephone calls multiplexed together in a 30 channel PCM system. Two such pairs are needed for a 4W link for 30 telephone channels, resulting in a 15:1 improvement in line usage for digital links.

Transmission line theory is also important for digital links, as we will see in the final part of this chapter when we look at 'reflections', where voltage and current pulses 'bounce' back from the end of a cable for the same reason that light is reflected by a mirror.

4.2.1 Characteristic impedance

The characteristic impedance is a characteristic, or property, of a cable that is independent of the cable length; it is also known as the surge impedance because it is the impedance seen by a high frequency transient.

Consider a cable with characteristic impedance Z_o, terminated by a load impedance, also of Z_o. Such a load is called a 'matched' load. The importance of this special case is that the impedance measured at the input to the cable is also Z_o.

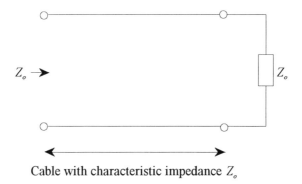

Cable with characteristic impedance Z_o

Figure 4.5 Cable terminated by a matched load

This is no coincidence: it follows that another length of cable can be connected to the input, as in figure 4.6, and the input impedance of the combined cable will still be Z_o. (Cable 1 with matched load can together be treated as the matched load for cable 2.) For a cable terminated by its matched load there is no discontinuity in impedance; the signal will not be reflected at any point and any residual signal which reaches the matched load will be dissipated in the load.

Figure 4.6 Two lengths of cable, both characteristic impedance Z_o

If there is a discontinuity in impedance then a reflection will occur; e.g. if the load is open circuit then no signal energy can be dissipated in the load (since there is no load). Any signal which reaches the open circuit will therefore be reflected back down the cable. This reflection is usually unwanted as it interferes with other signals in the cable. This is why, for example, the 50 Ω cable in an Ethernet LAN must be terminated with a 50 Ω terminating resistor.

To find an expression for the characteristic impedance Z_o we need to model a cable by electric circuit components. These components will depend on the length of the cable, so they are specified in terms of a unit length. The length units will cancel out, as Z_o does not depend on cable length, so the choice of units can be left open.

A cable of length x can be modelled as in figure 4.7 by a series resistance Rx and inductance Lx (with impedances Rx and $j\omega Lx$) and shunt conductance Gx and capacitance Cx (with impedances $1/(Gx)$ and $1/(j\omega Cx)$). (Conductance is the inverse of resistance and is measured in units of Siemens (S), hence a 100 Ω resistor has a conductance of 0.01 S.) For example, let $C = 0.1$ µF/km, $R = 100$ Ω/km, $G = 10$ µS/km and $L = 0.25$ mH/km, then for a 100 m length of cable $Cx = 0.01$ µF, $Rx = 10$ Ω, $Gx = 1$ µS and $Lx = 0.025$ mH.

We assume that the values for C, R, G and L do not vary with frequency, so they are called line constants. These values for the line constants will be used in many of the examples of this chapter as they are of the right order to represent a real cable. In fact, they are only constant over a restricted frequency range; the most important variation is due to the 'skin effect' where R increases with frequency as the current in the wire tends to concentrate at the surface at higher frequencies (rather than remain equally distributed over the wire's cross-section). The effect is caused by self-induction, i.e. a voltage, opposing the direction of current flow, is generated by the wire carrying a current in the magnetic field set up by that current. The skin effect is only significant at high frequencies and is ignored in the rest of this section. R is therefore the d.c. resistance per unit length of the cable. For a conductor of radius $r = 0.25$ mm and length $\ell = 1$ km, made of copper of resistivity $\rho = 1.7241 \times 10^{-8}$ Ωm, the resistance is

$$R = \frac{\rho \times \ell}{\pi r^2} = 87.8\,\Omega \text{ (hence } R = 87.8\ \Omega/\text{km).}$$

The conductance is a measure of the insulation between wires; the lower the conductance per unit length (G), the better.

In a cable, the components Cx, Rx, Gx and Lx are distributed evenly along the cable, but we can approximate the cable by making x very small (say length δx) and take many sections, each section having component values $C\delta x$, $R\delta x$, $G\delta x$ and $L\delta x$. If we make δx sufficiently small we will not be able to find any difference between the electrical behaviour of a length of cable and our model.

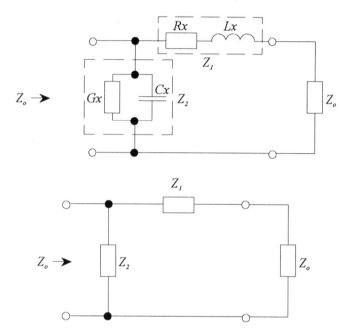

G = shunt conductance between conductors/unit length
C = shunt capacitance between conductors/unit length
R = series resistance of both conductors/unit length
L = series inductance of both conductors/unit length

Figure 4.7 Transmission line modelled by circuit components

From figure 4.7 and considering a single section of length δx,

$$Z_1 = R\delta x + j\omega L\delta x \qquad \Omega \qquad (4.1)$$

$$Z_2 = \frac{\dfrac{1}{j\omega C\delta x} \times \dfrac{1}{G\delta x}}{\dfrac{1}{j\omega C\delta x} + \dfrac{1}{G\delta x}} = \frac{1}{G\delta x + j\omega C\delta x} \qquad \Omega \qquad (4.2)$$

$$Z_o = \frac{Z_2(Z_1 + Z_o)}{Z_2 + (Z_1 + Z_o)} \quad \Omega \tag{4.3}$$

Rearranging equation 4.3

$$Z_o Z_2 + Z_o(Z_1 + Z_o) = Z_2 Z_1 + Z_o Z_2$$

$$Z_o(Z_1 + Z_o) = Z_2 Z_1$$

but, for a short length δx of cable, Z_o will be much greater than Z_1, i.e. $(Z_1 + Z_o) \cong Z_o$, hence

$$Z_o = \sqrt{Z_2 Z_1}$$

Substituting equations (4.1) and (4.2)

$$Z_o = \sqrt{\frac{R\delta x + j\omega L \delta x}{G\delta x + j\omega C \delta x}}$$

$$Z_o = \sqrt{\frac{R + j\omega L}{G + j\omega C}} \quad \Omega \tag{4.4}$$

In general Z_o is not constant but varies with frequency ω (rad/s). However, for analogue signals, as discussed before in section 4.2.1, it is important that the frequency characteristic of the communication channel (including any cable) is flat, so the cases where Z_o is constant with frequency are especially important. Two such cases are the lossless line and the distortionless line.

4.2.2 Lossless line

At high frequencies the inductive and capacitive terms $j\omega L$ and $j\omega C$ will be much greater than the resistance and conductance, which can therefore be neglected, i.e.

$$Z_o = \sqrt{\frac{R + j\omega L}{G + j\omega C}} \cong \sqrt{\frac{j\omega L}{j\omega C}} \quad (\omega L \gg R, \ \omega C \gg G)$$

hence $$Z_o = \sqrt{\frac{L}{C}} \quad \Omega \tag{4.5}$$

This is the case for TV broadcast signals, e.g. channels 21 - 35 in the 470 - 590 MHz frequency band. Using the same line constants as before, then $\omega L = 0.785$ MΩ/km at 500 MHz, which is much greater than R, and similarly $\omega C \gg G$. The value of the characteristic impedance Z_o is 50 Ω (N.B. for TV cable it should be 75Ω) whilst for a length of, say, 20 m the cable resistance is only 2 Ω

(the conductance can be ignored here, as 0.2 μS corresponds to a shunt resistance of 5 MΩ).

As will be shown in section 4.2.4 on the propagation coefficient, the velocity of propagation of a signal down a lossless line is $V_p = 1/\sqrt{(LC)}$ (note that the units of V_p are in unit lengths/s). For the same line constants then $V_p = 2 \times 10^5$ km/s $= 2 \times 10^8$ m/s. Clearly, the value of V_p depends on the electrical properties of the cable, which in turn depend on the cable material.

The attenuation factor of an ideal lossless cable is, by definition, zero. However, for practical cables it is not zero, but its effect on pulse distortion can be ignored above the frequency at which we can legitimately ignore R and G. As a rule of thumb a term may be ignored if it is only 10% of the dominant term, in this case when both $\omega L \geq 10R$ and $\omega C \geq 10G$, i.e. for our example cable when $\omega \geq 4 \times 10^6$ rad/s.

4.2.3 Distortionless line

At low frequencies the effects of resistance and conductance cannot be neglected, but there is still a way to make the characteristic impedance independent of frequency. Rearranging the equation for Z_o

$$Z_o = \sqrt{\frac{R + j\omega L}{G + j\omega C}}$$

$$= \sqrt{\frac{R(1 + j\omega L / R)}{G(1 + j\omega C / G)}}$$

If $\dfrac{L}{R} = \dfrac{C}{G}$ then the terms in brackets will cancel leaving

$$Z_o = \sqrt{\frac{R}{G}} \quad \Omega \tag{4.6}$$

To make the identity $L/R = C/G$ true for typical cables, e.g. our example cable, then either L or G can be increased (decreasing line constants is not an option). Increasing the leakage conductance can be expected to increase the attenuation and so is undesirable. Hence the only remaining option to make the identity true is to increase L to the new value

$$L_d = \frac{CR}{G} \tag{4.7}$$

For the given line constants this would require $L_d = 1$ H/km. In general $L_d - L$ H/unit length need to be added, but in this case the existing cable inductance of 0.25 mH/km can be ignored as it is small compared to L_d.

This extra inductance is usually added as a lumped component, e.g. a 1 H inductor may be inserted every kilometre in the cable, or a 0.5 H inductor every

500 m, etc. In principle, if the extra inductance could be added in a distributed fashion, and the line constants did not vary with frequency, the characteristic impedance would remain constant for all frequencies. Unfortunately, no one has yet found a method of doing this; even the so-called continuous loading, where a wire of high permeability material is wound around the cable, only works up to a few kHz.

Returning to the lumped loading case it will be shown in the next section that the velocity of propagation (V_p) is given by the same formula as for the lossless line (but noting that L_d rather than L is the appropriate constant to use), i.e.

$$V_p = \frac{1}{\sqrt{(L_d C)}} \qquad (4.8)$$

Hence, for our example cable $V_p = 3.16 \times 10^3$ km/s $= 3.16 \times 10^6$ m/s. This is only approximately 1% of the velocity of propagation in free space: i.e. the lumped inductance has significantly slowed the velocity of propagation. This is a drawback as a round trip delay of half a second corresponds to a distance of only 790 km, and a half second delay is about the maximum tolerable on a voice circuit.

The effect of adding the inductance as a lumped component is that the cable will have a high frequency cut-off, near which the attenuation will rise steeply. The high frequency cut-off occurs at the resonant frequency of the line which depends on the spacing *(d)* between lumped inductors. Continuing with the previous example, say 0.5 H of extra inductance is added every 500 m and using the symbols L_c and C_c for the inductance and capacitance per length $d = 500$ m, then $L_c = 0.5 + Ld / n = L_d d / n$ and $C_c = Cd / n$ (where n is the number of metres per unit length, 1000 in this example), see figure 4.8. The following method to find the resonant frequency of the cable is intuitive and needs bootstrapping (by assuming part of the answer to begin with) in order to start the process going. For a more algebraic approach see Glazier [GLA]; this has the benefit of enabling the impedance to be calculated at any frequency, but the derivation is longer.

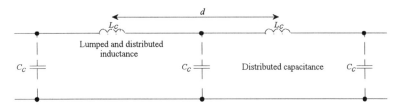

Figure 4.8 Lumped inductors in a cable

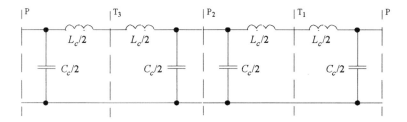

Figure 4.9 Half sections of lossless transmission line

Consider an infinite length cable divided into half sections as in figure 4.9. At resonance, let the impedance looking in each direction from the mid-series inductor points T_n be zero, i.e. a short circuit. This is called an image imped-ance because, although physically there is no wire link creating the short circuit, we will show that there is an apparent short circuit. Then to the left of point T_1 there is effectively a parallel combination of capacitor $C_c/2$ and inductor $L_c/2$. These resonate at a frequency

$$\omega_o = \frac{2}{\sqrt{(L_c C_c)}} \quad \text{rad/s}$$

and at the resonant frequency the impedance is infinite, i.e. the impedance looking in each direction from the mid-shunt capacitor point P_2 is infinite; this is also an image impedance. Thus to the right of point T_3 there is a series combination of inductor $L_c/2$ and capacitor $C_c/2$. This resonates at the same resonate frequency ω_o, but for a series combination the impedance at the resonant frequency is zero; hence the impedance at point T_3 is zero. For an infinite line this will apply to all other points T_n, confirming our original choice of zero for point T_1, and similarly the impedance at all points P_n will be infinite at resonance. The resonant frequency of the line is therefore confirmed as

$$\omega_o = \frac{2}{\sqrt{(L_c C_c)}} \quad \text{rad/s} \tag{4.9}$$

or, substituting for C_c and L_c

$$\omega_o = \frac{2n}{d\sqrt{(L_d C)}} = \frac{2V_p}{d} \quad \text{rad/s} \tag{4.10}$$

Where V_p is in units of m/s and the cut-off frequency is inversely proportional to d. Hence, for our example,

$$\omega_o = 12.6 \times 10^3 \quad \text{rad/s, or} \quad f_o = 2.01 \text{ kHz}$$

The wavelength at the cut-off frequency can be found from

$$\lambda_o = \frac{V_p}{f_o}$$

hence $\lambda_o = \pi d/n$ in unit lengths, or $\lambda_o = \pi d$ in m   (4.11)
which, for the case being considered, gives $\lambda_o = 1571$ m. Note that the
reduction in bandwidth makes such a distortionless line unsuitable for high
speed digital signals (as shown in chapter 3, channel capacity C is proportional
to bandwidth). For digital signals distortion is removed when the signal is
regenerated, hence the unloaded line is a far better channel.

In the next section the attenuation of a distortionless line is shown to be
$20\sqrt{(RG)}\,\log_{10}(e)$ dB per unit length of line. Using the same line constants as
before, the cable attenuation works out to be 0.275 dB/km.

Finally, putting together all the points considered in this section on the
distortionless transmission line, figure 4.10 shows an attenuation versus
frequency characteristic (using the numerical answers already calculated where
appropriate). In this case the addition of lumped inductors of 0.5 H every 500 m
has made the channel suitable for an analogue signal in the frequency range 0
to 2 kHz.

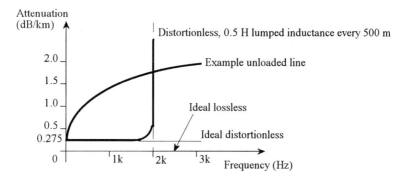

Figure 4.10 Attenuation versus frequency characteristic

4.2.4 Propagation coefficient

In this section we derive the results used before in the lossless and distortionless
line cases, i.e. that, in both cases, the velocity of propagation $V_p = 1/\sqrt{(LC)}$ and
that, for the distortionless line case, the attenuation per unit length of line is

$$20\sqrt{(RG)}\,\log_{10}(e)\ \text{dB}$$

The key to determining these relationships is the propagation coefficient,
usually represented by γ. The propagation coefficient is in general complex with
real part α, which is the attenuation (in units of neper per unit length), and
imaginary part β, which is the phase shift per unit length of line. This section

may be skipped at a first reading, if the reader is prepared to take these results on trust.

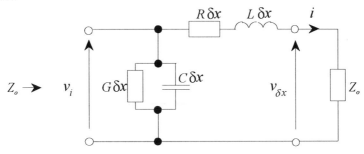

Figure 4.11 Small length of cable δx

Considering figure 4.11 for an input voltage v_i and line current i then the voltage $v_{\delta x}$ after a small length δx of line is $v_{\delta x} = iZ_o$; similarly

$$v_i = i\left(Z_o + R\delta x + j\omega L\delta x\right)$$

Hence

$$\frac{v_i}{v_{\delta x}} = 1 + \left(\frac{R + j\omega L}{Z_o}\right)\delta x$$

and substituting for Z_o gives

$$\frac{v_i}{v_{\delta x}} = 1 + \sqrt{(R + j\omega L)(G + j\omega C)} \times \delta x = 1 + \gamma\delta x \qquad (4.12)$$

where γ is the propagation coefficient $\sqrt{(R + j\omega L)(G + j\omega C)}$. For a longer length x there will be $x/\delta x$ elements in the line and v_i/v_x can be found by multiplying the elements together, i.e.

$$\frac{v_i}{v_x} = \left(1 + \gamma\delta x\right)^{x/\delta x}$$

Expanding by the binomial theorem

$$\frac{v_i}{v_x} = 1 + \gamma x + \frac{x}{\delta x}\left(\frac{x}{\delta x} - 1\right)\frac{\gamma^2\delta x^2}{2!} + \dots$$

In the limit as $\delta x \to 0$

$$\frac{v_i}{v_x} = 1 + \gamma x + \frac{\gamma^2 x^2}{2!} + \dots$$

By the definition of the exponential function, this is equivalent to

$$\frac{v_i}{v_x} = e^{\gamma x}$$

Rearranging and substituting for real and imaginary parts gives

$$v_x = v_i \, e^{-\alpha x} e^{-j\beta x} \tag{4.13}$$

with magnitude $|v_x| = |v_i|e^{-\alpha x}$ (4.14)

and phase $\angle v_x = \angle v_i - \beta x$ rad (4.15)

Hence the gain is $e^{-\alpha}$ per unit length, i.e. the amplitude decreases exponentially along the line. Taking natural logarithms of equation 4.14,

$$\log_e(v_x / v_i) = \ln(v_x / v_i) = -\alpha x \qquad \text{neper}$$

where α is defined as the attenuation in units of neper per unit length. In the more familiar decibel form the gain is

$$20 \, \log_{10}(v_x / v_i) = -20\alpha x \log_{10}(e) = -8.686\alpha x \qquad \text{dB} \tag{4.16}$$

The coefficient β determines the phase shift of the signal. Separating out α and β can be complicated, but there are two special cases where they can be found easily: the lossless line and the distortionless line cases again. For the lossless line $R = G = 0$ and we expect no attenuation of the signal along the line. Substituting $R = G = 0$ into equation 4.12 gives

$$\gamma = j\omega\sqrt{(LC)} \tag{4.17}$$

The attenuation is 0 dB as expected and $\beta = \omega\sqrt{LC}$. For the distortionless line the expression for the propagation coefficient (equation 4.12 again) can be rearranged as

$$\gamma = \sqrt{R(1 + j\omega[L/R]).G(1 + j\omega[C/G])}$$

But for such a line $L/R = C/G$. Hence

$$\gamma = \sqrt{(RG)} + j\omega\sqrt{(LC)} \tag{4.18}$$

Equating γ to $\alpha + j\beta$ gives $\alpha = \sqrt{(RG)}$ and $\beta = \omega\sqrt{(LC)}$. Note the expression for β is the same as for the lossless case (except that L is here defined by $L = CR/G$, i.e. L_d in the notation used in section 4.2.3). From equation 4.16 the attenuation is

$$A = 20 \sqrt{(RG)} \times \log_{10}(e) \qquad \text{dB per unit length of line} \tag{4.19}$$

Considering the phase shift relative to the input signal, from equation 4.15

$$\angle v_x = -\beta x \qquad \text{rad}$$

The wavelength (λ) can be found from this, since β is simply the phase shift per unit length of line and by definition one wavelength corresponds to 2π radians, i.e. $\qquad \beta\lambda = 2\pi \text{ or } \beta = \dfrac{2\pi}{\lambda}$ $\qquad\qquad\qquad$ (4.20)

Since for both the lossless and distortionless cases $\beta = \omega\sqrt{(LC)}$ the wavelength in both cases can be found from

$$\lambda = \frac{2\pi}{\beta} = \frac{1}{f\sqrt{LC}}$$ $\qquad\qquad$ (4.21)

The velocity of propagation (V_p) of the waves is given by $V_p = \lambda f$. Hence, for both the lossless and distortionless cases,

$$V_p = \frac{1}{\sqrt{(LC)}}$$ $\qquad\qquad$ (4.22)

Note that this is independent of frequency. The lossless and distortionless cases are special cases, albeit important ones. In general, the attenuation and velocity of propagation of a signal travelling down a transmission line will vary with frequency. Any signal, except a steady state sine wave, will then become distorted since different frequency components will travel at different velocities, become dispersed, and suffer different attenuation. This is the dispersive case and in such a case the velocity of propagation only has meaning when considering a steady state sine wave.

Unfortunately, although the sine wave will not be distorted it cannot carry any information since it is eternal. The presence of the sine wave can be predicted with certainty, so physically detecting the sine wave does not add anything to our knowledge. Also note that dispersion is distinct from attenuation, in that dispersion implies that the different signal components are 'scattered', but not dissipated.

For real signals (i.e. those which start and finish at some point in time) the simple velocity of propagation is inappropriate and instead the group velocity V_g is used. This is the velocity of propagation of the *envelope* of a group of sine waves, all at nearly the same frequency, see figure 4.12. From equation 4.21 an alternative expression for the velocity of propagation is

$$V_p = \frac{\omega}{\beta} \qquad \text{m/s}$$ $\qquad\qquad$ (4.23)

This is called the phase velocity. The group velocity is similar, being given as

$$V_g = \frac{\delta\omega}{\delta\beta} \qquad \text{m/s}$$ $\qquad\qquad$ (4.24)

i.e. the group velocity is the instantaneous slope of the graph of ω against β. The envelope will not be distorted if the group velocity is constant, the significance of this is that the envelope is the signal. For both the lossless and distortionless cases the phase characteristic is linear (i.e. the phase shift is proportional to frequency) so the slope of the graph of ω against β is a constant ω/β. Hence in these cases the group velocity is the same as the phase velocity which is why no distortion of the envelope occurs.

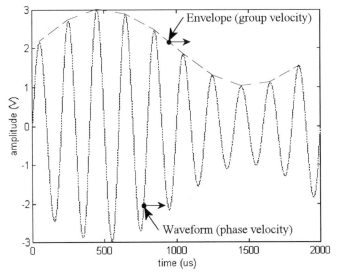

Figure 4.12 Group and phase velocities

4.3 Reflections

It was stated in section 4.1.2 that if cables and connectors do not have the same characteristic impedance, or the cable is not terminated in its matched load, signal reflections will occur which may interfere with the correct operation of the system. We investigate this effect in this section.

Consider figure 4.13, where subscript i refers to the incident voltage and current, subscript r refers to reflected signals, subscript L to signals dissipated in the load and A is taken as the point where any reflection occurs.

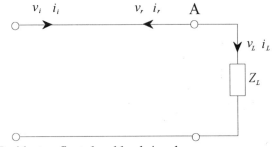

Figure 4.13 Incident, reflected and load signals

For a cable with characteristic (or 'surge') impedance Z_o, a signal travelling down the cable will 'see' this impedance (it cannot anticipate the load). Hence

$$\frac{v_i}{i_i} = Z_o \qquad (4.25)$$

$$\frac{v_r}{-i_r} = Z_o \qquad (4.26)$$

The minus sign for the reflected wave is because the reflected current always has the opposite sign to the reflected voltage. Similarly, for that part of the signal transferred to the load,

$$\frac{v_L}{i_L} = Z_L \qquad (4.27)$$

Considering the point A, the voltages and currents to left and right must balance. Hence

$$v_i + v_r = v_L \qquad (4.28)$$

$$i_i + i_r = i_L \qquad (4.29)$$

Substituting equations 4.25 to 4.27 into equation 4.29

$$\frac{v_i}{Z_o} - \frac{v_r}{Z_o} = \frac{v_L}{Z_L}$$

Eliminating v_L by using equation 4.28 gives

$$\frac{v_i - v_r}{Z_o} = \frac{v_i + v_r}{Z_L}$$

Collecting terms and rearranging

$$\frac{v_r}{v_i} = \frac{Z_L - Z_o}{Z_L + Z_o} = \rho \qquad (4.30)$$

where ρ is the voltage-reflection factor. Similarly, since from equations 4.25 and 4.26

$$\frac{i_r}{i_i} = -\frac{v_r}{v_i}$$

the current-reflection factor is

$$\frac{i_r}{i_i} = \frac{Z_o - Z_L}{Z_o + Z_L} \qquad (4.31)$$

For a lossless cable, taking decibels of the magnitude of the voltage-reflection factor gives the return loss, which is simply the attenuation of the reflected signal compared to the transmitted signal.

$$\text{Return loss} = 20 \log_{10} \left| \frac{Z_L - Z_o}{Z_L + Z_o} \right| \quad \text{dB}$$

There are three special cases: a matched load, an open circuit and a short circuit.

(i) *Matched load case*, i.e. $Z_L = Z_o$. From equations 4.30 and 4.31, v_r and i_r both equal zero (i.e. there are no reflections as expected for the matched load case). Since there are no reflections, all the energy of any signal which reaches the load must be dissipated in the load.

(ii) *Open circuit case*, i.e. $Z_L = \infty$. From equations 4.30 and 4.31

$$\frac{v_r}{v_i} = \frac{Z_L}{Z_L} = 1 \quad \text{and} \quad \frac{i_r}{i_i} = \frac{-Z_L}{Z_L} = -1$$

Hence $v_r = v_i$ and $i_r = -i_i$. At point A, as expected, $i_L = 0$ from equation 4.29 (current through an infinite impedance is zero), but note that $v_L = 2v_i$ from equation 4.28. To understand what this means consider a voltage pulse, of 5 V amplitude and 10 ns duration, as the incident signal travelling from left to right down a cable, as in figure 4.14. As previously determined, after being reflected the voltage signal will have the same amplitude but will be travelling from right to left; but when the signal is actually being reflected from the open circuit both incident and reflected pulses will be coincident and hence the voltage is the sum of the incident and reflected signals.

(iii) *Short circuit case*, i.e. $Z_L = 0$. From equations 4.30 and 4.31 $v_r = -v_i$ and $i_r = i_i$. At point A as expected for a short circuit $v_L = 0$ from equation 4.28; but note that no energy can be dissipated in an ideal short circuit (since the voltage across a short circuit is zero) and hence again the signal will be reflected. The difference to the open circuit case is that for the short circuit case the reflected voltage is of opposite sign to the incident voltage. Loosely, the voltage signal carries on through the short circuit and back along the return wire; but since it is now on the opposite wire it appears inverted.

From the maximum power transfer theorem and from the considerations above it is clear that the source, load and characteristic impedances of a transmission line should be the same in order to transfer the maximum power from the source to the load.

Consider an example of a more general case, where part of the signal is reflected and part dissipated, with a 100 Ω load impedance terminating a 50 m length of cable of characteristic impedance 50 Ω, as in figure 4.15. A step voltage of +15 V is applied from a generator with internal impedance 25 Ω. The cable is therefore mismatched at both source and load: the load impedance

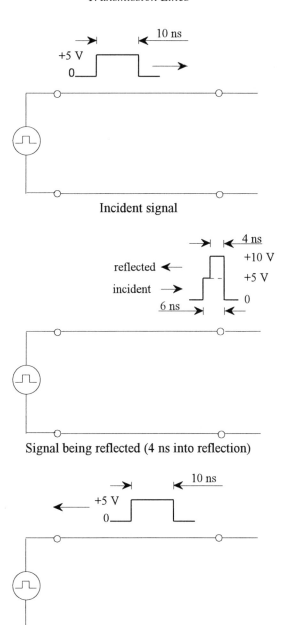

Figure 4.14 Incident and reflected pulses

being too high (so we expect a voltage reflection of the same sign as the incident signal) and the source impedance being too low (so we expect a voltage reflection of opposite sign). After steady state conditions have been reached, i.e. for d.c., the output voltage V_o can be found from voltage divider theory as

$$V_o = \frac{100}{100+25} \times 15 = 12 \text{ V}$$

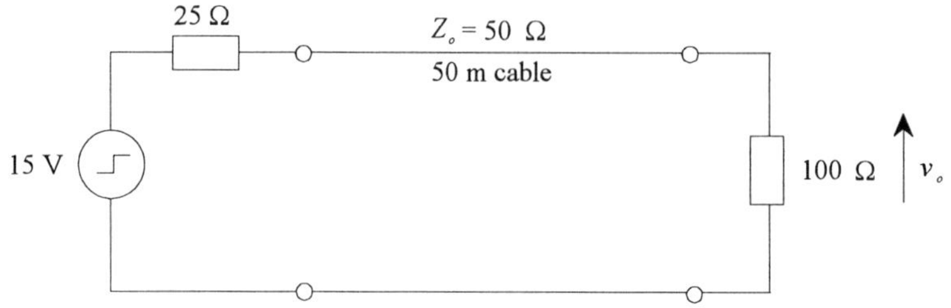

Figure 4.15 Mismatched cable

We want to investigate the transient response of this step waveform. The initial step launched into the 50 Ω cable will be

$$v_s = \frac{50}{50+25} \times 15 = 10 \text{ V}$$

The voltage-reflection ratio at the load will be $\rho_L = \dfrac{v_r}{v_i} = \dfrac{100-50}{100+50} = \dfrac{1}{3}$

Similarly, the source voltage-reflection ratio is $\rho_s = \dfrac{v_r}{v_i} = \dfrac{25-50}{25+50} = -\dfrac{1}{3}$

The 10 V step reaches the load and a signal of amplitude 10/3 V is reflected. Since the reflection is the same sign as the incident signal, the amplitude at the load is now $v_o = 10(1 + 1/3)$ V, see figure 4.16. When the reflected signal of 10/3 V reaches the source a signal of amplitude $(-1/3)(10/3) = -10/9$ is reflected back to the load. When this signal reaches the load it too will be partly reflected, the reflected signal being $(1/3)(-10/9)$ and the amplitude at the load is now

$$v_o = 10\left(1+\frac{1}{3}\right) - \frac{10}{9}\left(1+\frac{1}{3}\right) = 10\left(1+\frac{1}{3}\right)\left\{1-\frac{1}{9}\right\}$$

The signal continues to build up in this way, so the load amplitude becomes

$$v_o = 10\left(1+\frac{1}{3}\right)\left\{1-\frac{1}{9}+\frac{1}{9^2}-\frac{1}{9^3}+\ \cdots\right.$$

Substituting for the standard result for the sum of a geometric series

$$\frac{1}{1-r} = 1+r+r^2+r^3+\cdots \qquad\qquad (|r|<1)$$

gives $V_o = 10\left(1+\frac{1}{3}\right)\left\{\frac{1}{1+1/9}\right\} = 12$ V

The final result (in the limit as $t \to \infty$) of this method gives the same answer as the voltage divider equation, but this method also shows how the voltage builds up to the steady state value. The general result can be derived in exactly the same way, i.e.

$$V_o = V_s(1+\rho_L)\left\{\frac{1}{1-\rho_L\rho_s}\right\} \qquad\qquad (4.32)$$

where V_s is the amplitude of the initial voltage step and ρ_L, ρ_s are the voltage reflection coefficients at the load and source.

We can now define when a connection needs to be considered as a transmission line as opposed to when it can be considered as providing a simple electrical connection between two points. All practical signals have a non-zero rise-time (where the rise-time t_r is defined as the time it takes for the signal amplitude to go from 10% to 90% of its final value). If the time taken for a signal to propagate down a link is t_p the first reflection will arrive back at the source after $2t_p$ seconds. If this time is greater than the rise-time then the connection acts as a transmission line, i.e. say $2t_p > t_r/5$ to give some margin [TEX]. For example, taking the velocity of propagation of a signal on a Printed Circuit Board (PCB) as 2×10^8 m/s (it may well be slower than this due to capacitive loading), the maximum track length for which transmission line theory can be ignored for signals with rise-times of 15 ns is 30 cm. Hence a circuit which works well with a relatively slow Integrated Circuit (IC) technology may not work (because of the effect of signal reflections) if faster ICs are substituted (as t_r is reduced but $2t_p$ remains constant).

Figure 4.17 shows the result of an experiment where a 2 V pulse of duration 100 ns is sent down a 75 Ω cable of length 50 m. The top trace shows the voltage at the source, the lower trace the voltage at the load. The load is open circuit and, as expected, the pulse voltage at the load is double the incident pulse amplitude. The top trace allows us to calculate the velocity of propagation (i.e. the speed of light in this cable), since the time for the pulse to travel down and back the cable is 0.5 µs, i.e.

$$V_p = \frac{d}{t} = 2\times10^8 \quad \text{m/s}$$

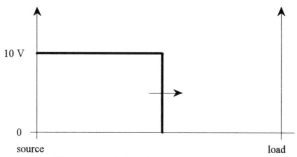

Initial 10 V step travelling towards load

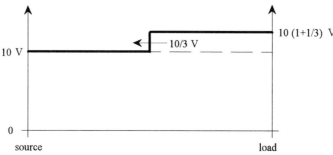

Reflection at load of 10/3 V

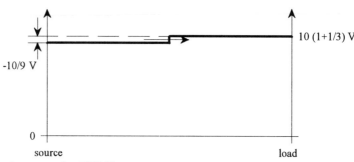

Reflection at source of – 10/9 V

Figure 4.16 Reflections with mismatched cable

This technique is used as the basis of an item of test equipment called a Time Domain Reflectometer (TDR). In this case the velocity of propagation in the cable is already known and hence the distance to a discontinuity can be calculated. A typical application would be using a TDR to find the location of a fault (i.e. a discontinuity) in an Ethernet LAN cable.

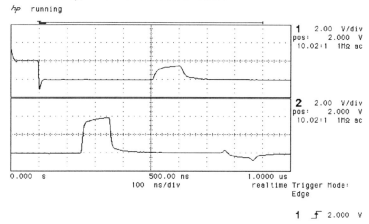

Figure 4.17 Experimental result for pulse propagation

Practical considerations
A problem sometimes met when developing or testing systems is that the test equipment has a 50 Ω impedance when the system under test is a 75 Ω system, or vice versa. A minimum loss pad can be used to interface between the two domains of impedance. This is a two resistor network that matches (both ways) with the minimum attenuation possible, see figure 4.18. If more loss is needed then a T or π network can be used, see figure 4.19. A T or π network can also be used as an attenuator section with the same characteristic impedance at both ends.

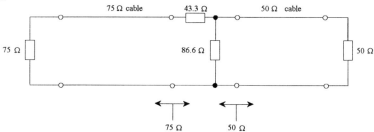

Figure 4.18 Minimum loss pad

Figure 4.19 T and π networks

4.3.1 PCB layout

The previous sections have concentrated on theory; this section, however, looks at the practical aspects of component layout to avoid problems caused by reflections and noise. Correctly laying out high frequency digital circuits is more of an art than a science, which means the theory of this chapter and the next on propagation has to be understood almost at an instinctive level. For many people, the first time they need to apply the theory will be when they have to design a Printed Circuit Board (PCB): this section aims to help them do that and demonstrate the importance of the theory. For example, tracks for clocks and data at 100 Mbps or more must be treated as transmission lines. Ideally, for a double sided PCB, the tracks should be of constant width on the top surface with a continuous ground plane on the other side – thus making a micro-strip transmission line. Bends should be gradual, i.e. right angles should be avoided, though unfortunately many PCB layout packages for low frequency circuits only allow right angle bends.

Each transmission line should be terminated by a matched load. The connecting tracks between components or IC pins should run as a single line (or bus) snaking past all the necessary connection points, rather than branching off (i.e. all branches from the main line should be kept as short as possible). This is because any branch line which is too long must also be treated as a transmission line and be correctly terminated. The line driver has to be capable of delivering a signal into all the loads; hence, to reduce the source power requirement, branch lines should be short and unterminated.

The characteristic impedance of the track will depend on its physical dimensions and the thickness and composition of the dielectric material, whilst the velocity of propagation depends only on the material. At high frequencies the load presented by an IC connection is principally capacitive. The more IC connections there are, the lower the characteristic impedance and the lower the velocity of propagation. Component leads on the other hand appear inductive, so they too should be as short as possible to minimize reflections.

The best termination for a PCB track is a series combination of a resistor and capacitor, between the last IC pin from the driver and earth, see figure 4.20 (a). This parallel a.c. termination causes no d.c. power drain. An alternative is to have two resistors connected to the IC pin, one going to earth and one to the power supply rail – see figure 4.20 (b); but this push-up/pull-down termination does cause a d.c. power drain. If branches cannot be avoided, it is better to terminate the line at source – with a single, series damping resistor (typically from 10 Ω to 75 Ω) between the line driver output and the line, see figure 4.20 (c), rather than have multiple terminations. Reflections will occur because the branches are not terminated, but they will be absorbed by the source. However, the possibility of incorrect logic operation during the time taken for the line to settle down must be taken into account (consider what will happen to a step voltage with an open circuit load).

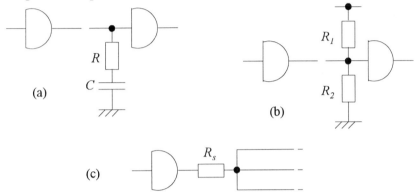

Figure 4.20 Terminations for PCB tracks

Often it is not possible with a double sided PCB to reserve one side solely for a ground plane. The alternatives are: 1) to use a multi-layer board; or 2) to set up a grid of power and earth lines to all the ICs on the PCB. It is conventional with digital circuits to set out the ICs in rows, with the earth and power tracks running parallel to each other and lengthwise under the ICs, on the other side of the board to the ICs. On a high frequency PCB, each IC will have a high performance decoupling capacitor of, say, 100 nF placed adjacent to it. This connects between the power rail and earth so that the power rail appears as a signal earth. These rails are connected together by tracks (on the same side as the ICs) running orthogonally to the rows. Arranging for these connections to be alternately power and earth, with approximately the same spacing as between the rows, results in a signal earth grid being set up. The grid spacing depends on the frequency, the higher the frequency the smaller the grid needed, e.g. for a 100 Mbps signal a grid spacing of two inches is possibly adequate whilst at microwave frequencies a ground plane is essential.

At high frequencies it is essential that all signal wires are treated as transmission lines, so coaxial cable or twisted pair should be used to bring signals and clocks on or off the board. Twisted pair is capable of working at 100 Mbps if the rules laid down for category 5 wiring are followed.

The situation is complicated if an analogue signal is present on the same PCB, a typical case being when using a high speed Analogue to Digital

Converter (ADC), as the design rules for earth connections for analogue signals are completely different. For analogue signals earth loops must be avoided, as a loop acts as an aerial and picks up noise (if a mains frequency 'hum' is heard on a hi-fi set an earth loop is a possible cause); instead, the analogue earths must be wired so that there is a single earth point to which all earths are connected by just one possible path (i.e. as in a tree topology). To enable common-mode noise to be rejected, it is important that the signal connection is accompanied as closely as possible by an earth wire, i.e. from where the signal arrives on the board an earth track should shadow it, this earth providing the earth return for any analogue ICs (making sure that the power rail does not create a signal earth loop). The analogue earths and digital earths should be kept separate, thus with an ADC they should only be joined where the signal changes from analogue to digital, i.e. at the ADC IC. Even with these pre-cautions it is difficult to prevent noise from the high amplitude, high frequency digital part of the circuit being radiated and picked up by the sensitive analogue circuitry (a shielded box may ultimately be necessary for either the analogue or digital part of the circuit).

If you need to make a high frequency PCB circuit find a good example of standard practice in your organization and base the design on that.

Exercises

(1)   State the differences between: a) unipolar signals; b) bipolar signals; c) differential; d) balanced mode signals.

(2)   Briefly explain the noise performance advantage of differential trans-mission compared to unipolar signalling.

(3)   State the number of wires required for six data circuits using:
 a) differential signals; b) unipolar signals with a common ground return.

(4)   State alternative ways for an analogue signal to be sent over a communication link without suffering distortion, assuming that the link is not distortionless to begin with.

(5)   State whether the characteristic impedance of a transmission line varies with the following parameters: a) line length; b) signal amplitude; c) signal frequency.

(6)   a) What is the correct terminating impedance for a line with a character-istic impedance of 120 Ω?

b) Determine the diameter of a copper wire with a resistance of 100 Ω/km, given that the resistivity of the copper is 1.7241×10^{-8} Ωm.

(7) Briefly explain why it is necessary for a high bit rate data communication link to be correctly terminated and why this is not important at low data rates. State a criterion to distinguish between low and high data rates in this context.

(8) Explain what is generally understood by 'lossless transmission line'.

(9) Explain what is generally understood by 'distortionless transmission line'. Show that the condition for distortionless transmission is given by $LG - RC$, where L, G, R and C are the primary line constants.

(10) The primary line constants of a particular type of twisted pair cable are $R = 200$ Ω/km, $L = 0.5$ mH/km, $G = 50$ μS/km and $C = 50$ nF/km. Determine the frequency above which this cable can be treated as 'lossless'. Calculate for this case: a) the cable's characteristic impedance; b) the velocity of propagation in the cable.

(11) The same cable type as in question (10) is required to be used as a distortionless transmission line for analogue transmission at a lower frequency than that found in question (10). Determine how this can be achieved, assuming that access to the cable can be gained every two kilometres. Calculate for this case: a) the cable's characteristic impedance; b) the velocity of propagation in the cable; c) the resonant frequency of the line; d) the attenuation in dB/km.

(12) Sketch a graph and briefly explain the attenuation versus frequency characteristics of the following types of cable: a) ideal lossless; b) ideal distortionless; c) realistic distortionless; d) the line of part c) without lumped inductors.

(13) Explain the advantages and disadvantages of a line made 'distortionless' by adding lumped inductors for: a) analogue signals; b) digital signals.

(14) A cable is to be installed between a radio station and a radio transmitting antenna 12 km away. The cable has the following primary line constants: a) $R = 100$ Ω/km; b) $L = 5$ mH/km; c) $G = 100$ μS/km; d) $C = 50$ nF/km. The signal to be transmitted is an analogue, high-fidelity (hi-fi), mono sound signal with a bandwidth from 50 Hz to 15 kHz. Calculate the lumped inductance required for a distortionless transmission line at the maximum spacing between lumped inductances.

(15) Briefly describe what happens when a line is terminated by: a) an open circuit; b) a matched load; c) a short circuit.

(16) Calculate the voltage reflection coefficient at the load for a cable with characteristic impedance 100 Ω when terminated by a 50 Ω resistance. Hence calculate the amplitude of the first reflected voltage, for a 12 V forward voltage travelling down the cable.

(17) Calculate the first reflected current for question (16).

(18) Calculate the characteristic impedance for a lossless transmission line with primary line constants $L = 0.1675$ μH/m and $C = 67$ pF/m. Briefly describe what happens when a +10 V pulse is generated by a source and applied to the line when it is terminated in: a) 100 Ω; b) 50 Ω; c) 10 Ω. The source impedance is a matched load.

(19) Calculate the forward and reverse attenuation in dB of the minimum loss pad required to match a 50 Ω cable to a 75 Ω cable.

(20) Considering figure 4.21, given that the terminating resistance is 27 Ω, the cable length is 50 m and assuming a lossless cable, determine:
    (i)   the characteristic impedance of the line;
    (ii)   the velocity of propagation.
    (iii) the source impedance;
    (iv) the capacitance and inductance per m.

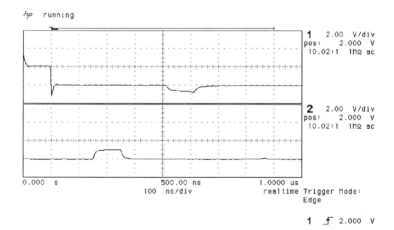

Figure 4.21 Pulse reflection experiment

(21) Compile a list of the more important equations used in this chapter.

(22) Write your own summary of what you have learnt in this chapter.

5 Propagation

In chapter 4 the treatment mainly concerned signals as voltages and currents, with voltage and current related by the circuit impedance. But associated with a current there is a magnetic field (e.g. consider an inductor) and associated with a voltage there is an electric field (as in a capacitor). It is therefore equally appropriate to consider a signal as consisting of magnetic and electric fields.

Whilst a steady state electric field can exist without a magnetic field, a changing electric field will generate a magnetic field (and vice versa). Since a signal must change to convey any information, an electrical signal has both electric and magnetic time-varying fields; such signals are called electro-magnetic waves.

5.1 Electromagnetic spectrum and light

The concept of electromagnetic waves is appropriate for the transmission of signals in free space and for certain types of transmission line (e.g. wave guides). The theory of electromagnetic waves was developed by James Clerk Maxwell (1831-79), a Scottish physicist, who worked in many areas of physics but whose greatest achievement was to unify electricity and magnetism.

At Cambridge University Maxwell had a bad reputation as a lecturer; his lectures were beyond most people, so he often ended up with a class of just three or four students. However, the brighter students (amongst whom was J. J. Thomson, the discoverer of the electron) were inspired by his lectures, so it cannot really be said that he was a bad lecturer. Between 1864-73 he developed his theory, which not only showed that electricity and magnetism were two aspects of the same force, but predicted the existence of electromagnetic radiation at frequencies other than visible light.

The theory today is based on just four equations, called Maxwell's equations, that determine the relationship between electric and magnetic fields. It is beyond the scope of this book to derive and explain these equations – the interested reader is recommended to study Bleaney and Bleaney [BLE] or Glazier [GLA]. However, we do need to consider the results. The velocity of such waves in free space is

$$c = \frac{1}{\sqrt{(\mu_o \varepsilon_o)}} \tag{5.1}$$

where μ_o (the Greek alphabet is given in appendix A) is the permeability of free space and is defined to be $4\pi \times 10^{-7}$ H/m, whilst ε_o is the permittivity of free space and was experimentally found to be 8.8547×10^{-12} F/m. The velocity of propagation of radio waves was hence found to be 3.0×10^{-8} m/s. It is not a coincidence that this is the same as the velocity of light, since light is an electromagnetic wave in a particular frequency range (the frequency range of visible light is from approximately 4.3×10^{14} to 7.5×10^{14} Hz). Nowadays, the velocity of light is defined to be 299 792 458 m/s and both the metre and ε_o are derived from this.

The reader may wonder why μ_o is defined as $4\pi \times 10^{-7}$ H/m, whereas the value for ε_o was found experimentally – this is explained in appendix B on units.

Radio waves, microwaves, infra-red light, visible light, ultra-violet light, x-rays and γ rays are all forms of electromagnetic waves, as is light. The range of such signals is called the electromagnetic spectrum, see figure 5.1, and for all such waves in free space the wavelength λ is related to the frequency f by

$$\lambda = \frac{c}{f}$$

A principle, or general law, of modern physics is that the speed of light in free space (c) is a constant. A consequence of this, from Einstein's special theory of relativity, is that signals cannot travel faster than the speed of light, i.e. in a material medium the velocity of propagation $V_p < c$.

Albert Einstein (1879-1955) was the greatest scientist of the twentieth century but he did not show great promise at school. When asked what profession Einstein should follow his headmaster reportedly replied 'It doesn't matter; he'll never make a success of anything'.

A minor change to equation 5.1 gives the velocity of propagation in a lossless material medium as

$$V_p = \frac{1}{\sqrt{(\mu\varepsilon)}} \qquad (5.2)$$

where μ is the permeability of the medium and ε is the permittivity. By definition $\mu = \mu_r\mu_o$ and $\varepsilon = \varepsilon_r\varepsilon_o$, where μ_r and ε_r are relative values (relative to the values for free space) and μ_o and ε_o are the values for free space. Another name for the relative permittivity ε_r is the dielectric constant, as capacitance is proportional to the relative permittivity of the dielectric material between the plates of the capacitor. Hence

$$V_p = \frac{c}{\sqrt{(\mu_r\varepsilon_r)}} \qquad (5.3)$$

where μ_r and $\varepsilon_r = 1$ for free space and μ_r and ε_r are both >1 for a material medium. In optics the velocity of light in a material of refractive index n is

$$V_p = \frac{c}{n} \qquad (5.4)$$

Hence $n = \sqrt{(\mu_r \varepsilon_r)}$, or for non-magnetic materials where $\mu_r \cong 1$ then $n \cong \sqrt{\varepsilon_r}$. The relative permittivity changes with frequency, so this expression is only valid if n and ε_r are measured at the same frequency.

Again, from Maxwell's equations, the characteristic impedance of a lossless medium is found to be

$$Z_o = \sqrt{\frac{\mu}{\varepsilon}} \qquad (5.5)$$

and for free space

$$Z_o = \sqrt{\frac{\mu_o}{\varepsilon_o}} = 377 \; \Omega$$

i.e. free space can be treated as a transmission line with a characteristic impedance of 377 Ω. Considering equations 4.22 and 4.5,

$$V_p = \frac{1}{\sqrt{(LC)}}$$

$$Z_o = \sqrt{\frac{L}{C}}$$

Clearly the inductance L per unit length and capacitance C per unit length have the same role in lumped systems as the permeability μ and permittivity ε in distributed systems.

Theories of light
The classical theory of light is the wave theory. This fully explains certain phenomena, such as refraction, diffraction and interference [see e.g. WHE] and is an assumption in the derivation of Maxwell's equations. This is the only theory needed to support the ideas put forward in this chapter, but it is only part of the story.

A wave is a disturbance propagating in some medium. Since a vacuum, by definition, is the absence of a medium, the first problem the wave theory has to face is: how can a wave propagate in a vacuum? The problem was solved by noting that for an electromagnetic wave both the electric and magnetic fields must exist, so it is supposed that they are self-supporting; i.e. the electric field is the medium in which the magnetic wave propagates and the magnetic field is the medium in which the electric wave propagates. The electric and magnetic fields are at right angles to each other and to the direction of travel, see figure 5.2. Such a wave is called a Transverse Electro-Magnetic wave (or TEM wave) because the direction of amplitude change of both the electric and magnetic fields is perpendicular to the direction of propagation, as opposed to e.g. a wave travelling along a coil spring, which is a longitudinal wave [WHE], or Transverse Electric (TE) or Transverse Magnetic (TM) waves in a waveguide [JOR].

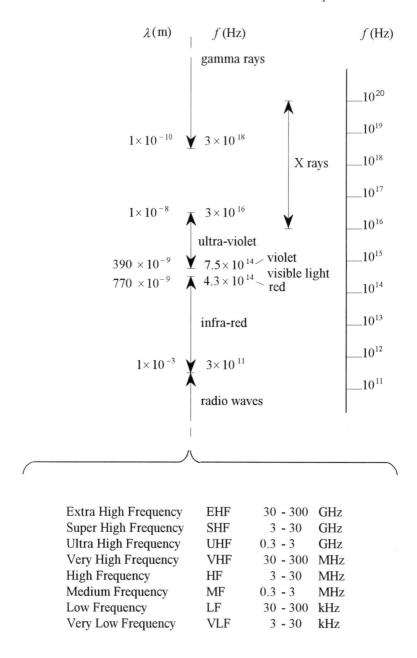

Figure 5.1 The electromagnetic spectrum

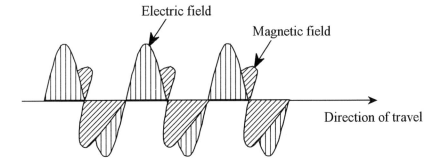

Figure 5.2 Transverse Electro-Magnetic (TEM) wave

There are, however, other problems that could not be explained by the wave theory of light. One such problem is the photo-electric effect, whereby light shining on a metal surface causes electrons to be emitted from the surface. It was found that the frequency of the light was critical for the effect to occur. If the frequency was too low then, no matter how intense the light, no electrons were emitted, but even a weak light source at the right frequency was sufficient for the effect to occur [WHE]. Einstein showed in 1905 (his miracle year when he also published papers on the special theory of relativity and the mathematics of Brownian motion) that the effect could be explained if light were considered to be made up of discrete particles (now called photons), with the energy of a single photon given by

$$E = hf \qquad (5.6)$$

where h is Planck's constant = 6.62620×10^{-34} Js and f is the frequency of the light. Thus a photon possesses a quantum of energy E. The photo-electric effect can now be explained in that if the light frequency is too low no photon will have enough energy to dislodge an electron; hence no amount of photons will enable a current to flow. Conversely, if the frequency is such that the photon's energy exceeds the minimum amount (or quantum) of energy needed to release an electron, a low intensity source will enable a current to flow. This was an important step in the development of the quantum theory and led to the particle theory of light.

The energy of a photon is set by the 'bandgap' of the light source, e.g. a red LED has a bandgap voltage of 1.55 V for a wavelength of 800 nm. A photon is emitted when an electron 'falls' from a higher energy state to a lower energy state. The energy of the photon is the same as the energy lost by the electron, which is the potential difference (i.e. the bandgap V_b) between the two states multiplied by the charge of the electron ($e = 1.60219 \times 10^{-19}$ C). Hence

$$hf = eV_b$$

or, in terms of the wavelength,

$$\lambda = \frac{c}{f} = \frac{ch}{eV_b} \qquad (5.7)$$

The particle theory of light can easily explain how light can travel in a vacuum but there are effects which cannot be explained by the particle theory. For example, experiments carried out with a *single* photon still show such effects as interference. This is of course impossible.

To cope with these problems the idea of light as a wave-particle duality was proposed. This meant choosing the appropriate theory to explain the particular effect. De Broglie (1892-1987), a French physicist, took this idea and consider-ed it the other way round, i.e. if light waves sometimes behave as particles could particles behave as waves? The idea was tested experimentally and diffraction and interference of electron beams was indeed observed. This demonstrated that in some circumstances electrons behave as waves, which is the principle of operation of the electron microscope. The theory of such interactions is the subject of quantum mechanics. However, having to choose between in-compatible theories depending on the application is not a satisfactory state of affairs.

The reader who wishes to take this topic on light further is recommended to read QED by Feynman [FEY], where the theory of Quantum Electro-Dynamics is used to explain particular light phenomena in terms of the sum of the complex probability amplitudes of all possible photon paths to a point. Richard Feynman (1918-88), an American scientist, was a joint winner of the Nobel Prize in 1965 for his work on quantum electro-dynamics.

5.2 Radio waves

Radio waves are at the low end of the electromagnetic spectrum, with a frequency range from 3 kHz to 300 GHz. Typical uses are in broadcasting commercial radio signals (AM and FM), broadcasting TV signals, and trans-mitting voice conversations over point-to-point links (for example radio amateurs' conversations). Very high frequency radio waves are limited to line of sight. It was a natural assumption that this would be true for all radio waves but, as Guglielmo Marconi (1874-1937) demonstrated in 1901, transatlantic communication is possible even though America cannot be seen from Europe!

Marconi was an Italian electrical engineer and businessman (founder of the Marconi group of companies) who pioneered work on radio transmission, receiving a Nobel prize in 1909 in recognition of his work. Many others had contributed to the development of radio: notably Maxwell, with his prediction of the presence of radio waves, and Heinrich Hertz (1857-94), a German physicist, who verified the prediction by demonstrating a transmitter and receiver in his laboratory in 1888.

There are several propagation modes besides line of sight, the most important being ionospheric propagation and ground wave propagation. It was ionospheric propagation that enabled Marconi to bridge the Atlantic.

5.2.1 Ionospheric propagation

Ionospheric propagation (or sky wave propagation) is the mode used for short-wave communications (from 3 MHz to 30 MHz), enabling signals from all over the world to be picked up on a short-wave receiver. The ionosphere is part of the earth's upper atmosphere where some of the molecules are ionized by the sun's radiation. Ionospheric propagation therefore varies with changes in solar radiation; changes occur over a daily cycle, with the seasons, and also over the roughly eleven year cycle of the sun known as the sunspot cycle. Peaks in radiation generally improve radio transmission; the most recent peak in the sunspot cycle was in 1990. During the day reception is best at higher frequencies (say above 10 MHz): whilst at night reception is best at lower frequencies (say below 10 MHz). However, finding the best conditions for reception can be more of an art than a science, which no doubt accounts for some of the fun people have in using short wave.

The ionosphere is subdivided into the D, E, F_1 and F_2 layers, ranging in height from about 50 km to 400 km above the earth's surface. The heights and the effects of these layers change with the daily cycle, accounting for the difference in night time and daytime reception. In a simple view the radio signal is reflected back from a layer, as in figure 5.3. Multiple skips are possible, where the signal is reflected back from the earth into the sky again.

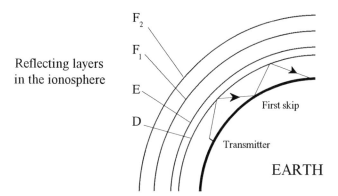

Figure 5.3 Reflections from the ionosphere

Of course this reflection does not occur at a single point and the interaction between the radio wave and the ionized air is complex. Basically, the direction of propagation of the radio signal is bent by refraction – which is an effect seen when visible light passes obliquely from one medium to another of different density (see chapter 6). The refractive index n of the ionosphere gradually decreases with height, so the radio wave is gradually bent downwards; and if bent far enough it will be reflected back to earth. This is a similar effect to the refraction of light in a graded index optical fibre (see chapter 6).

There is a critical angle (θ_c) at which the signal is just reflected back to earth (see figure 5.4, which ignores the curvature of the earth), where it touches earth again gives the first skip distance. Ionospheric reception is not possible if the receiver is *nearer* to the transmitter than the first skip distance, as radio waves transmitted at angles of incidence closer to the vertical than θ_c (i.e. smaller than θ_c) will not be reflected. Nearer to the station, ground wave reception (see following section) may enable the signal to be received, but a gap can exist (beyond the ground wave and before the first skip distance) in which no reception is possible.

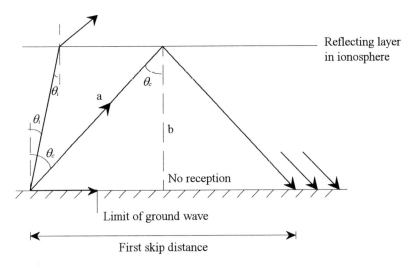

Figure 5.4 Critical angle and first skip distance

The critical angle depends on the frequency. The higher the frequency the less effective the ionospheric layers are at reflecting the signal and the greater the critical angle. Hence for a receiving station at a particular distance from a transmitting station, the maximum usable frequency (m.u.f.) is the frequency at which the signal is reflected at the critical angle and the receiver is at the first skip distance. At higher frequencies the signal will not be reflected by the ionosphere and at lower frequencies stations nearer to the transmitter can also pick up the transmissions.

If the frequency is decreased the critical angle will decrease, eventually becoming zero. The frequency at which this occurs is the critical frequency, i.e.

the maximum frequency at which reflection occurs when the signal is transmitted vertically upwards.

The m.u.f. can be estimated from the critical frequency (f_c) by noting the relationship between frequency and path length in figure 5.4, i.e.

$$\frac{m.u.f.}{f_c} = \frac{a}{b} = \frac{1}{\cos\theta_c}$$

hence
$$m.u.f. = \frac{f_c}{\cos\theta_c} = f_c \sec\theta_c$$

(5.8)

which is known as the secant law.

5.2.2 Ground wave propagation

Long range, ground wave propagation (or surface wave propagation) is limited to a frequency range up to 10 MHz. This is a relatively small bandwidth but it includes the medium and long wave radio broadcast stations (AM radio). The wave is guided along the surface of the earth or sea, propagating along the interface between the earth and the sky. The earth does not make an ideal lossless transmission line, so the signal is attenuated with distance; a typical range being 250 km with attenuation least over sea and greatest over desert. The radio waves are often vertically polarized transverse electromagnetic waves (i.e. the electric field is vertical) to minimize losses.

Reception of these ground waves can be investigated by tuning to an AM station on a portable radio [EHR]. Most portable radios pick up the signal primarily from an internal ferrite loop aerial that responds to the magnetic field, rather than from the external extendible aerial which responds to the electric field. Rotating the radio (with or without the external aerial extended) around a vertical axis should show that the reception is a minimum in two directions, 180° apart. These minima occur when the loops of the internal aerial are at right angles to the transmitter, see figure 5.5.

Repeating the experiment with an FM radio station (the radio is now receiving a line of sight signal) shows that an external antenna is normally needed, i.e. the receiver responds to the electric field rather than the magnetic field. It is difficult to detect a minimum with FM, because FM has good performance characteristics in the presence of noise, but the picture of a TV signal is transmitted as an AM signal, enabling line of sight reception to be investigated with a TV and portable aerial.

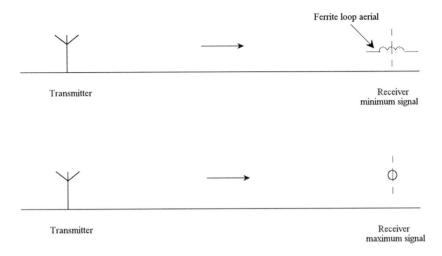

Figure 5.5 AM reception with a ferrite loop aerial

5.2.3 *Line of sight propagation*

Line of sight propagation (or space wave, or tropospheric propagation – because it takes place in the lowest layer of the atmosphere called the troposphere) is used for signals above 30 MHz. The distance is limited by the curvature of the earth, but is actually slightly greater than the optical line of sight, because the radio signal can travel some way over the horizon due to refraction.

Reflections from the ground or buildings, etc., can cause interference to the received signal; this type of distortion is called multipath distortion and can also be seen as 'ghosts' on a TV picture. The effect occurs because the reflected signal has travelled further and is therefore received slightly later. In addition reflection results in the reflected signal being inverted, a result first derived in chapter 4 where an incident pulse of positive voltage is reflected at a short circuit as a pulse of equal amplitude but opposite sign.

Line of sight propagation also occurs at lower frequencies, but its effect is usually cancelled out by an equal and opposite signal reflected from the ground. At high frequencies the difference in length between the two paths will be large compared to the signal's wave length, but at low frequencies the difference in path length will be small in terms of the signal wave length (see figure 5.6). Also, at low frequencies the earth acts as a good reflector and hence the reflected signal has almost the same power as the direct signal; therefore, at low frequencies the direct and reflected waves tend to cancel each other out, whilst at higher frequencies reflections give rise to multipath distortion.

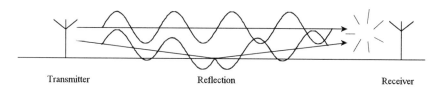

Transmitter   Reflection   Receiver

Figure 5.6 Loss of line of sight signal at low frequencies

5.2.4 Ducting

There are other modes of propagation, but only one more will be mentioned here because of its similarity to propagation in a monomode fibre optic cable (see chapter 6). At very low frequencies (i.e. below 30 kHz) the surface of the earth and the bottom of the ionosphere form a waveguide or duct. The signal is not 'bounced', or reflected, between the top and bottom of the waveguide but rather supported by them, and it can travel all the way around the earth with relatively little attenuation. Because of the long wavelength this mode of communication requires physically very large aerials to broadcast the signal. One use is to communicate with submarines, since the signal penetrates the upper sea layers, enabling it to be received by a submerged submarine.

Under certain weather conditions, ducting can also occur in the troposphere at much higher frequencies, say 30-200 MHz. This type of ducting is generally more of a nuisance than a reliable means of communication, as a signal can be carried long distances and interfere with other signals.

5.3 Antennas

An antenna (or aerial) is the interface between the transmitter (or the receiver) and the medium through which the signal is propagated. It is a purely passive device and as such cannot increase the overall power of a signal. However, antennas can be made directional so that they have a gain in a particular direction compared to an ideal non-directional (or isotropic) antenna. Since the overall power cannot be increased by the antenna, the directional antenna will also have a greater loss in some directions than a non-directional antenna. For broadcast services, such as FM radio or TV, it is usual to have an antenna with a uniform gain in the horizontal plane at the transmitter and directional antennas for the many receivers tuned to that transmitter.

The radiation from an antenna can be divided into two parts: the near field and the far field. We will only consider the far field, which is the dominant field at ranges greater than a few wavelengths of the signal (this is obviously the case for most applications). The power density from an antenna will decrease as the inverse square of the radial distance from the antenna; this is the same relationship as, for example, with a gravitational field and derives from the same reasoning, i.e. as the distance from the antenna increases, the surface of the sphere over which the field acts increases as the square of the radius.

Mathematically,

$$\rho = \frac{P_t G_t}{4 \pi h^2} \qquad (5.9)$$

where ρ is the power density, P_t the total transmitted power, h the radial distance and G_t the transmitting antenna's gain in the direction being considered. Note that no energy is being dissipated; the power density falls because the power is spread over a larger area.

The most basic type of antenna is called a dipole and is shown in figure 5.7. The most efficient coupling between the transmitter (or the receiver) and the antenna occurs if the electrical length of the antenna corresponds to an integer number of half wavelengths of the signal (i.e. $l_e = n\lambda/2$). The shortest antenna results when $n = 1$, giving the half-wave dipole. The physical length of a half-wave dipole is approximately 95% of the electrical length, assuming that the dipole cross-section is small.

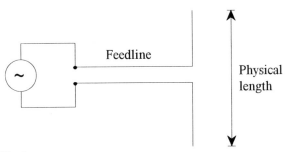

Figure 5.7 Dipole

The radiation pattern for a half-wave dipole compared to an isotropic antenna is shown in figure 5.8. It can be seen that this is a suitable antenna for a transmitter (it has a power gain of 1.64 in the horizontal direction compared to a non-directional antenna, see [GRI]).

plan views:

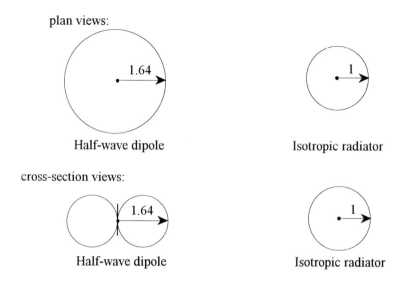

Half-wave dipole   Isotropic radiator

cross-section views:

Half-wave dipole   Isotropic radiator

Figure 5.8 Radiation patterns

Actually, there is a physically shorter antenna than the half-wave dipole: the quarter-wave monopole shown in figure 5.9; but this is electrically similar to the half-wave dipole. It relies on the ground acting as a good reflector at radio frequencies; hence the other arm of the half-wave dipole occurs as an image. The quarter-wave monopole is a suitable antenna for mobile communications receivers where a receiving antenna with uniform gain in the horizontal plane is needed and the vehicle's exterior acts as the ground. As a transmitter it launches a TEM wave polarized in the same direction as the dipole (i.e. a vertical dipole launches a TEM wave with the electric field vertical and the magnetic field horizontal).

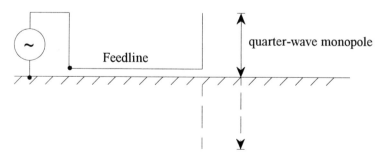

Figure 5.9 Quarter-wave monopole

For fixed TV receivers a highly directional antenna is common. This can be achieved using an array of dipoles. A common type of TV antenna is called a

Yagi (see figure 5.10) and has a dipole as the driven element (to which the TV aerial input is connected) with a reflector behind it and several shorter non-driven dipoles in front acting as directors. This is an endfire type of array as the direction of maximum gain is along the aerial.

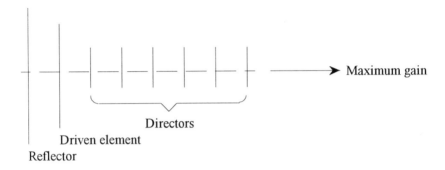

Figure 5.10 Yagi array

An alternative type of array is the broadside array, in which two or more dipoles (usually with a reflector behind) are mounted perpendicular to (i.e. 'broadside' on to) the direction to the transmitter.

Because half-wave dipoles and antennas based on them are tuned to resonate at a particular frequency, they can only be used for narrowband communication. Narrowband may be arbitrarily defined as the signal bandwidth being 10% or less of the carrier frequency (or resonant frequency). By contrast, if the signal bandwidth is over 10% of the carrier, the signal is termed broadband. The art of good antenna design is often to maximize the signal bandwidth compared to the resonant frequency.

5.4 Microwaves

Microwaves are radio waves (at frequencies > 1 GHz) which can be focused like visible light. Hence a common antenna is a metal dish shaped to have a parabolic surface (see below). In the transmitter the energy radiated from the source is reflected as a parallel beam, whilst at the receiver the incoming parallel beam is focused on to the detector. This is exactly the same principle as is applied in a Newtonian reflecting telescope for optical astronomy.

The definition of a parabola, see figure 5.11, is the locus of points P such that the distance of P from the focal point F is always equal to the distance of P from a fixed line. The antenna surface (or mirror for light) is generated by revolving the parabola about the x axis. Let the fixed line be at a distance $-a$ from the origin and the focal point F be at a distance $+a$ from the origin. Then, from the definition of a parabola,

$$x + a = PF = \sqrt{\left[(a-x)^2 + y^2\right]}$$

i.e. $y^2 = 4ax$ (5.10)

which is the equation of a parabola.

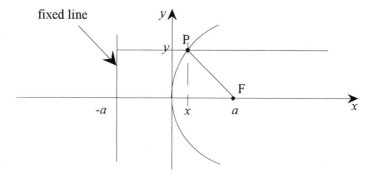

Figure 5.11 Parabola

Now move the fixed line to a position on the other side of the parabola, see figure 5.12, noting that the distance to the focal point is equal for all paths which are parallel to the x axis when they start at the line. From the wave theory of light, considering all points on the parabolic surface to act as sources of secondary wavelets when light strikes them (Huygen's construction [WHE]), all the light from a plane wavefront perpendicular to the x axis will arrive together at the focus, i.e. the light will be brought to a focus at point F.

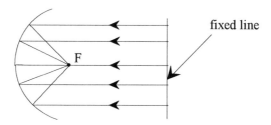

Figure 5.12 Parabolic antenna or mirror

It is worth considering what we are assuming about light here. The treatment of light so far has been that it is a wave. Waves do not necessarily travel in a straight line, for instance radio waves can bend around houses or other obstacles. However, this is only true if the wavelength is comparable to the dimension of the obstacle. If the wavelength is very much smaller than any obstacles then, to a good approximation, light travels in straight lines called rays. This way of treating light is called geometrical or ray optics; note that is based on the wave theory of light and not on the particle theory, i.e. it does not purport to show the paths of photons. Geometrical optics will be the principal way of treating light in the next chapter on fibre optics.

Microwaves can carry information at high data rates because their high carrier frequencies allow large signal bandwidths. They are used in a line of sight propagation mode; this means that a high capacity network can be set up in a city without cabling, or a long distance link can be set up by relaying signals, via towers or masts each in line of sight to the next tower. The antennas are usually situated on hill tops or high buildings to give a maximum line of sight distance of about 80 km, depending on the height and frequency of the signals.

Microwaves are also used to communicate with satellites. To avoid the need for continuous realignment of antennas, communication satellites are often in geosynchronous orbit, which means that they stay in the same position in the sky as their orbital period is exactly one day. This can only happen when the orbit of the satellite is 36,000 km above the surface of the earth and directly above the equator, see figure 5.13. So the round-trip delay for a message to go from ground station A to station B, via the satellite, and back is at least $t = 4h/c$ = 0.48 seconds (this assumes the shortest case when both A and B are directly under the satellite).

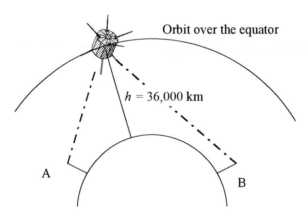

Figure 5.13 Geosynchronous satellite

Satellites act as transponders, receiving and retransmitting data signals up to one-third of the distance around the world – or even further when relayed via other satellites. The relatively long time before a reply is received can cause problems with speech. A half second delay is tolerable, but a delay of one second is not, as people begin to think that the message has not got through and start to repeat themselves. So speech circuits are limited to a single satellite hop, going the rest of the way over land or under sea if necessary. Any delay is expensive, because of the high data rates supported by commercial satellite links. For this reason, data communication protocols for use over satellite links have special features to minimize waiting time (e.g. see extended mode HDLC in chapter 7). Satellites are ideal for point-to-multipoint (i.e. broadcast) transmission and can provide a cost-effective solution to the need for communication in rural areas – especially in developing countries.

5.4.1 Free-space path loss

The area of a receiving dish antenna is $A = \pi d^2/4$, where d is the dish diameter. Allowing a factor η for the efficiency of the antenna in converting the incident signal power density (ρ) into signal power (for a parabolic antenna η is typically 55%) gives the effective area as

$$A_{\mathit{eff}} = \frac{\pi d^2}{4} \eta \qquad (5.11)$$

Hence the received signal power is

$$P_r = A_{\mathit{eff}} \times \rho \qquad (5.12)$$

substituting for ρ from equation 5.9 gives

$$P_r = \frac{\pi d^2 \eta}{4} \times \frac{P_t G_t}{4 \pi h^2}$$

where G_t is the gain of the transmitting antenna and h the distance between the transmitting and receiving antennas. Rearranging this gives the attenuation of free space (i.e. the ratio of the received to the transmitted power) as

$$\frac{P_r}{P_t} = \frac{d^2 \eta G_t}{16 h^2} \qquad (5.13)$$

The effective area of an antenna is also defined by its relation to the gain (G) and signal wavelength (λ)

$$A_{\mathit{eff}} = \frac{\lambda^2 G}{4 \pi} \qquad (5.14)$$

substituting this expression for the receiver antenna gain G_r into equation 5.12 gives an alternative expression for the attenuation of free space which is valid for all types of antennas, not just dish antennas,

$$\frac{P_r}{P_t} = \frac{\lambda^2 G_r G_t}{16\pi^2 h^2} \qquad (5.15)$$

Rearranging this in terms of the Effective Isotropic Radiated Power (EIRP = $P_t G_t$, i.e. the power needed with an isotropic antenna to give the same power at the receiver) and free-space path loss $(4\pi h/\lambda)^2$

$$P_r = \text{EIRP} \, / \, \text{free-space path loss}$$

$$P_r = P_t G_t G_r \left(\frac{4\pi h}{\lambda}\right)^{-2} \qquad (5.16)$$

The dependence on wavelength of the free-space path loss is due to the receiver antenna being defined in terms of gain rather than effective area. If G_r from equation 5.14 is substituted into equation 5.16, then the wavelength terms cancel, enabling equation 5.12 to be derived.

5.4.2 Link budget

From equation 5.16 the signal power at the input to the receiver depends on the EIRP and the free space path loss. But the most important factor in receiver design is not the received power level but its ratio to the noise at the input of the receiver, i.e. the Signal to Noise Ratio (SNR). The noise power N is given as

$$N = kT_{sys}B \qquad (5.17)$$

where k is Boltzmann's constant (1.38062×10^{-23} J/K), B is the receiver bandwidth and $T_{sys} = T_a + T_r$ is the system's effective temperature figure (K). This comprises the equivalent antenna noise temperature T_a (due to noise sources in the sky, e.g. cosmic sources at higher frequencies) and T_r (which represents noise due to the receiver, principally thermal noise from the first stage of amplification). These temperatures are not the actual temperatures of the equipment, but a convenient way of quantifying how much noise power a system component contributes to the overall SNR. Hence the SNR is

$$\text{SNR} = \frac{P_r}{N} = \frac{P_t G_t G_r}{kBT_{sys}} \left(\frac{4\pi h}{\lambda}\right)^{-2} \qquad (5.18)$$

$$= \text{EIRP} \times G_r \, / \, (\text{free-space path loss} \times N)$$

Usually the EIRP, bandwidth B, operating wavelength λ and distance h are given, so the remaining factor G_r/T_{sys} (called the 'receiver figure of merit') becomes very important in receiver design; hence, for critical applications, a large antenna and low noise receiver are required.

The link budget is worked out in dB, i.e.

$$\text{SNR} = \text{EIRP} - \text{free-space path loss} + 10\log_{10}\left(G_r\right) - 10\log_{10}\left(kT_{sys}B\right) \text{ dB} \quad (5.19)$$

For example, for a geosynchronous satellite with a transmitter power of 20 W, an antenna gain of 10 and transmitting at 15 cm, and a receiving station with an antenna noise temperature of 60 K, equivalent receiver noise temperature of 180 K, bandwidth of 1 MHz and needing a minimum SNR of 16 dB, find the required receiver antenna gain.

- The EIRP is 200 W or 23 dBW.
- The free-space path loss is 189.6 dB.
- The noise power is −144.8 dBW.
- The given SNR required at receiver is 16 dB.

Hence the minimum required receiver antenna gain is found from

$$23 - 189.6 + G_r - (-144.8) = 16 \text{ dB}$$

i.e. $G_r \geq 37.8$ dB.

This chapter has purposely highlighted the similarities between radio wave and light propagation, as the next chapter deals with light (but generally infrared rather than visible light) transmitted down fibre optic cables.

Exercises

(1)   Determine the wavelength of a radio station transmitting at 252 kHz in the long wave band.

(2)   A fibre optic cable has a core with refractive index of 1.5. Determine the relative permittivity at optical wavelengths and the velocity of propagation of light down the cable.

(3)   Determine the bandgap voltage across a green LED, given that the wavelength of the green light is 550 nm.

(4)   Check that the units of the equation $hf = eV_b$ are correct.

(5)   Determine the maximum usable frequency for a radio link between a receiver and transmitter, given the critical frequency is 5 MHz and critical angle is 30°.

(6)   For the radio link of question (5), determine the height of the reflecting layer in the ionosphere if the two stations are 100 km apart.

(7)   Determine the electrical and physical lengths of half-wave dipoles at (i) 100 MHz; (ii) 10 kHz.

(8)   An analogue telephone speech channel has a frequency range from 300 Hz to 3.4 kHz. This baseband signal is modulated on to a 1 MHz carrier frequency with the modulated signal bandwidth the same as the baseband signal. State whether the modulated signal is narrowband or wideband; justify your answer.

(9)   The bandwidth of a broadcast AM station on the medium wave band is 9 kHz in Europe (10 kHz in the USA).
    (i)   What is the maximum number of AM radio stations that can be received on the medium wave band from 526.5 kHz to 1606.5 kHz in Europe?
    (ii)   The modulated signal has twice the bandwidth of the baseband signal. State the frequency range of the baseband signal.

(10) Briefly explain some reasons for modulating a baseband signal. Your answers to questions (7), (8) and (9) may be of help.

(11) Discuss the advantages and disadvantages of different modes of radio propagation.

(12) Determine the gain of a parabolic antenna with radius 0.75 m at a frequency of 1 GHz.

(13) Determine the EIRP of a transmitter in units of dBW, given that it transmits 10 W signal power and has a directional antenna with a maximum gain of 10×.

(14) Find the electrical noise power due to the thermal noise generated by a 100 kΩ resistor at room temperature (say 20°C) at the input to a receiver, given that the signal bandwidth is 1 MHz and that absolute zero is −273°C.

(15) Determine the required receiver noise temperature for a satellite receiving station, given that the satellite is in geosynchronous orbit, transmitting 10 W at a frequency of 3 GHz and bandwidth 2 kHz from an aerial with gain of 2×, and that the ground station has a parabolic antenna of diameter 1 m and noise temperature of 100 K. The receiver requires a 20 dB SNR to operate successfully.

(16) The James Clark Maxwell telescope is an astronomical telescope for observing millimetre wavelengths (down to 0.5 mm). The main mirror has a diameter of 15 m, with a surface that follows an ideal parabolic dish shape with a positional error of less than 50 μm. Determine the diameter and surface accuracy required for the same gain and resolution for:

    (i)   an optical telescope for a wavelength of 400 nm;

    (ii)   a radio telescope for a frequency of 1 GHz.

(17) Compile a list of the more important equations used in this chapter.

(18) Write your own summary of what you have learnt in this chapter.

6 Fibre Optics

The light used for optical fibre communication is generally in the near and middle infra-red parts of the electromagnetic spectrum (near infra-red wavelengths range from 0.7 μm, the wavelength of visible red light, to 1.5 μm; middle infra-red ranges from 1.5 μm to 6 μm). It is customary to use units of wavelength rather than frequency in specifying fibre optic systems; alternatives to the micrometre (μm or 10^{-6} m) are the nanometre (nm or 10^{-9} m) and angstrom (Å or 10^{-10} m). The first wavelength range exploited for fibre optic communication was from 0.8 μm to 0.9 μm which was set by the available optical sources' emission characteristics; later, sources were developed for the frequency range from 1.1 to 1.6 μm to take advantage of the low loss characteristic of optical fibre cables at these wavelengths.

Light has traditionally been used for line of sight communications, e.g. signal beacons and semaphore, but these suffer from the disadvantage that fog or other vagaries of the weather could disrupt communications. It was only when fibre optic cables became available that light regained its importance in communications.

The principle of operation of a fibre optic cable is that a light beam is trapped in the cable and hence can be directed and bent (assuming the radius of the bend is not too small).

The effect can be demonstrated [EHR] by making a small hole (start with a pin prick) in a clear plastic bottle, filling the bottle with water, and shining a light through the bottle on to the hole. In a darkened room light should be seen emerging in the jet of water from the hole (if not, increase the size of the hole). The light may break out from the jet at a particular point; this point will change as the jet changes with the water level in the bottle.

High performance optical fibres are made from extremely pure silica glass. Silica is an abundant mineral (silicon dioxide) which occurs as quartz and is the main constituent of many rocks (e.g. sand). An easier material to use for manufacturing cables is plastic (e.g. Perspex), but the optical characteristics of plastic cable are not as good as those of glass fibre.

As discussed in chapter 5, the velocity of propagation of light in a material of refractive index n_1 is

$$V_p = c / n_1 \qquad (6.1)$$

where c is the velocity of light in a vacuum (3×10^8 m/s). For glass a typical figure for n_1 is 1.5 and for V_p it is 2×10^8 m/s. Clearly, the refractive index in a vacuum n_o is 1. The value for air is 1.00029 (usually taken as 1), whilst for water the value is 1.333 in visible light at room temperature. In physical terms the refractive index is a measure of the ability of the material to store energy; hence the refractive index will decrease as the density (i.e. the number of particles per unit volume) decreases. Particles (atoms and molecules) interact with electromagnetic radiation to store energy in various ways at different frequencies, hence the refractive index varies with frequency.

For light of a particular wavelength (λ) the frequency of the light in the cable is given by

$$f = \frac{V_p}{\lambda} = \frac{c/n_1}{\lambda} \tag{6.2}$$

Optical fibres have very small cross-section dimensions, comparable to the width of a human hair. A fibre consists of a central core, made of a solid dielectric material of refractive index n_1 and usually with a circular cross-section having a diameter, say, from 5 μm to 100 μm; this core is generally surrounded by a cladding (see figure 6.1) made of solid dielectric material of refractive index n_2 ($n_2 < n_1$). The core and cladding together provide the optically active part of the fibre, which is usually surrounded by supportive and protective layers or jackets. Even with these extra layers, a fibre optic cable is much smaller and lighter than a copper cable for the same data rate.

Current fibres are made either with plastic core and cladding, with glass core and plastic cladding (PCS or Plastic-Clad Silica), or with glass core and glass cladding (SCS or Silica-Clad Silica). SCS fibre has the best propagation characteristics but is the least rugged; plastic core and cladding is the cheapest but has the greatest attenuation characteristic, so is only suitable for short distance links. (In very cheap fibres a solid cladding can be omitted as the air acts as the cladding.)

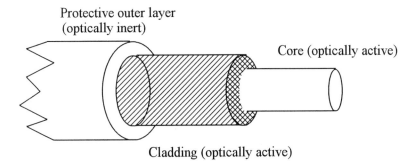

Figure 6.1 Fibre optic cable

Fibre optic cables are classified in two main ways. Firstly, by the number of possible modes by which light can travel down the cable: loosely such modes correspond to paths of light rays, i.e. fibres can be either monomode (single mode) or multimode. Secondly, they can be characterized by the profile of the refractive index (n) across the core, i.e. as either step index or graded index, see figure 6.2. In a step index fibre the refractive index is constant across the core before undergoing an abrupt (i.e. step) change at the core/cladding interface. In a graded index fibre the core refractive index varies gradually from the fibre centre to the cladding. Step index or graded index, as descriptions on their own, usually refer to multimode fibre; monomode on its own usually refers to a step index monomode fibre; these conventions will be followed in the rest of this chapter.

In terms of propagation characteristics, monomode fibre is best and step index worst, whilst in terms of cost, step index is usually cheapest and mono-mode the most expensive. Monomode fibres are generally wholly made of glass (i.e. SCS type), whilst multimode fibres can be of either SCS or PCS construction with either a step or graded index profile. Plastic fibres are norm-ally step index. The propagation of light down step index, graded index and monomode fibres is considered later in this chapter.

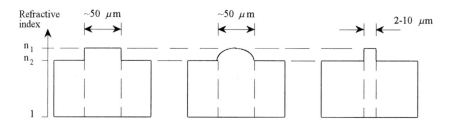

(i) Step index multimode   (ii) Graded index multimode   (iii) Step index monomode
n_1 refractive index of core; n_2 refractive index of cladding

Figure 6.2 Refractive index profiles

An optical fibre communication system is shown in figure 6.3. Optical sources are either lasers, usually a semiconductor laser (i.e. a Laser Diode, LD) or LEDs (Light Emitting Diodes). A laser produces purer light at higher power levels than a LED but is more expensive and generally has a shorter working life. The optical detector is usually a PIN diode (Positive Intrinsic Negative, which describes the diode's doping characteristics) or an APD (Avalanche Photo Diode, which has gain), although a photo transistor can also be used. The circuit symbols for these sources and detectors are also shown in figure 6.3.

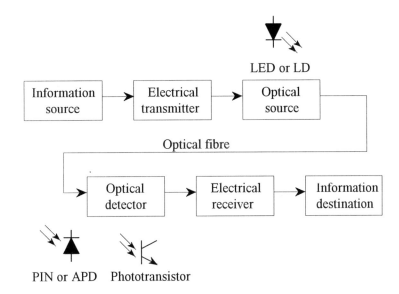

Figure 6.3 Optical fibre communications system

Fibre optic transmission is well suited to digital techniques as the light source is switched on or off (i.e. binary signalling). It is difficult to make the overall transmission characteristic of a fibre optic link linear, so it is not well suited to analogue signalling. Paradoxically, although fibre optics is a 'state of the art' technology, the actual technique of switching a light source on and off is very crude compared to the modulation techniques available in electrical communications.

The high frequency of the light used in optical fibre communications means that a very high bandwidth is available for the signal, i.e. very high data rates can be supported (of the order of hundreds of Mbps). To take advantage of such high data rates, baseband signals are often combined (i.e. multiplexed) using either FDM (Frequency Division Multiplexing) or TDM (Time Division Multiplexing).

In FDM, an analogue technique that generally needs some conversion process to produce a pulse stream suitable for driving the optical source, the link bandwidth is divided permanently between the channels (i.e. each channel has access to only a part of the link bandwidth but has that frequency slot all the time). In TDM, which nowadays is generally a digital technique, each channel has access to the entire link bandwidth but only for a short time (called the channel time slot) which recurs at regular times.

Another multiplexing technique is WDM (Wavelength Division Multiplexing). Although nominally this is the same as FDM, in that different frequency bands are used for different channels, the distinction is that WDM is a purely optical process. Multiple optical sources, operating at different wavelengths, are used to send signals down the same fibre with optical filters used to separate the signals at the receiver. WDM can also be used to set up a full duplex link over the same fibre using different wavelengths for the send and return paths.

The attractions of fibre optic communications can be summarized as below.

- The operating frequency is high, so the available signal bandwidth is large.
- With current cables the attenuation is very low, so long distances can be covered before the need for regeneration.
- The signal, being light, is immune to electrical interference (e.g. lightning or manmade impulsive noise).
- To a large extent the signal is contained in the cable, i.e. little energy is radiated, so crosstalk between signals in adjacent cables is minimal and the communication link is more secure.
- The cable is non-conducting, so the transmitter and receiver are electrically isolated and optical fibres can be used in hazardous environments without the risk of a spark igniting a fire.
- The cable is small and light and the raw material for the cable (silica or plastic) is cheap, unlike copper cables which are sometimes stolen for their copper.

To investigate fibre optic communication further it is necessary to know some basic optics: starting with Snell's law (Willebrord Snel, 1580-1626, Dutch mathematician and physicist) which is the fundamental law on which the theory in this chapter is based.

6.1 Snell's law

Consider what can happen to a beam of light at the interface between two media with refractive indices n_1 (in medium 1) and n_2 (medium 2). In figure 6.4 some of the light is reflected, with the angle of reflection θ_3 being equal to the angle of incidence θ_1 (the law of reflection), and some is transmitted. The direction of propagation of the transmitted light beam is in general different from the incident beam, the change of direction being due to refraction. The relationship between the angle of incidence θ_1 and angle of refraction θ_2 is given by Snell's law as

$$\frac{\sin \theta_1}{\sin \theta_2} = \frac{n_2}{n_1} \qquad\qquad (6.3)$$

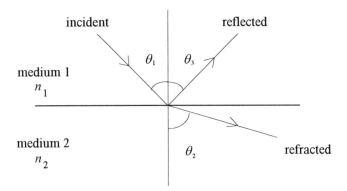

Figure 6.4 Reflection and refraction

To derive Snell's law consider figure 6.5 which shows a plane wavefront travelling from medium 1 to medium 2 ($n_1 > n_2$). All points of an incident wavefront (say line AB at time $t = 0$) will be refracted and form a wavefront in medium 2 (say line $A'B'$ at time $t = t_1$). From figure 6.5, light in medium 1 travels distance AA' in time t_1, whilst in medium 2 it travels distance BB' in the same time. From equation 6.1, the velocity of propagation is c/n_1 in medium 1 and c/n_2 in medium 2. Hence,

$$AA' = \frac{ct_1}{n_1} \tag{6.4}$$

$$BB' = \frac{ct_1}{n_2} \tag{6.5}$$

By inspection from figure 6.5,

$$AA' = BA' \sin\theta_1 \tag{6.6}$$

$$BB' = BA' \sin\theta_2 \tag{6.7}$$

Equating these equations,

$$BA' \sin\theta_1 = \frac{ct_1}{n_1} \tag{6.8}$$

$$BA' \sin\theta_2 = \frac{ct_1}{n_2} \tag{6.9}$$

and dividing equation 6.8 by 6.9 gives Snell's law $\dfrac{\sin\theta_1}{\sin\theta_2} = \dfrac{n_2}{n_1}$

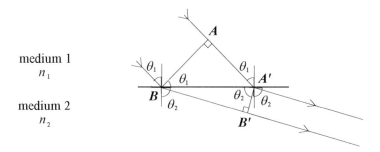

Figure 6.5 Refraction of a wavefront

The treatment of light here is an example of the use of light rays or geo-metrical optics which, as discussed in chapter 5, is a simplified treatment based on the wave theory of light. In essence, a light ray is the path of a wavefront; a wavefront being a surface of constant phase.

6.2 Total internal reflection

This is the phenomenon that makes fibre optic transmission possible by keeping light trapped in a fibre. Snell's law allows us to calculate the angle at which total internal reflection occurs. The smallest, or limiting, angle of incidence θ_1 for which all the light is reflected is called the critical angle θ_c. This occurs (see figure 6.4) when θ_2 is a right angle (as then the light remains in medium 1 and, by the law of reflection, the angle of reflection is equal to the angle of incid-ence). For example, if medium 2 is air ($n_2 \cong 1$) and medium 1 is silica glass with a refractive index $n_1 = 1.5$ then (since $\sin\theta_2 = 1$)

$$\sin\theta_c = \frac{n_2}{n_1} \qquad (6.10)$$

Hence, in our example, $\theta_c = 41.8°$. Note that total internal reflection can only occur in a fibre if the core refractive index (n_1) is greater than the refractive index of the cladding (n_2).

The effect can be experienced in a swimming pool, see figure 6.6. If you open your eyes underwater (preferably wearing goggles) then looking up you will be able to see out of the water, whilst looking obliquely at the water surface you will see a reflection of the bottom of the pool, i.e. the surface is acting as a mirror. The light reaching your eye when you look obliquely at the surface has undergone total internal reflection.

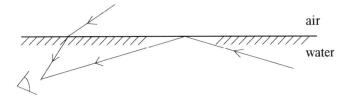

Figure 6.6 Total internal reflection in a swimming pool

6.3 Dispersion

The refractive index of glass or plastic generally varies with wavelength, which means that the velocity of propagation also changes with wavelength. Hence, from Snell's law, light of different colours will be refracted by a prism through different angles, causing white light to be split into a rainbow spectrum, i.e. the light is dispersed. A light pulse travelling down a fibre will similarly suffer from dispersion because the refractive index of the fibre varies with wavelength. This effect is called material dispersion and is one cause of pulse spreading. The material dispersion characteristic of a fibre is typically given in ρs, per km of fibre, per nm of source spectrum width (ρs.km^{-1}.nm^{-1}).

Other dispersion mechanisms are modal dispersion (see section 6.4.1), wavelength dispersion and profile dispersion [JAI, SEN].

The maximum data rate is limited by pulse spreading, because if a significant part of the pulse energy spreads into an adjacent data bit it degrades the Signal to Noise Ratio (SNR) by causing Inter Symbol Interference (ISI). Material dispersion can be reduced by using an emitter with a narrow spectrum of light emission, e.g. a laser – see figure 6.7. Since lasers produce a purer light than LEDs, lasers are used for high data rate or long haul links where material dispersion is a significant factor.

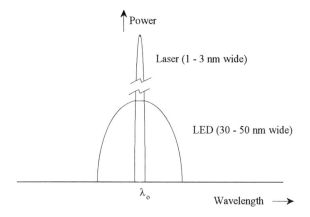

Figure 6.7 Spectrum of light emission for a laser and LED compared

Incidentally, refraction of light of different wavelengths through different angles is also the cause of an effect called chromatic aberration, in which the focal point of a simple lens varies with wavelength, e.g. the lens cannot bring both blue and yellow light to the same focus. Dispersion of light of different wavelengths does not occur with mirrors, since the angle of incidence is always equal to the angle of reflection; hence reflecting telescopes do not suffer from chromatic aberration.

6.4 Step index fibre

This derives its name from the profile of the refractive index across the cable, as shown in figures 6.2 and 6.8. Strictly this section deals with a step index multimode fibre. Considering light rays propagating down a step index fibre as in figure 6.8, if the angle of incidence is less than the critical angle θ_c (given by $\sin\theta_c = n_2/n_1$, equation 6.10), the light ray will not undergo total internal reflection and some light will leave the fibre core, resulting in the signal being rapidly attenuated. For long distance transmission a light ray following the path, or mode, with angle of incidence equal to the critical angle will propagate down the fibre as if between two parallel mirrors. This is one limiting case. The other limiting case is for the light ray passing directly down the centre of the fibre (i.e. the axial ray), which undergoes no reflections. In between there are many possible modes; hence this is a multimode fibre.

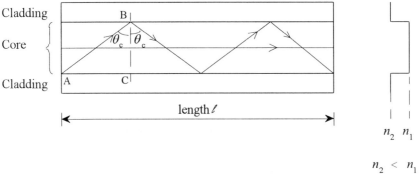

Figure 6.8 Step index fibre

6.4.1 Modal dispersion

A light pulse in a step index fibre will not only suffer pulse spreading from material dispersion, as described in section 6.3, but will also experience pulse spreading caused by modal dispersion (also known as modal spread or intermodal dispersion), i.e. the light travelling directly down the centre of the fibre will arrive first and the light reflected at the critical angle has furthest to travel and will arrive last. The pulse spreading caused by modal dispersion is, by definition,

$$\Delta t = t_{max} - t_{min} \tag{6.11}$$

where t_{min} is the time for the first part of the light pulse to arrive, i.e. the light directly down the centre of the fibre, and t_{max} is the time taken by light reflected at the critical angle. From figure 6.8,

$$t_{min} = \frac{\ell}{V_p} = \frac{\ell n_1}{c} \tag{6.12}$$

From triangle ABC, the distance travelled by light reflected at the critical angle will be in the ratio AB/AC ($= 1/\sin\theta_c$) compared to the direct path ℓ. Hence

$$t_{max} = \frac{\ell n_1}{c \, \sin\theta_c} \tag{6.13}$$

and $$\Delta t = \frac{\ell n_1}{c} \left(\frac{1}{\sin\theta_c} - 1 \right)$$

Substituting equation 6.10 gives the pulse spreading as

$$\Delta t = \frac{\ell n_1}{c n_2}(n_1 - n_2)$$ (6.14)

Referring to figure 6.9, if the width of the space in a Return to Zero (RZ) data bit is τ_s then $\Delta t = \tau_s$ defines the maximum length of cable (ℓ) that can be used before Inter Symbol Interference (ISI) occurs. (In figure 6.9 it is assumed that the optical power is constant across the core.) The optimum time to sample the received signal (and threshold the signal to regenerate the data) is when the transmitted signal has reached a peak and the ISI is a minimum; for the particular case shown in figure 6.9 the optimum time is clearly T/2. Note that the area of the pulse remains $A\tau_m$, which highlights the difference between dispersion and attenuation.

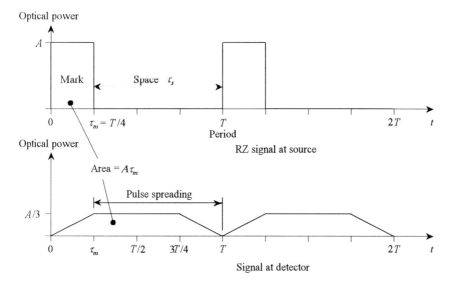

Figure 6.9 Pulse spreading due to modal dispersion

To demonstrate the effect of the cladding on pulse spreading, consider the results below for two types of step index multimode fibre, both with a core of refractive index $n_1 = 1.55$ but one with no cladding (i.e. $n_2 = 1.00$) and the other with a cladding of refractive index $n_2 = 1.50$.

(i)   No cladding, core $n_1 = 1.55$,
         $\theta_c = 40.2°$
         modal dispersion for 1 km = 2.84 µs

(ii)   Cladding $n_2 = 1.50$, core $n_1 = 1.55$
  $\theta_c = 75.4°$
  modal dispersion for 1 km $= 0.172$ μs

Clearly the fibre with cladding suffers significantly less from modal dispersion.

If Non Return to Zero data (i.e. standard binary signalling) is used, then ISI will occur. The limiting case is where a 1 occurs after a string of 0s, or vice versa. The optimum place to sample the received data is on the bit boundary at $t = nT$. In the case of the 1 the signal must rise to its maximum value in one bit period T (for the 0 it must fall to its minimum value), i.e. the maximum pulse spreading allowed is $\Delta t = T$ and hence the maximum bit rate is $1/\Delta t$.

6.4.2 Acceptance angle

This is a measure of how easy it is to couple a light source to a fibre. Referring to figure 6.10, the acceptance angle θ_{max} is the maximum angle at which a light ray incident to the air fibre interface can enter the core and be totally internally reflected at the core cladding interface. The acceptance angle is also known as the acceptance cone half angle, as rotating the acceptance angle around the fibre axis generates the acceptance cone. From figure 6.10 and using Snell's law,

$$n_{air} \sin\theta_{max} = n_1 \sin(90°-\theta_c) \qquad (6.15)$$

$$= n_1 \cos\theta_c$$

$$= n_1\sqrt{(1-\sin^2\theta_c)} \qquad (6.16)$$

but $n_{air} \cong 1$ and $\sin\theta_c = \dfrac{n_2}{n_1}$. Hence $\sin\theta_{max} = \sqrt{\left(n_1^2 - n_2^2\right)}$ (6.17)

where $\sin\theta_{max}$ is called the numerical aperture NA. Hence,

$$\theta_{max} = \begin{cases} \sin^{-1} NA = \sin^{-1}\sqrt{(n_1^2 - n_2^2)} & (NA \leq 1) \\ 90° & (NA > 1) \end{cases} \qquad (6.18)$$

Considering again the same two types of fibre as in the previous section,

(i)   No cladding, core $n_1 = 1.55$,
  NA $= 1.18$
  $\theta_{max} = 90°$

(ii)   Cladding $n_2 = 1.50$, core $n_1 = 1.55$
       NA = 0.391
       $\theta_{max} = 23.0°$

The acceptance angle for the fibre with no cladding is larger, which basically means that there are more modes in this type of fibre; it is easier to couple light into the fibre but the signal suffers more from modal dispersion.

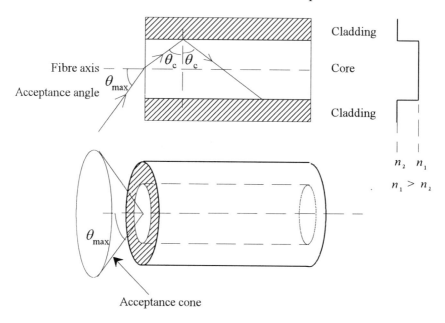

Figure 6.10 Acceptance angle

6.5 Graded index fibre

This derives its name from the profile of the refractive index across the cable, as shown in figure 6.2 (the profile is usually parabolic, or near parabolic). Like the step index fibre described in section 6.4 this too is a multimode fibre, but it suffers less from modal dispersion. Because the refractive index is less away from the centre, light will travel faster there, whilst the axial ray (i.e. the ray at the centre) will travel slowest, thus counteracting the effect of modal dispersion. Since the refractive index changes with wavelength this compensation effect is only possible at one wavelength. Ray paths which do not cross the fibre axis, i.e. helical or skew rays, are unwanted since these paths are difficult to compensate for.

For a ray that starts in the centre and penetrates into the outer parts of the core, as in figure 6.11, the situation is similar to the reflection of radio waves in ionospheric propagation (see chapter 5). The ray is continuously being refracted as it travels away from the centre until it is reflected back into the centre.

Although a graded index fibre is a more complicated structure than a step index fibre, it can be compared to a step index fibre with the same overall difference in refractive index between core and cladding. For example, consider the critical angle. If we approximate the refractive index profile to stepwise changes in refractive index, as indeed a real graded index fibre is built up, we can obtain a value for the critical angle θ_c at the fibre axis (see figure 6.11) by considering what happens to the light at each successive interface.

At the core layer adjacent to the cladding the light will undergo total internal reflection. Since θ_a is the critical angle for this layer

$$n_a \sin \theta_a = n_2 \tag{6.19}$$

The relationship between the light ray in layer a and layer b is given by Snell's law as

$$n_b \sin \theta_b = n_a \sin \theta_a \tag{6.20}$$

From equation 6.19 this reduces to

$$n_b \sin \theta_b = n_2 \tag{6.21}$$

This process can be repeated until the central layer is reached, when

$$n_1 \sin \theta_c = n_2$$

i.e.

$$\sin \theta_c = \frac{n_2}{n_1} \tag{6.22}$$

which is the same result as for a step index fibre with core refractive index n_1 and cladding refractive index n_2. Similarly, the numerical aperture varies across the width of the core, but from figure 6.11 it can be seen that at the fibre axis the numerical aperture will be the same as for a step index fibre.

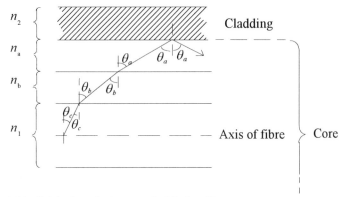

Figure 6.11 Critical angle in a graded index fibre

6.6 Monomode fibre

The refractive index profile across the cable is a step, as shown in figure 6.2, so sometimes this type of fibre is called a monomode (or single mode) step index fibre. The propagation of light through this cable is fundamentally different from that in either a graded index or a step index multimode fibre, as only a single light path is supported by the fibre. From the discussion in section 6.4.1 on modal dispersion it should be obvious that the advantage of a monomode fibre is that modal dispersion is eliminated. The main remaining contribution to pulse spreading comes from material dispersion.

It might appear that a monomode fibre just selects the axial ray but things are not that simple; since the core diameter is from 2 to 10 μm, which is of the same order as the wavelength of the light, the whole basis of geometric or light ray optics breaks down. A monomode fibre needs to be analysed as a waveguide, using propagation theory based on Maxwell's equations (see chapter 5). Such a treatment is beyond the scope of this book and [SEN] is recommended to the interested reader.

As an example of how ray optics breaks down, an appreciable part of the signal power propagates in the cladding, so the cladding must be of a suitable thickness and purity; this result cannot be derived by considering light as light rays. Propagation in a monomode fibre is similar to the ducting of very low frequency waves (see chapter 5). The cladding diameter needed is typically 100 μm, so the core and cladding of a monomode fibre need to be about the same overall diameter as for a multimode fibre. Another example of the limitations of ray optics is that the number of modes in a multimode fibre is not infinite (as might well be thought on considering figure 6.8). Both these results can be derived by using Maxwell's equations, where light is still considered as a wave but the treatment is more powerful than in the ray optics we have used.

6.7 Cable characteristics

Current silica glass fibre optic cables have losses of the order of 1 dB/km. Compare this with the attenuation of coaxial cable, which is of the order of 5 dB/km at 5 MHz, or twisted pair, which can be 25 dB/km at 1 MHz, and the advantage of fibre optics for high data rate, long haul transmission is apparent. To achieve such good performance the fibres are manufactured from extremely pure glass (with impurity levels below 1 part in 10^9), as impurities will cause the refractive index to change, thus scattering the light. Perspex cables have losses of the order of 500 dB/km, making them unsuitable for many communication applications.

Figure 6.12 shows the attenuation spectrum for a monomode glass fibre. The lowest attenuation occurs at a wavelength of 1.55 μm and is 0.4 dB/km for this fibre. This clearly shows the better performance characteristic at longer wavelengths compared to the first generation fibre technology that used wavelengths in the range from 0.8 to 0.9 μm.

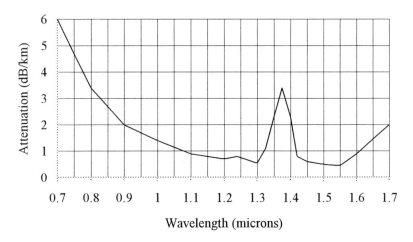

Figure 6.12 Attenuation spectrum

The peaks in the attenuation spectrum at 1.24 and 1.38 μm are absorption bands due to hydroxyl ions (OH⁻) from water dissolved in the glass, whilst the absorption above 1.7 μm is due to the molecular bonds of the glass itself. The attenuation at shorter wavelengths is principally due to Rayleigh scattering (with attenuation proportional to $1/\lambda^4$), where random fluctuations in the glass density and composition (resulting in changes in the refractive index) cause light to be scattered. Glass fibres today are approaching the fundamental limits set by Rayleigh scattering and the infra-red absorption due to the glass itself.

6.8 System considerations

Referring to figure 6.12, three 'windows' in the spectrum can be identified. The first one to be exploited was the waveband from 0.8 μm to 0.9 μm; currently wavelengths around 1.3 μm are being used in high performance links, whilst optical sources and detectors are being developed for the 'window' around 1.5 μm that has even lower loss.

Monomode fibres do not suffer from modal dispersion and graded index fibres minimize modal dispersion at one wavelength, hence to maximize their performance a laser source should be used because its narrow spectrum of light emission minimizes material dispersion. These types of fibres are more expensive than step index fibres and are used in applications that need their better propagation characteristics, e.g. long distance links. For such links a laser is needed anyway because of the increased optical power that it can deliver compared to a LED.

For multimode fibres there is a trade-off between modal dispersion and the ease of coupling light from the source into the fibre. Basically, the more modes allowed, the worse the modal dispersion but the greater the acceptance angle. The major coupling loss occurs between the light source and the fibre, as at the receiver the light from the fibre can be directed on to the detector. A LED can introduce, say, 13 dB of coupling loss to a multimode fibre because it has a large emitting area and produces a divergent beam, whilst the loss from a laser source, when correctly set up, can be taken as 0 dB into either monomode or multimode fibre. A LED would not normally be used as a source for a mono-mode fibre because of the difficulty of coupling light into the fibre. Monomode systems are generally more expensive than multimode systems: not only because of the greater cost of the cable, but also because of the greater accuracy needed by components such as cable connectors.

A power budget in decibels can be calculated for a system. The power available from the source (P_s – say 1 mW or 1 dBm), must be sufficient to deliver the required optical power at the detector (P_o), taking into account transmission losses (P_L) and a safety margin (P_m); i.e.

$$P_s = P_o + P_L + P_m \quad \text{dBm} \tag{6.23}$$

The transmission losses in a typical system include the light source to fibre coupling loss, connector and splice losses (a splice is a permanent joint between two cable segments with the advantage that it has a lower loss than a connector), and fibre loss (i.e. the product of the attenuation in dB/km and the distance); as stated above the fibre to detector coupling loss can usually be ignored. Connectors can be taken as each introducing a loss of 1 dB, whilst each splice introduces, say, 0.1 dB. The safety margin provides for an adequate Signal to Noise Ratio (SNR) at the receiver, so that the signal can be recovered with errors occurring at an acceptable rate; it must also take into account factors such as component tolerances and ageing. For systems using a LED an appropriate figure for P_m is 6 - 8 dB, whilst for a laser source the figure is 8 - 10 dB to take account of the greater variability that can occur with a laser. Figure 6.13 from [GHA] contrasts two power budgets, one for a short link using a LED and step index fibre, the other for a long distance telecommunication link using a laser source and monomode fibre.

(a) Short link using LED and step index fibre:

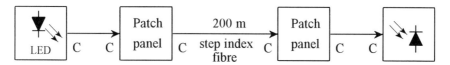

C connector (6 off)

LED power into fibre	−13.0 dBm
Connector loss (6 × 1.0 dB)	6.0 dB
Fibre loss (200 m @ 5 dB/km)	1.0 dB
System margin	8.0 dB
Hence required receiver sensitivity	−28.0 dBm

(b) Long distance link using laser diode and monomode fibre:

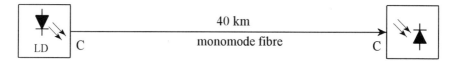

C connector (2 off)
1 splice every 2 km (19 off)

Laser power into fibre	0.0 dBm
Connector loss (2 × 1.0 dB)	2.0 dB
Splice loss (19 × 0.1 dB)	1.9 dB
Fibre loss (40 km @ 0.5 dB/km)	20.0 dB
System margin	10.0 dB
Hence required receiver sensitivity	−33.9 dBm

Figure 6.13 Power budgets

A further important point to note in system design is that the electrical and optical system bandwidths are not the same (the optical −3 dB bandwidth corresponds to the electrical −6 dB bandwidth). This is because there is a linear relationship between optical power in the fibre and the currents in the optical source and detector. Hence, in terms of the optical source and detector currents, the optical −3 dB point occurs when the detector current has fallen to half its maximum value. This means the electrical power at the optical −3 dB point has fallen to a quarter of its d.c. value, corresponding to −6 dB. Thus the electrical bandwidth is less than the optical bandwidth, which is a point to be wary of when comparing systems.

Fibre optic technology seems to offer more bandwidth than can be consumed, i.e. we are in an era of cheap bandwidth, and this affects the way the whole communication industry will develop; e.g. there is little justification for expensive terminal equipment as bandwidth can be traded for cost. Reverting from an optical signal to an electrical signal in order to regenerate or switch the signal reduces the data rate, as electronic circuits cannot operate at the speeds made possible by fibre optics, i.e. the electronics is a 'bottleneck'. Hence the intense interest in optical switching and regeneration. Although we appear to be near the limit in terms of reducing the attenuation per kilometre, the limit of fibre optic technology has not been reached. Propagation using solitons should give rise to another step increase in the data rates of fibre optic systems (essentially a soliton is a pulse that keeps itself together, i.e. it resists dispersion). Also the Erbium Doped Fibre Amplifier (EDFA) now gives optical gain in the 1.5 μm window, resulting in zero attenuation fibre systems. For example, a submarine cable EDFA optical system is being planned to cross the Atlantic ocean in 1997. Operating at 2.4 Gbps, the only electrical pulse regenerators will be at either end of the cable.

Exercises

(1)   Explain the difference between step index multimode, graded index multimode and monomode fibre.

(2)   Compare the following types of fibre in terms of optical quality and cost: plastic, Plastic-Clad Silica and Silica-Clad Silica.

(3)   Explain why total internal reflection of a light beam occurs at the interface between two materials.

(4)   Discuss causes of dispersion in optical fibre systems.

(5) Give reasons for choosing an appropriate type of optical fibre (step or graded index, multi- or monomode, plastic/PCS/SCS) and light source (LED or laser diode) for the following applications:

    (i)   a long haul, high capacity telecommunications link;

    (ii)   a short distance, low speed, minimum cost link.

(6) A step index multimode optical fibre has a core of refractive index 1.5, a cladding of refractive index 1.4 and a loss of 4 dB/km. For a length of 3 km:

    (i)   determine the overall cable attenuation as a power ratio.

    (ii)   estimate the pulse spreading;

    (iii) determine the maximum data rate for this channel using NRZ data.

(7) A step index multimode optical fibre has a core of refractive index 1.51 and a cladding of refractive index 1.49. Determine for this cable:

    (i)   the numerical aperture;

    (ii)   the acceptance angle;

    (iii) the critical angle;

    (iv) the maximum length of cable for a 2.048 Mbps data channel using NRZ data.

(8) Explain why there is a trade-off between acceptance angle and pulse dispersion for a step index multimode fibre.

(9) For a graded index fibre with a core of refractive index 1.5 and cladding of refractive index 1.48:

    (i)   determine the acceptance angle;

    (ii)   determine the critical angle.

(10) Estimate the required receiver sensitivity for a 2 km length of step index multimode fibre with attenuation of 4 dB/km – connected via patch panels to a LED source, which outputs 1 mW of optical power, and a PIN detector.

(11) Estimate the required receiver sensitivity for a 50 km length of monomode cable with attenuation of 0.5 dB/km, assuming that the cable is spliced every 2 km and the source is a laser diode with an output of 2 mW of optical power.

(12) Compare laser diodes with LEDs as light sources for optical fibres, stating their suitability for different types of fibre.

(13) State how modal dispersion can be minimized or eliminated.

(14) Variation of the refractive index with wavelength causes material dispersion in fibre optics. Variation of the characteristic impedance with frequency causes distortion in transmission lines (see chapter 4). Discuss the similarities between the two phenomena.

(15) Investigate current manufacturing techniques for optical fibres and write a 1000 word essay on how they are made, include specifications for current 'state of the art' glass and plastic fibres.

(16) Investigate current research on optical regeneration, optical switching and solitons. Use trade, research and professional body journals, and the Internet (see chapter 8). Quote the references used and use more than one type of source for your references.

(17) Compile a list of the more important equations used in this chapter.

(18) Write your own summary of what you have learnt in this chapter.

7 Data Link Protocols

A communication protocol is a set of rules to ensure the successful transfer of data between two terminals. These rules are analogous with the rules governing human conversation, e.g. only one person should speak at one time, things not understood can be repeated, etc. Data link protocols are one type of communication protocol and govern the transfer of data over both point-to-point links and multi-drop links. A point-to-point link is analogous to a conversation between two people, whilst a multi-drop link, between e.g. a mainframe computer and many terminals, is analogous to the way a TV presenter takes questions from an audience for a panel of experts.

In terms of the communication channel introduced in chapter 1, a connection is made by means of the physical interface, e.g. V.24 or X.21, as covered in chapter 3. A data link protocol 'sits' on top of this physical link in order to actually transfer data. In terms of protocol layers, the bottom layer – layer 1 – is the physical interface, whilst layer 2 is the data link protocol. Higher layers will be added in chapter 8 but this chapter is primarily concerned with how to get data across a single link; the multi-drop link really being an extension of this in that only one call can be set up on the link at any one time.

A simple data link protocol, the asynchronous protocol, was covered in chapter 3. The problem with this protocol is that it is inefficient, as it only sends a single character at a time. For example, sending a 7 bit ASCII character with one start bit, a parity bit, and two stop bits means that the protocol is only 63.6% efficient. This chapter deals with synchronous protocols: synchronous meaning that the receiver circuitry is clocked at the same clock rate as the transmitter. This allows many characters to be sent consecutively, i.e. as a block, without errors being caused by clock slip. Generally no minimum block length is specified and the maximum is typically one or two kilobytes. The common features of all synchronous protocols are:

- the use of a common clock at transmitter and receiver;
- the transmission of data in blocks;
- a means of identifying the start and end of frames;
- some means of detecting errors;
- a way of automatically requesting retransmission of any faulty data blocks (such a process being known as Automatic Repeat reQuest, ARQ).

The user data must either be collected together in a block, e.g. for a user typing in at a terminal, or segmented into blocks, e.g. to transfer a large file. The user data and the protocol overhead make up a frame or Protocol Data Unit (PDU), the protocol overhead being carried in a header and trailer either side of the data, see figure 7.1.

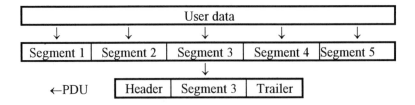

Figure 7.1 Synchronous Protocol Data Unit (PDU) or frame

To achieve synchronism a direct link may be set up from the transmitter clock circuit to the receiver, e.g. using the timing signals in RS-232. However in many cases, especially for long distance links, a separate channel is not appropriate. In these cases the clock signal is combined (i.e. multiplexed) with the data signal, transmitted over the channel, and recovered at the other end by a clock extraction circuit, see figure 7.2. The receive clock is set by transitions in the received signal; since these transitions were set at the transmitter the receive and transmit clocks will be in step, i.e. synchronous.

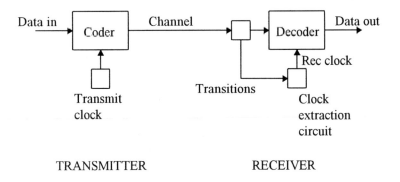

Figure 7.2 Synchronous transmission

Synchronous protocols can be divided into character oriented and bit oriented. The older protocols, represented by bisync, are character oriented whilst the newer protocols, represented by HDLC (High-level Data Link Control), are bit oriented. We will briefly review bisync, partly because it is still used but mainly to draw out the contrasts between it and HDLC. The main focus of the chapter however will be HDLC, as it is not only a commonly used protocol but is also the basis for many other protocols, e.g. LAP-B (Link Access Protocol-Balanced, used in X.25), LAP-D (used in ISDN), etc. The differences between these protocols and HDLC are minor; hence an understanding of how the HDLC protocol works will also enable the workings of many other modern protocols to be understood. For HDLC the header and trailer are three bytes each: hence, for a 1024 byte block of data, the protocol is 99.4% efficient, which highlights the advantage of synchronous protocols over the asynchronous protocol.

The principal advantage of HDLC compared to bisync is the adroit way it achieves 'data transparency', which allows it to transmit any type of data in any format, e.g. graphic characters, control characters or numerical data. A bit oriented protocol is by definition transparent to data, as it treats the data as a bit stream. On the other hand a character oriented protocol relies on control characters to regulate the exchange of the data. Control characters simulated by the data would upset the correct operation of the protocol; hence a character oriented protocol is not transparent to data unless special procedures are taken (as is done for bisync).

7.1 Character oriented protocols

The most common character oriented protocols are bisync and Basic Mode. At the most basic level an information exchange between two DCEs is the same for all variants of bisync and Basic Mode. The most common control characters used to control the transfer of data are listed below:

ACK	Acknowledge
NAK	Negative acknowledge
ENQ	Enquiry
EOT	End Of Transmission
ETB	End of Text Block
STX	Start of Text
ETX	End of Text
SYN	Synchronous idle
DLE	Data Link Escape

N.B. although the acronyms for many of the control characters are the same in ASCII (see appendix D) and EBCDIC, their binary values are not necessarily the same.

The use of these control characters is illustrated below in an example information exchange between a master and slave station, with the master transmitting first. The only acronym of the exchange not yet mentioned is the Block Check Sequence (BCS), which is used in the detection of errors. The BCS is either a two byte Cyclic Redundancy Check (see section 7.3.2) or a one byte Longitudinal Redundancy Check (see section 7.1.3).

	Master	**Slave**
(1)	←SYN SYN ENQ	←SYN SYN ACK
(2)	←SYN SYN STX ... data ... ETB BCS	←SYN SYN ACK
(3)	←SYN SYN STX ... data ... ETX BCS	←SYN SYN NAK
(4)	←SYN SYN STX ... data ... ETX BCS	←SYN SYN ACK
(5)	←SYN SYN EOT	←SYN SYN EOT

In (1) a call is established. The data to be transferred consists of two blocks: in (2) the first block is successfully transferred; in (3) an error has occurred in transmitting the second block, so an ARQ request is made to repeat the transfer (by sending NAK, which should, but does not, stand for 'knackered'); in (4) the second block is successfully retransmitted. In (5) the call is cleared down.

This exchange illustrates several points:

- the two SYN characters enable the receiver to lock on and identify the start of the frame (i.e. achieve frame, character and bit synchronization);
- a NAK is used to initiate an Automatic Repeat reQuest (ARQ), an ACK is used for a positive acknowledgement;
- a stop-and-wait ARQ scheme is used, as every data block must be successfully acknowledged before the next one is sent;
- although a full duplex link is often used, the protocol essentially operates in the half duplex mode as, at any one time, one channel is for data in one direction and the return channel for acknowledgements;
- the last block is signalled by ETX, all others being terminated by ETB;
- the exchange consists of three phases: call set up, data transfer, call clear down.

Note that another name for stop-and-wait ARQ is idle ARQ.

7.1.1 Bisync

Bisync, also known as Binary Synchronous Control or BSC, is the name for a proprietary standard protocol developed by IBM as its version of Basic Mode; or rather for a number of protocols all sharing some common features. Reputedly there about 50 distinct variants of bisync alone; this highlights another advantage of HDLC in that far fewer variations to the standard have been found necessary to accommodate different applications. Considering the information exchange above, the variant of bisync considered in this chapter has the following features:

- it uses the EBCDIC character code;
- it is transparent to data;
- the Block Check Sequence (BCS) is two bytes and uses a similar Cyclic Redundancy Check (CRC) process to that used by HDLC (see section 7.3.2);

- it uses ACK0 and ACK1 alternately instead of ACK.

Data transparency is achieved by adding a DLE character before every valid control character. In this way control characters simulated in the data can be ignored as they will not normally be preceded by a DLE character. If the DLE character is simulated in the data then, before transmission, another DLE character is inserted before it. At the receiver a DLE DLE pair is recognized as a single DLE data character. For example, if the data happened to contain the sequence DLE DLE ETX this would be transmitted as DLE DLE DLE DLE ETX; at the receiver each DLE pair would be recognized as a single DLE data character and ETX without a DLE control character would also be taken as data. Although this makes the protocol transparent, it increases the protocol overhead, as a typical message would be as in figure 7.3:

| DLE | SYN | DLE | SYN | DLE | STX | ..data.. | DLE | ETX | BCS (2 bytes) |

Figure 7.3 Bisync frame

The DLE character is also used to enable extra control sequences to be defined: e.g. WACK (DLE ';') can be used as a positive acknowledgement which signals that the receiver is not ready to receive any more data; and ACK0, ACK1 (DLE decimal 112, DLE '/') are used alternately instead of ACK, which can be useful in identifying that a whole frame has gone missing.

7.1.2 IBM 3270 master/slave protocol

Among the variants of bisync is IBM's 3270, which is designed for a main-frame computer communicating with many DCEs, attached in a multidrop configuration, as in figure 7.4. A CCU is a Cluster Control Unit which allows several terminals and printers to share a line to a mainframe computer; it achieves this by multiplexing frames from the terminals one after another down the line to the mainframe and distributing frames from the mainframe to the correct terminal. The 3270 version of bisync is an example of a master/slave protocol, where the mainframe is the master and the CCUs are the slaves. In order to send data to a terminal the mainframe must 'select' the appropriate CCU. To send data back to the mainframe a CCU must wait until 'polled' by the mainframe. Hence all data transfers are controlled by the mainframe. To offload such communication tasks from the mainframe a Front End Processor (FEP, or communications processor) is often used. The protocol needs a single address field: when a reply is received from a poll by the mainframe the field carries the address of the terminal which is the source of the data; when the mainframe makes a select it carries the destination address for the data. The master/slave mode of operation has been superseded by the peer-to-peer protocols of Local Area Networks (see chapter 9), where in principle any node can send data to any other node and all nodes are equal in terms of gaining access to the network.

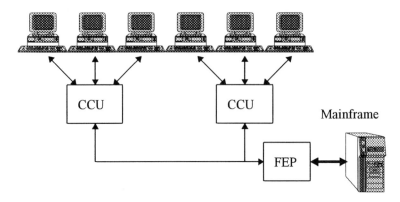

Figure 7.4 A multi-drop line and Cluster Control Units

7.1.3 Basic Mode

Basic Mode also has many variants. The principal differences between Basic Mode and the bisync variant considered above are that Basic Mode normally uses the seven bit ASCII character set, in which case it uses a one byte Block Check Sequence, and it is not transparent to data. When using eight bit characters it uses the same CRC as bisync.

For the one byte BCS, Basic Mode adds an odd parity bit, called a Vertical Redundancy Check (VRC), to each 7 bit character, see figure 7.5. It then adds the single byte BCS, called a Longitudinal Redundancy Check (LRC), of even parity. Theoretically this enables any single bit error to be corrected by using the row and column with the wrong parity to indicate the bit to be flipped. However, this error detection method is not as powerful (i.e. it cannot detect as many errors) as the Cyclic Redundancy Check (CRC) used by bisync and HDLC. In practice it is used solely to detect errors rather than correct them.

In data communications burst errors are more important than single errors, e.g. a lightning strike which lasts for 1 ms would corrupt 10 bits on a 9.2 kbps line. The length of an error burst is defined by the first and last bits which are in error (if all bits in between are random then half of them can be expected to be correct). The matrix parity check of Basic Mode can detect but not correct any two bits in error. All odd numbers of errors will be detected, but it is possible that the parity checks would fail to detect, say, four bits in error.

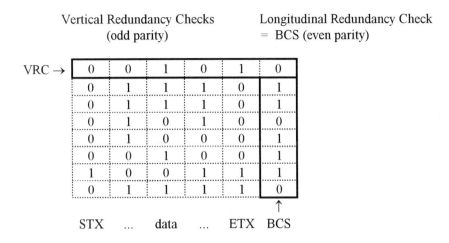

Figure 7.5 Longitudinal Redundancy Check

7.2 HDLC

A High-level Data Link Control frame [ISO/IEC 3309] (see figure 7.6) provides the standard features of synchronous protocols: a means of identifying the start and end of frames (the flag); a means of detecting errors (the Frame Check Sequence); a way of automatically requesting retransmission of faulty data blocks (using the control byte); and a block of (transparent) data. In addition it has an address byte, which can be extended in multiples of bytes, for use on multi-drop lines. The Frame Check Sequence is a two byte Cyclic Redundancy Check, see section 7.3.2. The control byte is a very powerful means of acknowledging data; it is considered in detail in section 7.2.1.

| Flag | Address | Control | ... data ... | FCS (2 bytes) | Flag |

Flag	01111110
FCS	Frame Check Sequence
Control byte	see figure 7.8

Figure 7.6 HDLC frame

The important difference between HDLC and bisync is that HDLC is a bit oriented protocol and hence inherently transparent to data. The flag is the key to this, as it is a unique bit pattern of 01111110; unique because the protocol ensures that it does not occur in the data. It does this by use of a process of 'bit stuffing' at the transmitter and the reverse process of 'bit stripping' at the receiver.

All of the PDU between the flags marking the beginning and end of a frame at the transmitter is sent as a bit stream via the 'bit stuffing' process. The algorithm for this is very simple: after every 5 consecutive 1s a 0 is inserted (stuffed). Hence if a flag was simulated in the data it would be transmitted as 011111010 and would not be received as a flag.

At the receiver the true flags mark the beginning and end of the frame. All the data between these flags is sent via the 'bit stripping' process. This is simply the reverse of the process at the transmitter, i.e. a bit is deleted (stripped out) after every consecutive group of five 1s (the bit will be a 0 but the algorithm does not need to check this). Hence a received pattern of 011111010 will be recovered as 01111110, i.e. the same bit sequence as input to the transmitter.

A common line code used with HDLC is NRZI (Non Return to Zero, Inverted) which has the same format as NRZ binary (see chapter 1) with the difference that the polarity changes whenever a 0 bit is encountered. Since (i) bit stuffing and stripping ensures that there are never more than five consecutive 1s in the data, and (ii) NRZI ensures that the line code toggles for every zero sent, this line-code guarantees transitions for the receiver's clock extraction circuitry.

HDLC is a bit oriented protocol because of these processes. Note that the data is considered as a bit stream rather than a string of characters. This means that the receiver uses a sliding 'window' to inspect the received data; e.g. to detect the flag, eight bits of data are inspected at a time, the data is then clocked on one bit and the new eight bits of data are inspected to see if they correspond to the flag, see figure 7.7. Once the flag pattern is detected the receiver has achieved frame synchronization, which means it will also have achieved character and bit synchronization.

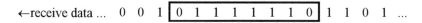

←receive data ...   0   0   1 | 0   1   1   1   1   1   1   0 | 1   1   0   1   ...

Figure 7.7 Eight bit sliding window to detect the flag

7.2.1 *HDLC control byte*

The control byte enables HDLC to use continuous ARQ, rather than stop-and-wait ARQ as with bisync, i.e. with HDLC the transmitter does not have to wait for an acknowledgement from the receiver. In addition, positive acknowledgements can be sent 'piggy-backed' on a data frame; hence HDLC can be operated in a full duplex mode. This means that it is possible for a link using the HDLC protocol to be sending continuous streams of data in both directions at once. Trying to unravel what is happening on such a link is complicated, so we will restrict ourselves to the half duplex mode in explaining the operation of the protocol.

There are three types of frame in HDLC, which can be distinguished by their control bytes, see figure 7.8 [ISO/IEC 4335]: information frames to send data and two types of supervisory frames, used for commands rather than data. Numbered supervisory frames (bits 7, 6 = '10') are used to acknowledge the data and unnumbered supervisory frames (bits 7, 6 = '11') are used to set up, clear down the link, etc.

Different standards use different bit numbering schemes. For the sake of consistency, in this book the lsb is always bit 0, the leftmost bit in a figure is transmitted first, and where there are multiple bytes the topmost byte is transmitted first.

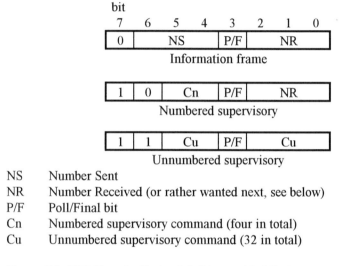

NS   Number Sent
NR   Number Received (or rather wanted next, see below)
P/F   Poll/Final bit
Cn   Numbered supervisory command (four in total)
Cu   Unnumbered supervisory command (32 in total)

Figure 7.8 HDLC control bytes, bit 7 transmitted first

The information frame control byte contains a three bit field (NS) for the number of the frame being sent; hence the transmitted frames can be numbered from 0 to 7. After frame 7 has been sent the frame numbers wrap around so that frame 0 is sent next.

Considering next the control byte for numbered supervisory frames: the control byte has a three bit field (NR) to acknowledge received frames. The number in this field is the number of the frame that the receiver wants next. Hence the master might send four information frames consecutively, numbered 0 ... 3, and the slave would acknowledge correct receipt of all these frames by sending just one numbered supervisory frame with NR = 4.

The information frame also has an NR field; hence in the normal case (no errors) both ends can send acknowledgements 'piggy-backed' on to an information frame. If an error is detected or there is no data to send, a numbered supervisory is returned instead.

The Poll/Final bit has various functions depending on the link configuration. Its main function is in the normal response mode (see section 7.2.2), where it is used by the master to poll the slaves (as a 'poll' bit) or to signal the end of data (from the slave as a 'final' bit). The use of this bit is illustrated in section 7.2.3 but for the present we will ignore it.

A number must be sent in the NS and NR fields; hence if nothing has changed the last number sent is repeated. This means that only 7 frames (rather than 8) can be sent before waiting for an acknowledgement, i.e. the send window for HDLC is 7 frames. This can be explained by considering figure 7.9, where the master transmits first:

Master		**Slave**		**Master**		**Slave**
NS		NR		NS		NR
0	←	1		0	←	1
1				1		
2				2		
3				3		
4				4		
5				5		
6				6		
7				7	←	0
0	←	1		0	←	1
(a)				(b)		

Figure 7.9 Seven frame send window for HDLC

In both cases (a) and (b) frame number NS = 0 is sent and positively acknowledged by NR = 1. In case (a) the master then sends eight frames (1 ... 0) before asking for an acknowledgement. The slave acknowledges correct receipt of all eight frames with NR = 1. However, this acknowledgement is ambiguous. If the receiver had not received any of the eight frames it would still have sent NR = 1, as this was the last NR value set. This ambiguity is avoided in case (b) by the master asking for an acknowledgement after *seven* frames. The next acknowledgement, for frame NS = 0 with NR = 1, must apply to the second NS = 0 frame sent since the NR field has changed in between. Hence the send window for HDLC is limited to seven frames, not eight.

In some cases, e.g. for satellite links, a send window of 7 frames is not sufficient. To ensure that the transmitter does not have to waste time waiting for an acknowledgement, an extended mode of HDLC can be used, with seven bits for the NR and NS fields. This means that the send window is 127 frames, or $2^7 - 1$.

7.2.2 *Supervisory commands*

As explained above, HDLC uses continuous ARQ. However, if an error is detected, HDLC has two options to govern retransmission of faulty frames: either go-back-N or selective reject, also known as selective repeat. The simplest option to implement is go-back-N, as it does not require any extra buffers at the data destination. In this case, an ARQ (negative) acknowledge-ment of NR = n is interpreted by the data source as go back to the frame number n and start again from there. The alternative ARQ process, of selective reject, means retransmit the frame in error (i.e. with NS = n) and then continue transmitting from where left off. There is less data to retransmit but it does require the destination to buffer all the frames received since the frame in error.

On detection of an error, the ARQ method is set by the command field of the numbered supervisory control byte. There are two bits available to signal a reply, i.e. four commands can be sent:

- Receiver Ready (RR) for acknowledging frames with no errors but with no data to be returned;
- Receiver Not Ready (RNR), again acknowledging error-free frames but also signalling back that no more data should be sent for the moment (e.g. because the receiver's buffers are full);
- REJect (REJ) for go-back-N ARQ;
- Select REJect (SREJ) for selective reject ARQ.

Different modes of operation are allowed in the standard. In the Normal Response Mode the address field is used to identify the destination in command frames (when the master selects a device to transmit data to), or the source device in response frames (after the master has polled the slaves). There is no provision for slaves to communicate directly with each other. In the Asynchronous Balanced Mode a peer-to-peer protocol is set up over a point-to-point link, i.e. the terminals have equal status. There is no need for polling or the address byte but it is included for uniformity. These are the two most common modes of operation. The unnumbered supervisory commands (with five bits, 32 commands are possible) are concerned with setting up these modes, recovering from fault conditions, etc. For example:

- a multi-drop link using a master/slave protocol can be set up using the Set Normal Response Mode (SNRM) command;
- a point-to-point, peer-to-peer link can be set up using the Set Asynchronous Balanced Mode (SABM) command;
- the disconnect (DISC) command allows a link to be cleared.

7.2.3 HDLC conclusion

Putting together the explanations above the reader should be able to understand how the control byte and, in particular, the poll/final bit organize the data exchanges below:

Master Type of byte	NS	P/F	NR			Slave Type of byte	NS	P/F	NR
Information	0	0	0	→					
Information	1	0	0	→					
Information	2	0	0	→					
Information	3	P	0	(1) →					
					←(2)	Unnumbered S go-back-N	-	F	2
Information	2	0	0	→					
Information	3	P	0	→					
					←(3)	Information	0	0	4
				←		Information	1	0	4
					←(4)	Information	2	F	4
Information	4	P	3	→					
					←(5)	Unnumbered S RR	-	F	5

This exchange illustrates several points:
(1)   the master uses a poll to force an acknowledgement;
(2)   the slave has detected an error in frame NS = 2 from the master: it asks for this frame and all subsequent frames to be repeated;
(3)   the slave 'piggy-backs' a positive acknowledgement on the data;
(4)   the slave signals it has no more data to send by setting the final bit;
(5)   the slave replies with an unnumbered supervisory (command: Receiver Ready) if it has no data to send itself.

For satellite links a 127 frame send window and selective reject ARQ should be used. For a more down-to-earth application, say a 20 km link between a computer centre and a branch office, a seven frame send window would be used with go-back-N ARQ. Both these cases, being point-to-point, would use the Asynchronous Balanced Mode.

HDLC is successful as a standard because it can be used for many applications, including master/slave and point-to-point links. A measure of its success is its use as the basis for new protocols, e.g. LAP-B for X.25, LAP-D for ISDN, LAP-M for modems, etc. Indeed these new protocols are often just a subset of HDLC. IBM's SDLC (Synchronous Data Link Control) is also based on it. In this it is superior to bisync and Basic Mode, where often new variants were devised for minor modifications to applications.

7.3 Error detection and correction

A major function of the data link protocol is to detect and correct errors, so the subject is covered here although error checks are used in other protocols too. A check sequence enables some errors in a block of data to be detected, in the same way as the parity check in the asynchronous protocol (see chapter 3) enabled some errors in a character to be detected. Once detected appropriate action needs to be taken, e.g. the data might be ignored or corrected. There are two alternative ways of correcting errors: the message may be repeated using backward error control, as in ARQ, or Forward Error Control (FEC) may be used to correct errors directly. Error detection and correction are only possible if there is some redundancy in the message, more redundancy being required for FEC than for error detection. Hence error correction using forward error control is less efficient, in terms of protocol overhead, than error detection with ARQ to correct the data. Also, if a forward error control scheme is used then some detected errors will be incorrectly corrected; hence the error rate in the recovered data will be higher than when using ARQ. Generally, therefore, ARQ is the preferred means of error correction in data communications, but there are some circumstances where ARQ is not appropriate, e.g. for a link to a space probe where, since the link is operated in the simplex mode, forward error control is the only possibility.

A simple type of check sequence is a one's complement check, as used in the TCP/IP suite of protocols (see chapter 8). For a one's complement check with a two byte check sequence, the data is split into 16 bit words which are added together using modulo-2^{16} arithmetic (i.e. carries into bit position 16 are ignored). The required check sequence is simply the negative of this sum. Hence, adding up the received data and check sequence will give a zero result if there are no errors. To make the result negative in one's complement the binary data is simply inverted. A modulo-2^{16} addition at the receiver on the received data and check sequence will generate an all 1s result if there are no errors (all 1s corresponds to zero in one's complement, as inverting it gives all 0s, i.e. there are two zeros in one's complement). The following example for a four bit check sequence should make this clear:

	Transmitter	Receiver
	bit 3 2 1 0	
	1 1 0 1	1 1 0 1
	1 0 0 0	1 0 0 0
	0 1 1 0 +	0 1 1 0
(1)	1 0 1 1	0 1 0 0 +
		1 1 1 1

Normal binary is used to add the four bit words of the data, but the carry into bit position 4 is ignored (i.e. modulo-16 arithmetic is used for a four bit check sequence). The sum is then inverted, resulting in the four bit check sequence 0100 which is appended to the data before transmission. Modulo-16 addition at the receiver will give a result of 1111 if the data has not changed.

To investigate error detection and correction further, consider a simple case where the data (d) is either 00, 01 or 11 and an even parity check bit (c) is used, i.e. there are three valid code words with message format ddc and 8 possible permutations which can be received:

transmitted code word (ddc)	possible received messages
000	000
	001
	010
011	011
	100
	101
110	110
	111

Note that the minimum 'distance' (in terms of the number of code word bits that are different between valid code words) is 2 bits, e.g. between 000 and 011. The minimum distance between any two valid code words is called the Hamming distance and is an important property of the code. A Hamming distance of two signifies that at least two bits must be in error for a message to be incorrectly accepted as correct, e.g. if the message 000 was sent and the two errors happened to be in the second and third bit positions then the message 011 would be received. By definition, the receiver must accept a valid message as valid, so the system will not detect this error. Note though that if the errors were in the first and third positions then 101 would be received which is not a valid code word, i.e. these two errors would be detected. In general, a Hamming distance of $e + 1$ allows at least e errors to be detected, i.e. the minimum requirement is a Hamming distance of 2 to enable 1 error to be detected. A Hamming distance of 1 means that a single bit in error could change a valid code word to another valid code word, i.e. error detection is not possible.

To correct e errors using forward error control requires a Hamming distance of at least $2e + 1$; this is because all received messages within a distance of e code words on either side of a valid code word, plus the valid code word itself, will be taken as the valid code word. To correct one error therefore requires a Hamming distance of three. A very simple code for forward error control is given below, where the single data bit (d) is simply repeated twice for the check bits (c) to ensure that the Hamming distance is three.

transmitted code word (dcc)	possible received messages
000	000
	001
	010
	011
	100
	101
	110
111	111

Assume the message 000 was sent and the first bit is received in error, i.e. 100 is received. This is not a valid code word so an error has been detected. 100 is nearer to 000 than 111 in terms of the Hamming distance, so it is reasonable to assume that 000 was actually sent. Hence the error is corrected and the data 0 output by the receiver. Notice, however, what happens if two bits are received in error, e.g. 000 is received as 110. Although an error is detected in this case too, the wrong data will be output (since 110 is nearer to 111 than 000 the assumption that 111 was sent will be made). This highlights the point that error detection followed by an ARQ process results in fewer errors getting through to the destination than forward error control.

7.3.1 Hamming single bit code

This code detects any single bit error and pinpoints its position, enabling the bit to be flipped to correct the error. It is an example of a FEC code. The check bits can be arranged to occupy all bit positions that are powers of two in the message. For example, consider the message with bits $m_a = m_1 \ldots m_{10}$, the check bits c_j occur when a in m_a is a power of two.

m_{10}	m_9	m_8	m_7	m_6	m_5	m_4	m_3	m_2	m_1
d_6	d_5	c_4	d_4	d_3	d_2	c_3	d_1	c_2	c_1

At the receiver incorrect check bits are used to pinpoint the position of the error, e.g. say c_4, c_2 and c_1 are inconsistent when recalculated at the receiver: the position of the error is therefore message bit m_7 ($7 = 4 + 2 + 1$).

For a code of length n and with source data of length k the efficiency will be $E = k/n$. These codes are known as block codes, the particular type being indicated as (n,k), e.g. the 10 bit code considered above is a (10,6) block code with an efficiency of 60%. Because the check bits occupy positions that are powers of two, the code efficiency has multiple peaks which occur for message lengths $n = 2^j - 1$ (for $j \geq 2$, where j is the number of check bits), i.e. for $n = 3$, 7, 15, etc. Since $k = n - j$, the code efficiency $E = 1 - j/n$, hence $E = 33.3\%$, 57.1%, 73.3%, etc. The problem with these codes, as with other forward error control codes, is that they are not efficient for small message lengths, whilst for long message lengths the probability of multiple errors may become too high.

From the above, the minimum number of check bits for 4 bits of source data is 3, i.e. a (7,4) code. To prove this result consider the general case. There are 2^k valid code words for a source data length of k bits. For a single bit error correcting code of length n each valid code word will differ in one bit position from n invalid code words, i.e. there must be at least $(n + 1)2^k$ code words. Since there are 2^n possible code words

$$(n + 1)2^k \leq 2^n \tag{7.1}$$

With j check bits then $n = k + j$, i.e. for a single bit error correcting code,

$$(k + j + 1) \leq 2^j \tag{7.2}$$

Hence, for $k = 4$ then $j \geq 3$, as before.

An example is the best way to explain how the code works. Consider a (7,4) block code again, the actual data to be transmitted being 1011. Hence there is a data one in position m_7, m_5 and m_3 and a zero in position m_6. The binary numbers corresponding to the values of a in m_a where the data is a one are added together, using modulo-2 arithmetic (i.e. ignoring any carry into bit position 1 out of the lsb 0).

Modulo-2 arithmetic was introduced in chapter 3, when discussing Trellis Coded Modulation (TCM); which is a convolutional coding scheme, as opposed to the block coding technique of Hamming discussed here. To add binary numbers using modulo-2 arithmetic, the numbers are simply added up, column by column, ignoring any carries.

$$
\begin{array}{r}
111 \\
101 \\
\underline{011+} \\
001
\end{array}
$$

The result gives the three check bits as $c_3 = 0$, $c_2 = 0$ and $c_1 = 1$. Thus the transmitted message is:

m_7	m_6	m_5	m_4	m_3	m_2	m_1
d_4	d_3	d_2	c_3	d_1	c_2	c_1
1	0	1	0	1	0	1

At the receiver the binary numbers corresponding to all message positions (including the check bits) with a one are added together, again using modulo-2 arithmetic:

$$
\begin{array}{r}
111 \\
101 \\
011 \\
\underline{001+} \\
000
\end{array}
$$

The result is zero indicating no error detected.

Now suppose an error is introduced, say m_3 is received as 0 instead of 1. Going through the same process at the receiver now gives:

$$
\begin{array}{r}
111 \\
101 \\
\underline{001+} \\
011
\end{array}
$$

Notice that the result now points to message bit m_3 as being wrong, hence the single bit error can be corrected. The process works just as well for an error in a check bit.

As explained before, burst errors are more of a problem in data communications than single bit errors. Interleaving is a refinement of the Hamming single bit code which enables it to cope with burst errors. Suppose the maximum length burst error that the code is designed to cope with is 8 bits: then, using the coding scheme in the example above, the m_7 bits from eight code words are transmitted consecutively, followed by eight m_6 bits, etc. The result is that any two bits from the same block check are separated by at least eight other bits, i.e. a burst error of up to eight bits will only affect up to one bit in any one code word, hence a burst of up to eight errors can be corrected.

7.3.2 Cyclic Redundancy Check

At the transmitter the data is processed to generate a Cyclic Redundancy Check (CRC) sequence, which is appended to the data before transmission. At the receiver, the recovered message, *including* the check sequence, is processed in the same way. The result should be a predetermined pattern (e.g. zero), anything else indicating that an error has occurred.

To explain how a CRC works is best shown by way of an example. Note that the data and check sequences are sequences of binary digits, i.e. they are binary numbers. The CRC operates on these numbers using the rules of modulo-2 arithmetic. Initially, for ease of explanation of the algorithm, decimal notation and the normal rules of arithmetic will be used.

Suppose the data to be transmitted is decimal 14562 and a 'key' of say 13 is to be used. The algorithm can be broken down into three stages at the transmitter:

(1)   zeros (2 in this case) are appended to the source data (i.e. the data is multiplied by 100 to give 1456200);

(2)   the result of stage (1) is then divided by the key (13 in this case) to find the whole number remainder (r = 5);

(3)   the remainder is then subtracted from the result of stage (1) (i.e. 1456200 − 5 = 1456195).

This number is then transmitted: it can be broken down into source data − 1 (= 14561) and an appended check sequence (95). At the receiver if the received message with no errors (i.e. 1456195) is divided by the same key as at the transmitter, the remainder will be zero; hence the data (14561 + 1 = 14562) can be accepted as valid. A non-zero remainder indicates that an error has occurred. Note that errors will not be detected if their effect results in a number that is a multiple of the key, e.g. 1456208 is incorrect (the recovered data would be 14563) although it passes the test.

The actual algorithm uses modulo-2 arithmetic operating on binary numbers. Clearly, the value of the remainder is of no intrinsic interest, all that is required is some value to allow the algorithm to work. Modulo-2 arithmetic has the advantage that there are no carries. A minor advantage of this is that the data will not be altered by the process (in the decimal example above, the data 14562 was transmitted as 14561 because of a carry in the subtraction) but the major advantage is speed, as the electronic circuit which actually does the operation can operate on all bits in parallel without considering carries from one bit position to another. The type of circuit used is usually a serial shift register with XOR gates providing feedback from the output to different stages of the shift register (as also used to generate a PRBS − Pseudo Random Binary Sequence). Clearly, the key must be the same at transmitter and receiver. Standard keys, which get the best out of the algorithm, have been specified: bisync uses CRC-16 whilst HDLC uses CRC-ITU.

CRC-ITU is 1 0001 0000 0010 0001, a 17 bit number which generates a 16 bit check sequence that can detect burst errors up to 16 bits in length. The standard way of writing such keys is as a polynomial, hence their alternative name of 'generator polynomials'. The bit positions which are 1 are indicated by powers of x, the power indicating the bit position. Thus CRC-ITU is $x^{16}+x^{12}+x^5+1$. The last 1 (i.e. x^0) is important as it generates a parity check, thus detecting all odd numbers of errors; all the other bits are there to detect even number bursts of errors up to the limit of the check. Other standard keys are:

- CRC-16 $= x^{16}+x^{15}+x^2+1$
- Ethernet and Token Ring, CRC-32
  $= x^{32}+x^{26}+x^{23}+x^{22}+x^{16}+x^{12}+x^{11}+x^{10}+x^8+ x^7+x^5+x^4+x^2+x+1$
- ATM and DQDB $= x^8+x^2+x+1$

These keys can detect burst errors up to the length of the check sequence. They can also detect all double bit errors (not necessarily in a burst) and will detect many burst errors with burst length greater than the length guaranteed to be detected. For the mathematics to prove these properties see for example [PET].

As an example of a CRC check using binary and modulo-2 arithmetic consider the parity check, i.e. the generator polynomial is $x^1 + 1$, with data 11001. Modifying the algorithm given above for a decimal CRC:

(1) as the length of the key is 2 bits the check sequence will be one bit long, so append one zero to the data giving 110010;

(2) divide this number by the key to find the remainder (1 in this case) using modulo-2 division;

$$
\begin{array}{r}
10001 \\
11\,)\,110010 \\
\underline{11} \\
00 \\
\underline{00} \\
00 \\
\underline{00} \\
01 \\
\underline{00} \\
10 \\
\underline{11} \\
r = 1
\end{array}
$$

(3) subtract the remainder from 110010; however, subtraction in modulo-2 is the same as addition, so the transmitted data is simply the original data with the remainder appended, i.e. 110011.

$$
\begin{array}{r}
110010 \\
1- \\
\hline
110011
\end{array}
$$

The check bit here is simply an even parity bit. The name Cyclic Redundancy Check arises because if the data is rotated another valid code word will result. This is obviously true for parity, e.g. rotating the transmitted data one bit right results in 111001, which is still a valid code word for even parity.

The algorithm described above is sometimes modified, for example in the case of HDLC [ISO/IEC 3309]:

• the serial shift register used to generate the FCS is preloaded with all ones;
• the one's complement of the remainder is appended to the data at the transmitter;

- the serial shift register used to check the FCS at the receiver is also pre-loaded with all ones;
- the remainder with no errors is 0001 1101 0000 1111.

7.4 Link utilization

Network latency (L) is the elapsed time between when the first bit of data from an information source enters the transmitter to when the last bit is received at the destination. The communication channel may be routed over many links, so the latency is given by $L = t_p + H + t_s + t_q$, where t_p is the end-to-end propagation delay, H is the message holding time, t_s is the processing time and t_q is the queuing time. The propagation delay is given by

$$t_p = \frac{\ell}{V_p} \tag{7.3}$$

where ℓ is the end-to-end distance across the channel and V_p is the velocity of propagation. The holding time H is the time during which the whole PDU occupies the channel, i.e.

$$H - \text{frame length (in bits) / channel bit rate} \tag{7.4}$$

The processing time t_s can generally be ignored, as with modern high speed processors this time is generally small compared to the other times. It is the cumulative time taken in processing the message, including time taken in error detection (e.g. performing the CRC algorithm at the transmitter and receiver), putting the PDU together, selecting a link (i.e. switching or routing the message, see chapter 8), etc. The queuing time t_q is the cumulative time that the message spends in buffers waiting to be processed; ideally this time should be zero, so we will ignore this time too. Thus the latency can be approximated by

$$L = t_p + H \tag{7.5}$$

The network latency is important as it is the fundamental distinguishing feature between Wide Area Networks (WANs) and Local Area Networks (LANs), which are the subjects of the next chapters. Loosely, a LAN is a network that occupies a small geographical area, e.g. an office building or a factory, whilst a WAN covers a greater area, e.g. a country, continent or indeed the whole world.

In-between a LAN and a WAN comes a Metropolitan Area Network (MAN), which is designed to provide a backbone network covering an extended area up to the size of a city, e.g. linking the various sites of a university.

The concept of network latency allows a more meaningful differentiation (in terms of communication processes) between LANs and WANs than the geographical area covered. For WANs the end-to-end distance ℓ is generally large, so the propagation delay t_p is generally much larger than the holding time H and to a first approximation the holding time can be ignored. Defining

$$a = \frac{t_p}{H} \tag{7.6}$$

then for WANs, say $a \geq 10$. For LANs on the other hand ℓ is smaller, so both the holding time and propagation time must be considered, i.e. say $a < 10$. As bit rates increase in the future the holding time H will decrease, so it will become appropriate to consider networks covering smaller areas as WANs. The trend is therefore for future networks to be designed as WANs, whilst LANs will be restricted to smaller and smaller areas. Ultimately, as the data rate or the end-to-end distance increases, all networks are limited by the velocity of propagation of signals in the particular transmission medium; which gives an alternative definition of a WAN as a network whose performance is limited by the velocity of propagation of the signals that it carries.

Consider the link utilization U of a stop-and-wait ARQ process such as bisync. The definition of the link utilization is the ratio of two times, both measured from when the first bit of data from the information source enters the transmitter,

$$U = \frac{\text{time for transmitter to transmit a frame}}{\text{elapsed time until acknowledgement is received}} \tag{7.7}$$

The time for the transmitter to transmit a frame is the message holding time H. Again ignoring processing and queuing times, and also ignoring the holding time for a positive acknowledgement signal (as it is much less than the message holding time), the elapsed time until the acknowledgement is received is the holding time plus twice the propagation delay (once for the message and once for the acknowledgement), i.e.

$$U = \frac{H}{H + 2t_p} = \frac{1}{1 + \left(\dfrac{2t_p}{H}\right)} = \frac{1}{1 + 2a} \tag{7.8}$$

The discussion above has implicitly considered error-free transmission. Consider now random (i.e. not burst) errors with an error probability p, where $p = 1 \times 10^{-3}$ means that the Bit Error Rate (BER) is one error in every 1000 bits (i.e. one error is to be expected, on average, in every 1000 bits). The probability of one bit *not* being in error is $1 - p$ and the probability of receiving a frame of length n bits without errors is

$$P(\text{no errors in frame}) = (1 - p)^n \tag{7.9}$$

The expected number of transmissions (N) required for a frame to be success-fully received is the inverse of this, i.e.

$$N = \frac{1}{(1-p)^n} \tag{7.10}$$

whilst the probability of receiving a frame in error is

$$P(\text{errors in frame}) = 1 - (1-p)^n \tag{7.11}$$

For example, for an error-free link p is zero, hence $P(\text{no errors}) = 1$ and $N = 1$, whilst if it is certain that a bit will be wrong then $p = 1$, hence $P(\text{no errors}) = 0$ and $N = \infty$. Actually, the receiver is acting idiotically here, as if the probability of error is 1 then simply inverting the received bit gives the correct data. For a more realistic case assume the received data is random, i.e. $p = 0.5$; then for a frame length of $n = 1000$ bits the $P(\text{no errors}) = 0$ to a very close approximation and $N = \infty$ again.

To take account of random errors, the value for the link utilization given in equation (7.8) must be divided by the expected number of transmissions until the frame is successfully received. Hence the link utilization with errors $U' - U \times P(\text{no errors in frame})$, i.e.

$$U' = \frac{1}{\left(1 + \left(\dfrac{2t_p}{H}\right)\right)N} = \frac{(1-p)^n}{1 + \left(\dfrac{2t_p}{H}\right)} \tag{7.12}$$

For a continuous ARQ scheme, as with HDLC, the link utilization should be greater. Indeed, for a send window sufficient to ensure that there is no need to wait for acknowledgements and no errors $U = 1$ or, with random errors and selective reject (i.e. not go-back-N), then

$$U(\text{selective reject}) = \frac{1}{N} = (1-p)^n \tag{7.13}$$

This implies that the send window in time is $\geq H + 2t_p$ seconds or in terms of frames the send window is

$$W \geq 1 + \frac{2t_p}{H} \text{ frames} \tag{7.14}$$

If the send window is less than this then

$$U(\text{selective reject}) = \frac{W}{\left(1 + \dfrac{2t_p}{H}\right)N} = \frac{W(1-p)^n}{\left(1 + \dfrac{2t_p}{H}\right)} \tag{7.15}$$

These equations give quantitative comparisons between stop-and-wait and continuous ARQ methods, and of their expected performance with random errors. For further discussion on these comparisons see [STA]. Note that burst errors are actually more common but, since the effect of a burst error will probably lead to only one frame having to be repeated, the performance figures for random errors can be expected to be worse than for burst errors, i.e. these expressions give a conservative design.

The advantage of the stop-and-wait ARQ scheme is that only the single frame being transmitted needs to be buffered; hence, stop-and-wait ARQ is used for links where *a* is small or, despite its obvious inferiority in terms of link utilization, for long distance links where the cost of bandwidth is of less concern than the cost of the terminal devices.

Exercises

(1) Describe, in general terms applicable to all synchronous protocols, how such protocols detect and correct errors over a duplex link.

(2) State the common features of synchronous protocols.

(3) Explain the difference between polling and selecting on a multi-drop link.

(4) State the two functions of the DLE character in bisync.

(5) Given the following sequence, in which an error has been detected, continue the transmission sequence assuming that no further errors occur:

Master	Slave
←SYN SYN ENQ	←SYN SYN ACK
←SYN SYN STX ... data ... ETX BCS	←SYN SYN NAK

(6) Determine the Vertical and Longitudinal Parity Checks that would be formed by the Basic Mode protocol for the following block of ASCII characters:

100 0101   100 0011   100 0110   100 0100

(7) The following data is received on a link using the Basic Mode protocol. Detect and correct the single bit error. The format is the same as figure 7.5.

0	1	1	1	0
0	1	1	0	0
0	0	1	0	1
0	0	0	0	0
0	1	1	0	0
0	0	0	0	0
1	1	0	1	0
0	0	1	1	0

(8) State whether two bit errors can be detected and corrected by the error detection scheme of Basic Mode.

(9) Compare and contrast the following: Basic Mode; the variant of bisync described in this chapter (IBM 3270); and HDLC.

(10) Explain what is meant by character oriented and bit oriented protocols.

(11) What does HDLC stand for?

(12) Sketch and explain the general format of an HDLC information frame.

(13) State how HDLC can simultaneously achieve both a unique synchronization sequence and data transparency; and explain how the process works by way of an example.

(14) Explain the terms 'piggy-backing' and continuous ARQ and state which improvement they make possible in protocol operation.

(15) State how errors are detected and corrected in HDLC.

(16) Complete the following HDLC transmission sequence, assuming that no more errors occur and there is no more data to transmit:

Master				**Slave**	
Type of byte	NS			Type of byte	NR
Information	0	→			
Information	1	→			
Information	2	→			
		←		Unnumbered S: go-back-N	1

(17) Discuss the advantages and disadvantages of different sized send windows, and the continuous ARQ modes selective reject and go-back-N, when applied to: (i) a short distance, terrestrial link; (ii) a satellite link.

(18) List other protocols based on HDLC.

(19) Determine (in hex) the 8 bit check sequence using one's complement for the hex data: A0 BB C8.

(20) State the Hamming distances required to (i) detect and (ii) correct all double bit errors. State the Hamming distance required for a parity check scheme.

(21) Determine the minimum number of check bits required to correct all single bit errors in a 16 bit message.

(22) Determine the transmitted message for a single bit Hamming code for the source data d_4 ... d_1 = 1010.

(23) With a single bit Hamming code, a message m_7 ... m_1 = 1000010 is received. Determine the source data.

(24) Determine the transmitted frame (i.e. source data and appended check sequence) for a CRC, performing the calculations in decimal for a generator polynomial 17 and source data 24835, to give a remainder of zero at the receiver. Check that the remainder is indeed zero at the receiver.

(25) (a) Determine the transmitted frame (i.e. source data and appended check sequence) for a CRC, to give a remainder 0 at the receiver, using the generator polynomial $x^3 + 1$ operating on the binary source data 11001 (msb ... lsb).
    (b) Check that the remainder is indeed zero at the receiver.

(26) For the transmitted frame of question (25) show that a double error (in the first and fourth data bits from the left, i.e. the received data sequence is 01011) is detected by the receiver.

(27) For the transmitted frame of question (25) show that it has even parity and state the bit sequence in the generator polynomial which generates the parity.

(28) (a) For the transmitted frame of question (25) cycle the bits one position to the right (e.g. for four bit words 1011 would become 1101) and show that this received frame also results in a zero remainder.
    (b) State another class of received messages which would give zero remainder for the generator polynomial of question (25).

(29) Discuss the importance of latency in terms of network design.

(30) Derive the link utilization for a selective reject, continuous ARQ protocol, assuming no errors and that the send window is $< 1 + 2t_p/H$.

(31) For a frame length of 100 bits, a velocity of propagation of 2×10^8 m/s, an end-to-end path of 10,000 m, a data rate of 10 Mbps, and no errors, determine the link utilization for the following cases: (i) stop-and-wait ARQ; (ii) selective reject ARQ with a seven frame window. Comment on your results.

(32) Repeat question (31) for a BER of 1 in 100.

(33) Confirm the following observations: (i) with no errors, go-back-n behaves as selective reject ARQ; (ii) with a one frame window, selective reject ARQ behaves as stop-and-wait ARQ; (iii) for a short link, stop-and-wait ARQ behaves as selective reject ARQ.

(34) Compile a list of the more important equations used in this chapter.

(35) Write your own summary of what you have learnt in this chapter.

8 Wide Area Networks and Open Standards

The previous chapter concentrated on point-to-point links. In this chapter we use these links to build a Wide Area Network (WAN). WANs are to be contrasted with Local Area Networks (LANs), which are discussed in the next chapter. A simple distinction between WANs and LANs is that WANs are designed to cover a large geographical area, whilst LANs are designed for a restricted area, e.g. an office building or factory. Another way of distinguishing between WANs and LANs, this time in terms of the network parameters t_p (end-to-end propagation delay) and H (holding time), is that the factor $a = t_p/H$ is, say, ≥ 10 for WANs and < 10 for LANs, as discussed in chapter 7 on latency.

The mode of routing or switching principally considered in this chapter is packet switching. Messages are first segmented into packets or frames, as in HDLC, see chapter 7. A wide area network, see figure 8.1, is made up of point-to-point links between network nodes. Packets are routed over these links by the nodes, hence the nodes are called Packet Switching Exchanges (PSEs). The messages share the use of the network by interleaving packets over the same links. Note that this is a form of multiplexing, but it differs from Time Division Multiplexing (TDM), where the time slots for each channel come at regular, preassigned intervals.

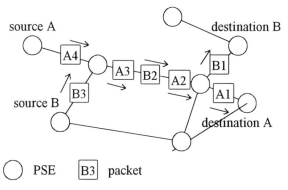

Figure 8.1 Multiplexing by packet switching

Alternatives to packet switching are:
- Circuit switching, where there is a continuous channel for the duration of the call. Sometimes the channel is a continuous physical link, but it may be a TDM link, where the physical channel only exists at regular intervals. Calls sent over the PSTN (Public Switched Telephone Network) use circuit switching, see section 8.4.
- Message switching, which is similar to packet switching except the whole message is sent in one go, essentially as one – possibly large – packet. This is

179

not a common switching mode, as it is unwieldy compared to packet switching. For example, other messages will have to wait until a message has finished using a link before they can continue, which means that the latency of the network is unpredictable and can be excessive.

Communication costs can be split between the channel and the terminal equipment. The cost of a channel can be expressed in units of Hertz per unit cost. Terminal costs partly depend on the cost of the processing required to prepare a message for transmission. Traditionally, the fixed allocation of time slots in TDM is usually a better choice when bandwidth costs are less than computing costs; the dynamic allocation of packet switching is usually better when computing is cheaper than bandwidth. Computing power is now very cheap, in comparison with what it has been, but with the new fibre optic systems bandwidth has become even cheaper. This does not mean to say that cabling costs can be ignored, but rather that the potential bandwidth of a fibre optic cable is so large that currently most of it is not used. This unused bandwidth means that we are now in an era of cheap bandwidth and attention will focus on the terminals: e.g. to trade bandwidth for improved signal quality or cheaper terminals, or to use the extra bandwidth to send more signals.

Packet switching
There are two main modes of operation for packet switching: either virtual circuit (also called connection oriented) or datagram (also called connection-less).

When operating in a virtual circuit mode all the packets follow the same route through the network. This has similarities to circuit switching in that there is a connection set-up phase, an information transfer phase, and a call clear-down phase. The difference between a virtual circuit and circuit switching can be inferred from the word 'virtual', as in circuit switching the channel is a physical circuit. With a virtual circuit a link is only assigned to a call when necessary to send a packet; hence in-between the links are free to be used by other calls, allowing packets to be multiplexed over the links.

When operating in the datagram mode each packet is treated as a message and will be sent via the best route as determined by each network node as the packet arrives, see figure 8.2. As conditions on the network change so the route may change. Hence in a datagram network the packets may travel different routes. This mode has obvious similarities to message switching, except that the packets will not exceed a fixed length.

Consider the consequences of these two modes for the operation of the network:
• In a virtual circuit the first packet transmitted will be the first packet received, i.e. the order of the packets remains unchanged.
• In a datagram circuit the packets may arrive in any order, as an earlier packet may be sent over a longer route.

Also, a datagram must contain the complete destination address information whilst a virtual circuit packet follows a route set up in each network node, i.e. it need only contain the information to identify which virtual circuit it is to follow. The trend today is towards virtual circuit operation but datagrams are still used, e.g. datagrams are needed to set up the connection for a virtual circuit!

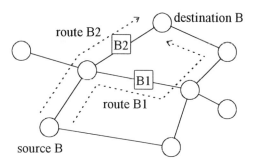

Figure 8.2 Datagram mode of operation

In section 8.2 a particular WAN standard called X.25 is described. This is a virtual circuit, packet switching WAN which is a common standard, following the seven layer reference model. However, before considering the X.25 protocol, it would be helpful to discuss the seven layer reference model, as this is the most influential set of standards in communications.

8.1 Seven layer reference model

The International Standards Organization (ISO) is responsible for the development of standards in many areas. In communications it was concerned at the way communication protocols were developing, in that suppliers were 'locking' customers into proprietary systems. It therefore developed (and is still developing) standards that are 'open', i.e. equipment from different manufacturers to the same standard should be able to work together, creating an open market in communications equipment. This has obvious benefits to the customer: in that they are not dependent on one supplier and can obtain good value for money. The benefit to the supplier is a larger market. However, even though customers can obtain equipment from many different suppliers they often buy from one supplier, as trying to pin down a fault among equipment from different manufacturers can be a difficult process.

Another justification for the need for standards can be seen in the network of figure 8.3, where four machines from four manufacturers are connected to each other in a fully connected network. Without a standard interface each manufacturer will have to provide an interface program for every other range of

equipment; hence, as shown in figure 8.3 (a), twelve individual two-way interface programs have to be written. With a common set of standards only one
interface program needs to be written for each range of machines; hence only
four interface programs are required as in figure 8.3 (b).

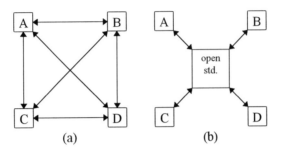

(a)   (b)

Figure 8.3 Advantage of a common set of standards

The result of this work on standards is the ISO Reference Model (RM) of
Open Systems Interconnection (OSI), which differentiates the task of a network
architecture into seven layers, hence the alternative name of the seven layer
RM.

In the seven layer RM the various functions of the communication hardware
and software are hierarchically organized into layers. Although the placing of
functions was straightforward in the lower layers, the boundaries between the
higher layers are somewhat arbitrary. Indeed, IBM has a proprietary network
architecture, called SNA (System Network Architecture), which also has a
seven layer architecture. However, only the lower two layers follow the same
grouping of tasks as the seven layer RM; the higher layers, although having
obvious similarities in their aims, are not divided in the same way.

Although there is little to justify the particular division of layers chosen by
the ISO, it is important that some such choice is made. For example, a
computer program written for one layer can be modified or replaced by a new
program without rewriting all the communication software in the layers above
and below. This means that the communication software is written in reusable
modules, with considerable savings in development and maintenance costs.

The standards do not so much specify what must be done in each layer as
specify the interfaces between the layers, which leaves manufacturers free to
develop their own communications equipment as long as they provide the
expected interfaces.

The first three of the seven layers have already been met, they are as follows:
• Physical layer (layer 1), which is concerned with the electrical and
mechanical properties of the interface, e.g. V.24/V.28, X.21, X.21 *bis* and X.20
bis, all mentioned in chapter 3, are ISO physical layer standards. Note that RS-
232 is a US national standard rather than an ISO standard.

• Data link layer (layer 2), which is concerned with how data is transferred over the physical link set up by a layer 1 standard. HDLC (High-level Data Link Control, covered in chapter 7) is the prime example of an ISO data link layer standard. Other examples are the derivatives of HDLC, such as LAP-B (Link Access Protocol - Balanced), LAP-D, and LAP-M. Note however that SDLC is IBM's SNA layer 2 standard (called Data Link Control layer in SNA) and is not an ISO standard.

• Network layer (layer 3), which is responsible for routing messages over a network. X.25 is the prime example of a layer 3 protocol, see section 8.2. Note that here X.25 refers specifically to a network layer protocol; at other times it can refer to the stack (or set) of protocols required for a WAN running X.25, see figure 8.4. An X.25 network needs an X. series (i.e. a standard for a public data network) physical layer interface; one of those from figure 8.4 should be chosen depending on the terminal capabilities. LAP-B is the protocol responsible for transmitting data over any of the point-to-point links of the network, whilst X.25 is the layer 3 protocol responsible for transferring data from end-to-end over the network.

ISO RM layer	X.25 protocol stack
3 – Network layer	X.25
2 – Data Link layer	LAP-B
1 – Physical layer	X.21, X.20, X.21 *bis*, or X.20 *bis*

Figure 8.4 X.25 protocol stack

The remaining ISO RM layers are briefly described below for completeness. Note that these layers are concerned with the communication functions that need to take place at the end stations.

• Transport layer (layer 4), which has to compensate for different network layers, e.g. for a datagram network layer the transport layer must order the packets into the correct sequence before passing them on to layer 5, but this is unnecessary with a virtual circuit layer 3.

• Session layer (layer 5), which has to organize and synchronize the call or session, e.g. this layer is responsible for setting-up and clearing-down a call. Another function of this layer is to ensure consistency between databases at either end of the network. For example, if an electronic fund transfer is made between two banks both computers must agree that a transaction has been made. It would not be acceptable for a communication fault to result in a debit being recorded by one bank but no corresponding credit recorded by the other bank. To achieve consistency the session layer organizes synchronization points during the progress of the call; if a fault occurs then both ends roll-back to the previous synchronization point (where the data is consistent at both ends).

• Presentation layer (layer 6), which is responsible for converting between data formats so that the host machine can read the data. This is needed for example to convert between the ASCII and EBCDIC character sets when a PC (which uses ASCII) is connected to an IBM mainframe (which uses EBCDIC). Another function of this layer is data security, by encrypting the message at the source and decrypting it at the destination.

• Application layer (layer 7), which provides a set of programs, each of which offers a particular network service. The application program names are given below for reference. Given the types of services (e.g. file transfer, E-mail, etc.) supported by a network, the names are mostly self-explanatory; discussion of these services is held over until TCP/IP applications are covered in section 8.3.

FTAM (File Transfer, Access and Management), Virtual Terminal (VT) protocol, MOTIS (Message Oriented Text Interchange Standard), CMIP (Common Management Information Protocol), JTM (Job Transfer and Manipulation), MMS (Manufacturing Messaging Service), RDA (Remote Database Access), DTB (Distributed Transaction Processing).

The seven layer RM is a strict hierarchy in that higher layers use lower layers to transport data, but each layer can only communicate with a corresponding layer in another machine, see figure 8.5 (i.e. the information flow is from layer 7 in host 1, down through all layers in host 1, across at layer 1, and up through all layers in host 2). The actual end-user application is running in code native to the host machine above layer 7.

native system		HOST 1 end-user ↓		HOST 2 end-user ↑	
host	7	Application	↔	Application	7
user oriented	6	Presentation	↔	Presentation	6
layers	5	Session	↔	Session	5
host	4	Transport	↔	Transport	4
network	3	Network	network	Network	3
layers	2	Data link	service	Data link	2
	1	Physical	layers	Physical	1

↑ physical connection

Figure 8.5 The seven layer RM hierarchy

To summarize the relationships between the layers:

• Layer 1 is a physical interface whilst all the other layers are protocols.

• Layers 1 and 2 are generally hardware layers (layer 1 is wholly concerned with hardware, whilst the bit-stuffing/stripping and CRC processes of HDLC are usually performed in hardware for speed, although they can be done in software), whilst the higher layers are generally carried out in software.

- Layers 1 through 3 are concerned with the end-to-end transfer of data across a network, whilst layers 5 through 7 are concerned with the preparation and organization of the data at the end stations.
- Layers 3 and 4 together provide a common interface to layer 5, although some of their functions overlap.

The seven layer RM is not the only way to achieve open standards: an alternative is TCP/IP, the protocol suite used for the Internet, which is introduced in section 8.3 and compared to the seven layer RM in section 8.3.3.

8.2 X.25

X.25 is really a network access protocol rather than a network protocol, with a maximum data rate of 2 Mbps. This means that X.25 is an open standard that defines the interface to a Public Data Network (PDN). The network itself is the responsibility of the operating agency, which may well decide to use a proprietary system. It is of no concern to the customers of a PDN how the network is built; all they require is that the network reliably transports their data across the network. Since the PDN must support all the functionality of X.25, it is usually sufficient to assume that the network itself uses the X.25 protocol stack.

8.2.1 X.25 protocol

The X.25 packet consists of a header, described below, and a data field up to 4096 bytes long; there is no trailer. The default length for the data field is 128 bytes. This layer 3 packet is sent in the information field of the LAP-B information frame at layer 2. LAP-B is a subset of HDLC, using the Asynchronous Balanced Mode of operation. Since HDLC was discussed in chapter 7 LAP-B need not be considered further.

The X.25 header is 3 bytes long when using 3 bit fields for NR and NS, see figure 8.6 [ISO/IEC 8208]; the extended mode with 7 bit fields is recognized by bits 2 and 3 in the first byte being reversed.

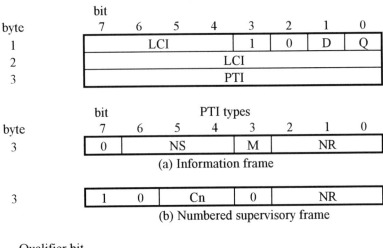

Figure 8.6 X.25 packet header and PTI byte

Q   Qualifier bit
D   Delivery confirmation bit (i.e. acknowledgement required when set)
LCI   Logical Channel Identifier
PTI   Packet Type Identifier
NR   Number Received (i.e. wanted next)
NS   Number Sent
M   More bit (i.e. more data follows when set)
Cn   Numbered supervisory commands:
        00 – Receiver Ready (RR)
        01 – REJect (REJ, go-back-N ARQ)
        10 – Receiver Not Ready (RNR)

bit 7 of the top byte is transmitted first

Figure 8.6 X.25 packet header and PTI byte

The header has a Packet Type Identifier (PTI) which has essentially the same format as the control byte in HDLC. However, there is no Frame Check Sequence at level 3 as there is no trailer, so the PTI is concerned more with flow control than error control. Nevertheless, errors such as missing frames will be detected and corrected using the PTI. As with HDLC the maximum send window is 7 frames (or 127 frames in extended mode). However, the default value on Public Data Networks is set to 2. This normally only applies between a terminal and the local Packet Switching Exchange (remember, X.25 is a network access protocol); it does not mean that a maximum of only two packets can be in transit over the network. The M bit has the same function as the P/F bit – used as the Final bit – in HDLC. Apart from these points, the operation of the PTI is as explained in chapter 7 for the operation of the control byte for HDLC.

Considering the rest of the header, bits 0 to 3 of the first byte of the header make up the General Format Indicator (GFI) and the remaining twelve bits of the header represent the virtual circuit number or Logical Channel Identifier (LCI). The GFI contains the Q and D bits.

When set, the Q (or Qualifier) bit indicates that the packet contains data which is intended for the network (to select facilities or options, etc.) and so should not be delivered to the end user.

When set, the D (or Delivery) bit indicates that a confirmation of delivery is required from the other end of the network. The D bit is only used for important information, because of the overhead in time and the extra network traffic generated. With a small value for the send window it would also severely limit throughput (e.g. a send window of 2 would mean that a maximum of 2 packets could be in transit across the whole network if this bit is set).

The LCI allows 4096 simultaneous virtual circuits to be set up by one DTE over one physical link. The address range is allocated in contiguous blocks, starting with address 1 (address 0 is reserved for diagnostic packets) and numbered upwards for permanent virtual circuits, followed by incoming calls from the network. Outgoing calls from the DTE are allocated downwards from a predefined maximum number. There is a region in the middle that can be allocated to either incoming or outgoing calls as required.

There are other options for the PTI field, corresponding to the unnumbered supervisory commands of HDLC [HAL].

8.2.2 PAD

A specialized packet terminal can be used to access an X.25 network; although a more common access method, with an existing terminal or PC, is to use a Packet Assembler Disassembler (PAD). The PAD assembles the user data into packets and disassembles the received packets. It adds the X.25 layer 3 protocol header to the data to be transmitted over the network and strips off the header from the received packets, thus keeping the operation of the network invisible to the user.

There are three standards which together specify how a PAD operates in the network. Collectively, these are known as the 'Triple X' standard, see figure 8.7 which shows their relationship to the X.25 protocol:

- X.3 specifies the functions of the PAD itself and the various commands to enable its mode of operation to be set.
- X.28 describes the protocol used to communicate between a terminal and the PAD. This enables the terminal to send commands to the PAD, e.g. asking the PAD to establish a virtual circuit.

- X.29 describes the protocol used to communicate between the PAD and a remote PAD across the network, e.g. to establish a virtual circuit. The X.29 control information is carried in the data field of an X.25 packet with the Q bit set to indicate that the information is not user data.

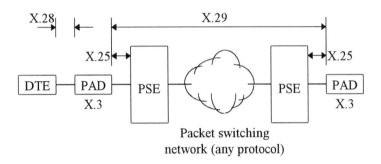

Packet switching
network (any protocol)

Figure 8.7 Triple X standards

There are two main ways to access a PAD: either making use of a private PAD or a public PAD (see figure 8.8, which also shows the application of other X.25 protocols). If users have their own private PAD it is usually placed next to their terminal in their office. They access a Public Data Network via a leased line to their nearest Packet Switching Exchange. Alternatively, a user can use the PSTN and a modem to connect their terminal to a public PAD at the nearest PSE. Note that both examples require just a local (i.e. short distance) connection to the PSE. The pricing regime for a PDN is often determined solely by the amount of data sent, i.e. distance is no object. Hence the user has to pay only for a local link but has access to everywhere covered by the WAN.

Users can employ private PADs to build up a private X.25 data network to multiplex data from several terminals over a leased line, say from a branch office to a head office where another PAD demultiplexes the data. X.25 is being used here for its ability to multiplex data streams rather than for packet switching.

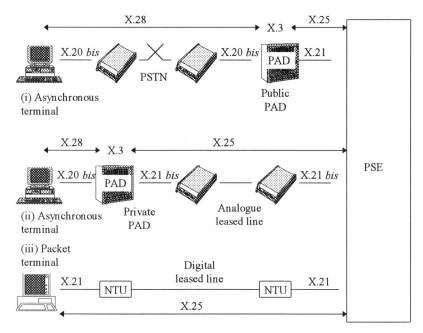

NTU   Network Terminating Unit

(i)   Asynchronous terminal to public PAD.
(ii)   Asynchronous terminal to PSE using private PAD.
(iii)   Packet terminal to PSE via digital leased line.

Figure 8.8 Public and private PADs and packet terminal

8.2.3 X.25 summary

Collecting together some of the points mentioned above about X.25, the major
functions of a network protocol are:

- Control of the connection, e.g. call set-up and clear-down of a virtual circuit.
- Addressing, i.e. identifying the channel by means of the virtual circuit
  identifier.
- Segmentation of the data into packets, up to the maximum length set for the
  network.
- Flow control, to ensure that the source address sends data no faster than the
  slowest link or node can accept.
- Multiplexing of data streams over a single link.
- Acknowledgement of data.

- Distinguishing between end-user information and control messages.
- Identification and reporting of error conditions (not mentioned before but also an important function).

8.3 TCP/IP

This is a WAN protocol suite using packet switching which takes it name from its two key protocols: the Transmission Control Protocol and the Internet Protocol. It supports both datagrams (using IP) and virtual circuits (using TCP, which in turn uses IP). It is a *de facto* open standard, but it has a different philosophy about layering and network evolution compared to the seven layer RM; these differences, discussed in section 8.3.3, justify the existence of a second set of open standards. Its best known use is as the protocol suite used for the Internet: the public global system of many LANs and packet switched networks connected together to allow internetworking. Access to the Internet is gained from any network that is part of the Internet. For example, a modem can be used to access an on-line information service over the PSTN. The on-line service acts as a gateway to the Internet and should provide all the software mentioned later (and more). Alternatively, if an organization's network is connected to the Internet, then access can be gained from every networked workstation by running the applications supplied with the network operating system.

Network applications can be divided into those providing a service (servers) and those wanting to use a service (clients). Many open system applications are based on this client-server model, including the majority of TCP/IP applications. The point about this division is that server applications must run continuously, as a client may request the service at any time, whilst client applications need only run when requested by the user. The servers can be further divided into two classes: iterative servers, where the server processes one client at a time before dealing with the next; and concurrent servers, where a new server is started for each new client (i.e. many clients may be using the service concurrently). The new server handles a client's request and terminates when finished. The drawback to iterative servers is that the client may have to wait in a queue for the server to be finished, whilst with a concurrent server the client will not have to wait long, if at all, to be given a new server.

The TCP/IP protocol stack was originally developed in the late 1960s for the US Department of Defense (DOD). The standard TCP/IP implementation is from the University of California at Berkeley; the first widely available release was in 1983 [STE].

The TCP/IP protocol suite is divided into four layers, see figure 8.9 which shows the position of some of the many protocols in the suite. Note that this division into layers is not as strict as in the seven layer RM, e.g. routing is considered a network layer function, but the routing protocols RIP and OSPF use a transport layer protocol (hence they are not shown as belonging to any particular layer in figure 8.9).

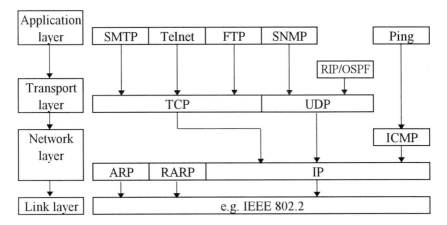

SMTP   Simple Mail Transfer Protocol
Telnet   remote terminal protocol
FTP   File Transfer Protocol
SNMP   Simple Network Management Protocol
Ping   Packet Internet Groper
RIP   Routing Information Protocol
OSPF   Open Shortest Path First
TCP   Transmission Control Protocol
UDP   User Datagram Protocol
ICMP   Internet Control Message Protocol
ARP   Address Resolution Protocol
RARP   Reverse Address Resolution Protocol
IP   Internet Protocol

Figure 8.9 TCP/IP protocol suite layers

The lowest or link layer corresponds to layers 1 and 2 of the seven layer RM, so it is not considered further here. Hence TCP/IP can run on Token Ring or Ethernet LANs, see chapter 9.

The network layer contains IP and associated protocols. IP provides a best effort but unreliable datagram service (i.e. delivery is not guaranteed) and, being a datagram service, packets may be delivered out of sequence. This is the layer at which packets are routed, i.e. it is the four byte IP address that identifies the source and destination.

The transport layer contains TCP and UDP. TCP provides a virtual circuit service. It takes a stream of data from an application layer protocol and performs the following operations:

- Segments the data to make a TCP Protocol Data Unit with TCP header and application data.
- Sends each packet using IP.
- Reassembles the application data.

It must compensate for the service provided by IP by ensuring that lost packets are retransmitted and by resequencing the IP packets if necessary. Applications that only need a datagram service use an alternative host-to-host protocol called UDP, which provides a minimum overhead service with no guarantee of delivery.

Finally, the application layer provides a set of programs, each of which offers a particular network service, e.g. SMTP, Telnet, FTP, SNMP and Ping, which are explained in the next section. They offer the same types of service as with the seven layer RM (see section 8.1), although the TCP/IP and seven layer RM applications differ in the detail of their provision.

The protocols of figure 8.9 that have not been mentioned yet are:

- ICMP, which communicates error and control messages, etc. (e.g. as used for the Ping application).
- RIP and OSPF, which are dynamic routing protocols, see section 8.3.5.
- ARP and RARP, which provide the address mapping between the 4 byte IP address (see section 8.3.2) and the address used at the data link layer to identify the particular terminal device (e.g. in Ethernet, the 6 byte address which is the unique identifier of an Ethernet card in a PC, see chapter 9).

When a network terminal is first switched on, it needs to obtain its IP address. For a terminal with a hard disk the address is normally in its configuration file, but a diskless workstation must send an RARP request to obtain its IP address from the server. Once the IP address is obtained the two types of terminal behave in the same way.

If a source has a message to send to a station on its network but does not know the physical address it broadcasts an ARP request. This request contains the IP address of the required destination. The station with this IP address sends back an ARP reply which contains both the IP and the physical address. The source then puts these addresses into its address translation table so that next time it has the address ready. A table entry is deleted if no use is made of it for some time.

Thus RARP provides address resolution from a physical address to an IP address for a diskless workstation, whilst ARP provides address resolution for all terminals from an IP address to a physical address.

8.3.1 TCP/IP application layer services

Example commands for some TCP/IP applications are given below for NOVELL NetWare 3 'LAN WorkPlace' running under Windows version 3.11 on an IBM compatible PC. Although these applications are started from

Windows some of them are command line versions, i.e. the user must type a command after the application prompt. What the user should type is shown **bold** in single quotes and ***address*** is either the hostname or IP address of a site that allows the service, see section 8.3.2 (which also indicates how to find such addresses). To end the application program type '**quit**'.

The examples should give sufficient clues to run other versions of the applications and, more importantly, to enable the reader to know what to expect. For a more detailed explanation of the commands see [STE].

- **SMTP** (Simple Mail Transfer Protocol) is the protocol used to support E-mail which, measured by the number of connections made, accounts for about half of all TCP connections [STE]. It provides a connection between two Message Transfer Agencies (MTAs), one of which is the client whilst the other is the server. These provide a common interface for the different E-mail application programs running on users' networks. To send an E-mail message over the Internet the first thing to know is the destination E-mail address (see section 8.3.2), which is also, somewhat obscurely for many people, called the SMTP address.

E-mail stands for Electronic-mail which, as its name suggests, is the electronic equivalent of the letter post. The user has a 'mailbox' at the server that can only be accessed with a password. However, messages can be put in a user's mailbox by anyone who has access to the system. It is very easy to send the same message to many mailboxes at the same time; overuse of this facility is frowned upon. E-mail is almost as fast and far more convenient than the telephone, since both people need not be at their desks at the same time, which is especially important for international communications.

- **Telnet** allows a client terminal to login to a remote server or host. It is designed to work between hosts and terminals using any operating systems by defining a Network Virtual Terminal (NVT), which both ends of the link use to map to and from the particular terminals they support. For example, keystrokes entered at the client keyboard are changed to NVT keystrokes, when transmitting to the server, and NVT replies are changed back to commands that the client's display unit will recognize. To run Telnet type '**telnet**' at the network's command line prompt; or double-click on the 'TNVT220' icon in 'LAN WorkPlace' and then click on 'OK'. Type '**help**' for a list of Telnet commands. To use Telnet type '**open** ***address***' at the TNVT220> prompt, e.g. login to NASA's Spacelink by typing
  '**open spacelink.msfc.nasa.gov**'.
- **FTP** is the protocol used to copy a file from a server to a client, i.e. to download a file. Measured by the number of bytes sent, this accounts for more data than even SMTP [STE]. To run FTP type '**ftp**' at the network's command line prompt or double-click on the 'ftp' icon in 'LAN WorkPlace'. A client must login to the server first. An anonymous FTP server allows anyone to access and download any of its files in the anonymous FTP area. Before running

FTP you need to know the file name you wish to transfer and the address of the site where it is held (see section 8.3.2 for ways of searching for interesting files). To login to anonymous FTP:

(1) type 'open *address*' at the ftp> prompt;

(2) type 'anonymous' at the login (or Remote User Name, etc.) prompt;

(3) finally, it is conventional (i.e. polite) to use your E-mail address for the password.

Once logged in, use standard UNIX commands to change directories, etc. at the remote site and commands prefaced by 'l' for your local site. For example, to transfer a file named *f* in the remote directory \remotedir to a local directory \localdir: (1) type 'ls' (or 'dir') at the ftp> prompt to list the contents of the current remote directory; (2) type 'cd *remotedir*' to change to directory *remotedir*; (repeat steps (1) and (2) until the directory listing shows the file you wish to transfer, N.B. 'cd ..' changes to the next higher directory in the directory tree); (3) set up the local directory you wish the file to be transferred to, e.g. by typing 'lcd *localdir*'; (4) type 'hash' so that you can monitor the file transfer process; (5) you must type 'binary' to transfer the file as an exact copy, otherwise the file will be transferred as 7 bit ASCII characters with the msb of the byte set to 0 (having typed 'binary' type 'ASCII' to get back to text mode if your computer cannot read a text file transferred in binary mode); and finally (6) copy the file by typing 'get *f*'. Type 'help' for a list of FTP commands.

• **SNMP** is the protocol supporting TCP/IP's solution to network manage-ment. Compared with CMIP (Common Management Information Protocol) of the seven layer RM, SNMP has been taken up by more users because it was available first, probably because it was designed to be simpler than CMIP. SNMP uses UDP as a transport layer protocol, as the overhead is less than with virtual circuit operation. Network management is designed to improve network performance rather than degrade it!

• **Ping** is commonly used as a diagnostic aid to see if another host is reachable (note though that the host may have security checks that allow E-mail but not Ping). Ping sends an ICMP echo request and waits for an ICMP echo reply. To run ping, type 'ping *address*' at the network's command line prompt or double-click on the 'ping' icon in 'LAN WorkPlace' and enter '*address*'.

8.3.2 IP addressing

The IP address is used for routing. It is actually a pair of addresses: netid and hostid, i.e. the address of the network and the address of a host on the network together make a unique address. The netid is allocated by the Internet Network Information Center in the USA, whilst the hostid is the responsibility of the system administrator. The four bytes of the IP address are conventionally written in a dotted decimal notation, each field being the representation of one byte of the address, e.g.

1000 0000.0000 1010.0000 0010.0001 1110_2 is written as 128.10.2.30.

There are several classes of address (see figure 8.10). For example, class A refers to large networks and since the netid is only 7 bits long there can be a maximum of 128 such networks in an internet. Class D is used to multicast or broadcast messages, where broadcast means the message is for every host and multicast means the message is for a selected subset of destinations. No hostid can be all ones or all zeros, as all zeros refers to the network itself whilst all ones refers to all hosts on the network. Note how each class begins with a sequence of 1s (a null sequence for class A) followed by a 0.

Hence, when written in dotted decimal notation:

- Class A addresses start with a number between 0 and 127;
- Class B addresses start with a number between 128 and 191;
- Class C addresses start with a number between 192 and 223;
- Class D addresses start with a number between 224 and 239.

A subnet id can be substituted for part of the hostid. The number of bits for a subnet id is a matter for the system administrator. A subnet mask, which in binary is all ones for the net and subnet id and all zeros for the remaining hostid, is used to determine the boundary between the subnet and hostid, whilst the boundary between the net and subnet id is given by the address class.

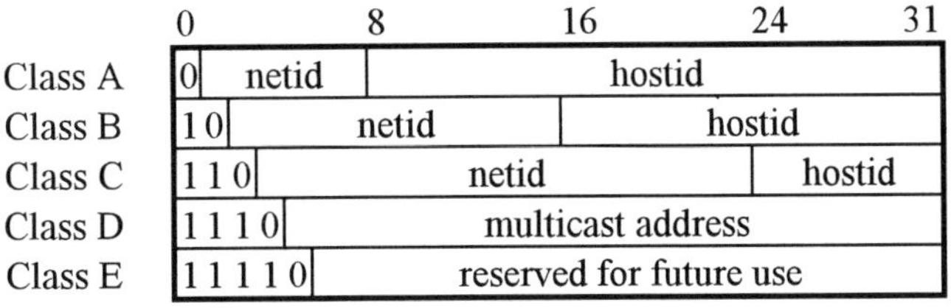

	0	8	16	24	31
Class A	0 netid		hostid		
Class B	1 0	netid	hostid		
Class C	1 1 0	netid		hostid	
Class D	1 1 1 0	multicast address			
Class E	1 1 1 1 0	reserved for future use			

Figure 8.10 Classes of IP addresses

There is a more easily remembered form of Internet address called a hostname, e.g. the hostname of my mail server (but not my E-mail address) is **marconi.eit.shu.ac.uk**, where **marconi** is the name given to a particular machine, **eit** is a work group, **shu** refers to Sheffield Hallam University, **ac** refers to the Academic Community (e.g. universities, research institutions, etc.) and **uk** refers to the UK (hostname addresses are not case sensitive). Note how the address forms a tree structure, with the lowest level in the hierarchy on the left (i.e. the opposite way round to the IP address hierarchy). Hostnames are part of a distributed database [CAR, STE] called the Domain Name System (DNS), which enables an IP address to be found from a hostname address and vice versa. Most applications can use a hostname, as well as an IP address in dotted decimal format, by running a resolver to find the IP address from the hostname.

The Domain Name System is based on a tree structure of domain names. The root node is unnamed. There are three types of domains in the next level down (i.e. the first level):

1. Country domains, all of which are two characters, e.g. **.uk**.
2. Generic or organizational domains, which are three characters long and of which there are seven:

    .com for commercial organizations

    .edu for educational institutions

    .gov for US governmental organizations

    .int for international organizations

    .mil for US military organizations

    .net for networks

    .org for other organizations

Note that apart from the **.gov** and **.mil** domains, these are not reserved for US organizations and many US organizations are in the **.us** country domain.

3. The **.arpa** domain. This has a second level domain **in-addr** used for IP addresses so that they also form part of the DNS. The most significant byte of the IP address is the third level domain, etc., so that the addresses can be looked up and resolved in the same way as hostnames, i.e. by running a resolver.

The mail server on a network is defined by a Mail Exchange (MX) record in the DNS. Hence, if for any reason the server needs to be changed, all that is required is that the DNS record is updated and the E-mail will get through. My E-mail (or SMTP) address is **a.simmonds@shu.ac.uk**. A message sent to this address would first need to be resolved to give the IP address of the mail server at **shu.ac.uk**, so a name server is queried. If this cannot resolve the name it passes the query on to another name server, and so on (remember that DNS is a distributed database).

There is a great deal of information on the Internet; a problem is how to find a relevant piece of information rather than just 'surfing' the Internet. Three possibilities are briefly mentioned here (there are other ways):

An **Archie** server allows anonymous FTP servers to be searched. Archie databases contain lists of files and directories that can be searched by keyword, to give the full filename and the hostname where a file is stored. The file can then be downloaded by anonymous FTP.

Gopher (it is not an accident that it sounds like 'go-for') is a menu based distributed document search and retrieval system with a search tool called Veronica.

The **World Wide Web** (WWW) is a hypertext service initially developed at CERN, the European Centre for Nuclear Research. A hypertext page has, within its text, connections or pointers to files containing related information. The connections are sometimes called 'hyperlinks', sometimes 'hotlinks'; and are made visible to the user, e.g. by underlined and highlighted text. Clicking with the mouse on such a connection causes the related file to be fetched and run. The file can be a text file, an image file, a sound file, etc. Running a text or image file will display it, running a sound file will output sound to speakers. Strictly, such a system is a hypermedia system, i.e. hypermedia is hypertext plus multimedia. The link can be to another Web server, thus allowing a virtual web of connections to be created. The ease with which such cross-links can be followed from within documents is the great advantage of the WWW compared to using services such as Gopher.

The WWW hypertext pages are written using HTML (Hypertext Markup Language). This contains text in ASCII plus specifications for the placement of the text and objects such as pictures. Hence HTML is a presentation layer standard which enables different types of machines to communicate hypertext pages. Web browsers are necessary for reading HTML (example browsers are 'Mosaic' and 'Netscape') and a HTML author can help greatly in creating a hypertext document.

The actual file transfer of hypertext pages is carried out using HTTP (Hypertext Transfer Protocol), which is a TCP/IP application layer service like FTP. The user runs a Web browser, which is a HTTP client, to access a Web server and get a hypertext page as HTML source code. This can be displayed as a hypertext page by the client. The initial page of a Web server is usually called the home page and often appears as a contents page with links to more detailed information held anywhere on the Internet.

A Uniform Resource Locator (URL) allows files to be accessed in a common way. For example, a Web browser may have a field with 'URL' or 'Location'. This is the information needed to run the file: the appropriate application, the hostname where the file is stored, the path to the file, and the file name. The format is

   '*protocol*://*hostname*[:*port*]/*path*/*filename*'

Where *protocol* is **ftp**, **gopher**, **http**, **telnet** or **file**. In the case of **file** the filename extension will define how the file is to be run, e.g. a **.gif** extension means that the file is to be displayed as a picture. The square brackets around **:*port*** indicate this is an optional field, i.e. [and] are not part of the URL. This optional field is for the port number, e.g. 23 for Telnet. Note that there are no spaces in a URL. As an example, NASA's Spacelink URL for hypertext is

   '**http://spacelink.msfc.nasa.gov/**'

Behind every hyperlink in a hypertext page is a URL, which creates a link to the related file when the mouse clicks on the hyperlink.

Generally, the first thing to find on the WWW is a server with a search engine, where keywords can be entered and the server comes up with a list of pages which may be relevant. If you want to come back to any page it can be marked by a 'bookmark', where the URL is simply added to the list kept by your browser. Clicking on a URL in your list of bookmarks takes you straight to the wanted page. These aids, and the 'back' and 'forward' buttons of your web browser, help you navigate the 'information super-highway'.

8.3.3 Comparison of the seven layer RM and TCP/IP

TCP/IP does not fit the seven layer RM exactly, but loosely IP corresponds to layer 3 (the network layer) and TCP corresponds to layer 4 (the transport layer). Apart from the obvious difference that TCP/IP only has three layers above the data link layer, note from figure 8.9 that TCP/IP is not a strict hierarchy. This means that protocols can use a protocol below them without necessarily having to go through an intermediate layer, e.g. ping uses ICMP directly, which is part of the network layer, without using a transport layer protocol. Another example of TCP/IP not being a strict hierarchy is when a lower layer protocol closes down a higher layer protocol without requiring the higher layer protocols at both ends to communicate.

The primary aim of TCP/IP is to facilitate internetworking. It would be unwise to assume that all intermediate networks are reliable and it would be restrictive if only virtual circuits were allowed to be connected. However, even if just one datagram circuit is connected to an internet, then all end-stations must be able to cope with the consequences, e.g. with packets missing or arriving out of sequence. Thus IP provides a datagram service and TCP builds on this to provide a virtual circuit. Currently, the seven layer RM emphasises virtual circuits, e.g. initially X.25 supported both datagram and virtual circuit modes of operation, but the datagram option has been deleted from later versions of the standard.

TCP/IP is predominantly user driven, whilst the seven layer RM is predominantly supplier driven. This is because the seven layer RM is an official international standard. It is only bodies such as national standards organizations, or large manufacturers through their national PTTs, who have the weight to contribute to the specification of new standards. It also means that the standardization process usually takes longer with the seven layer RM than with TCP/IP (compare the fortunes of the two network management protocols: CMIP and SNMP). On the other hand the discussions on seven layer RM standards are usually thorough, so the standard changes little when made public, whilst TCP/IP can take a more experimental approach. For example, several protocols may be tested, some of which will be unsuccessful, which can lead to problems of compatibility with legacy systems (i.e. systems that have not been updated to use the latest protocol or technology).

TCP/IP protocols and standards are defined by Request For Comments (RFCs). In addition, other RFCs are published for information, e.g. as part of the standardization process by asking for comments on a proposed new standard. RFCs are available on the Internet and, indeed, the extensive use of the network is another reason why TCP/IP standards can be written relatively quickly. When accessing a TCP/IP standard, make sure that the latest RFC is obtained, as revised standards are given new RFC numbers rather than replacing older versions. A current index should indicate which RFCs are obsolete and point to the RFCs which have replaced them.

8.3.4 TCP and IP protocol headers

TCP is used to establish a reliable point-to-point connection across a network. The TCP header is normally 20 bytes, as shown in figure 8.11. There are options in TCP, but it would be inappropriate to attempt to cover them all, so the discussion here is restricted to the normal 20 byte header. The two byte source and destination port numbers identify the application in the host. Note that the four byte source and destination IP addresses in the IP header identify the actual hosts. The TCP port address and the IP address together are sometimes described as a 'socket' and the source and destination sockets as a socket pair. The socket pair uniquely identifies the two ends of the TCP connection.

'Sockets' is the name of an Application Programming Interface (API), also called 'Berkeley sockets' after where the interface was developed. An API is the appropriate interface for programmers developing network applications. Alternative APIs are TLI (Transport Layer Interface) and XTI (effectively a superset of TLI) [STE].

Standard port numbers are known as 'well-known' port numbers, e.g. the FTP server is on port 21, Telnet on port 23.

The four byte sequence and acknowledgement numbers are used in the same way as the NS and NR numbers in HDLC's control byte, except they refer to byte numbers not frame numbers (which is why a range from $0 \ldots 2^{32} - 1$ is required), i.e. the acknowledgement number contains the number of the next byte wanted by the destination. The mode of operation is FDX, continuous ARQ, go-back-N (see chapter 7). The two byte window length allows the send window to be set; it too refers to the number of bytes. Hence a maximum of $2^{16} - 1$ bytes can be outstanding before an acknowledgement is required.

The four bit header length refers to the length of the header in four byte words (e.g. its value is normally 5).

The two byte checksum covers the header and the data in the TCP PDU. Note that it is a simple one's complement check (see chapter 7) and is not as powerful as a CRC.

There are six flags in the flag field:

- URG signifies that the two byte urgent pointer is valid. This allows urgent data to be given top priority.
- ACK signifies that the acknowledgement number is valid (always set once a connection is established).

- PUSH is the push flag, meaning pass all the data to the destination application.
- RST means reset the connection.
- SYN synchronizes the sequence numbers when establishing a connection.
- FIN indicates that the source has finished sending data.

bytes	bit 31			bit 15	bit 0
1-4	source port number			destination port number	
5-8	sequence number				
9-12	acknowledgement number				
13-16	header length (4 bit)	reserved (6 bits)	flags (6 bits)	window size	
17-20	TCP checksum			urgent pointer	

bit 31 of the top bytes is transmitted first

Figure 8.11 TCP header

The format of an IP datagram is shown in figure 8.12. Again, the normal size of an IP header is 20 bytes and options will not be covered here. Relating the explanation to the TCP header, the most important parts of the header are the four byte source and destination addresses, which are the network addresses of the hosts at either end of the network. There is a two byte header checksum, which is a one's complement check as with TCP, except with IP only the header is checked. The four bit header length refers to the length of the header in four byte words, as with TCP. The two byte identification field is the send packet sequence number (referring to frames not bytes).

Considering the other fields:

The four bit version field refers to the version number of IP being used.

Only four bits of the Type Of Service (TOS) field are used today; they are: minimize delay, maximize throughput, maximize reliability, and minimize cost. The routing protocol OSPF can use this field in making decisions as to where to route the packet.

The total length field gives the length of the IP packet in bytes, which can be from 0 ... 65,535 bytes. However, long packets would probably be fragmented into a sequence of smaller packets at the link layer; indeed the minimum requirement for a host is to be able to receive a 576 byte IP packet. The flags and fragmentation offset fields deal with such fragmentation.

The one byte Time To Live (TTL) field is set by the host and decremented by one each time the packet passes through a network node. When the value in this field reaches zero the packet is discarded and an ICMP error message returned to the source. This prevents the network from becoming clogged with messages which for some reason or other cannot reach their destination.

The one byte protocol field identifies the next protocol up, i.e. it demultiplexes the IP data to the relevant protocol (e.g. TCP, UDP, etc.).

byte	bit 31				bit 0
1-4	vers-ion (4 bit)	header length (4 bit)	TOS (8 bit)	total length	
5-8	identification			flags (3 bit)	fragmentation offset (13 bit)
9-12	TTL		protocol	header checksum	
13-16	source IP address				
17-20	destination IP address				

bit 31 of the top bytes is transmitted first

Figure 8.12 IP header

TCP starts a timer when it sends a packet, and then waits for the destination to return an acknowledgement. If no acknowledgement is received before the timer times out, then the packet is retransmitted. If an error is detected using the TCP checksum the faulty packet is discarded and no acknowledgement is made; the packet will be automatically retransmitted when the source timer times out. Since IP datagrams may be received out of sequence, TCP must be able to correctly sequence the received packets. Note that there are no acknowledgements at the IP level.

8.3.5 Routing

Routing is a function of every wide area network. The TCP/IP protocol RIP (Routing Information Protocol) is considered in this section as representing other routing protocols, but a possible point of confusion about the word 'gateway' needs to be cleared up first. The equipment that performs the routing function is called a router. Since the network layer in the seven layer RM is a layer three protocol then routers fit into layer three (or the equivalent in the case of TCP/IP). Unfortunately, in TCP/IP terms a router is often called a gateway; however, this is confusing as the more common use of the term gateway is to describe the equipment used to interface between two dissimilar networks (which is how the term is used in this book).

If two networks are totally dissimilar, then a gateway between them would consist of two complete network protocol stacks, placed back-to-back, to recover the user data from one network and then put it into a form suitable to send over the next network. A minimum gateway would consist of two network protocol stacks of the lower four layers of the seven layer RM; this would be needed to interface a datagram WAN to a virtual circuit WAN. For example, consider that packets with sequence numbers 1, 2, 3 are sent over the datagram network. At the gateway they may well arrive in the order 3, 1, 2. If the packets are simply passed on in this order to the virtual circuit WAN then, at the other end of the virtual circuit, the layer 4 protocol will be presented with packets arriving in the sequence 3, 1, 2 and will probably reject them. Hence the gateway must have a datagram layer 4 protocol to resequence the packets ready to send them over the virtual circuit WAN.

In all forms of TCP/IP routing, the netid in the IP address is used to look up an entry in the router's routing table. If the router is attached to the network then the packet can be transmitted directly to the Destination Address (DA); assuming the router knows the physical address of the DA; if not, it must first send an ARP request to find the physical address. If the netid refers to a remote network then the entry in the routing table will give the address of the next router to send the packet to. For a small network the routing tables could be set by the systems administrator. But a large internet may change frequently, e.g. due to a fault occurring or a new network being attached. Hence, for large networks an automatic, distributed procedure is needed in which the routers exchange information between themselves to update their routing tables. Such routing protocols are called dynamic, in comparison with a static routing protocol whose tables are set by the system administrator. A common dynamic routing protocol used on the Internet is the Routing Information Protocol (RIP) [RFC 1058 and RFC 1723].

RIP is based on the distance-vector algorithm. The term distance need not mean the physical distance between routers, e.g. it could mean the delay (as measured by the time taken to get a response from neighbouring routers) but the simplest case is that the distance is measured in 'hops' (a 'hop' being across a network). The distance-vector algorithm seeks to minimize whichever measure has been chosen; hence in the example below the routers adjust their routing tables to minimize the number of 'hops' to the destination. Although RIP has a four byte field for the distance vector it defines the maximum distance as 15; any value greater than 16 is set to 16 which indicates that the destination is unreachable (i.e. $16 = \infty$ in RIP). Obviously, RIP is not suitable as a routing protocol for the whole of the Internet, but it is still the most common routing protocol on the Internet; this is because the Internet is divided into areas or domains inside which a protocol such as RIP can be used. Hence RIP is an Interior Gateway Protocol (IGP) in TCP/IP terms. Exterior Gateway Protocols (EGPs) are needed to route between these domains.

Considering the network in figure 8.13, the initial routing tables are set by the system administrator and give the netids of the networks to which the router is directly connected. The hop count is one from the router to these networks. Earlier versions of RIP had a value of zero for directly connected networks but RFC 1058 has redefined this to be more consistent when dealing with metrics other than hops. The routing tables show the netid, the distance x (in hops in this example) and the router IP address (RA) to send the packet to. These tables are exchanged periodically between immediately neighbouring routers, enabling the tables to be updated. The exchanged tables have the address of the router sending the table placed in the RA field and all the hop counts incremented by one. The shortest distances are then entered in the router's own table. Stages of this process are shown in figure 8.14.

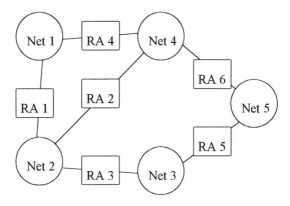

RA n router with IP address n NET n LAN with netid n

Figure 8.13 Example internet

In practice the exchanges occur asynchronously; indeed special precautions are taken to ensure that they occur at different times to avoid overloading the network. The algorithm works by ratcheting down to the shortest distance. An entry remains in the table unless a shorter distance is found or the network changes. To allow changes the protocol must 'forget' entries if they are not periodically confirmed. It will also update an entry if the router to which the entry points sends a message with a changed distance for that route. In the example below the exchanges occur synchronously, so for the sake of example in case of a tie then the entry with the smallest RA is chosen.

The routing is performed on a hop-by-hop basis. For example, to go from router RA 5 to Net 1 the netid is looked up in router RA 5's table. This gives RA 3 as the address to send the packet to. Router RA 3 then looks up Net 1 in its table and sends the packet on to router RA 1, which recognizes that the

Initial routing tables:

Net	x	RA		Net	x	RA		Net	x	RA		Net	x	RA		Net	x	RA		Net	x	RA
RA 1				**RA 2**				**RA 3**				**RA 4**				**RA 5**				**RA 6**		
1	1	1		2	1	2		2	1	3		1	1	4		3	1	5		4	1	6
2	1	1		4	1	2		3	1	3		4	1	4		5	1	5		5	1	6

Routing tables, after exchanging initial routing tables and choosing shortest x (lowest RA if equal x):

Net	x	RA		Net	x	RA		Net	x	RA		Net	x	RA		Net	x	RA		Net	x	RA
RA 1				**RA 2**				**RA 3**				**RA 4**				**RA 5**				**RA 6**		
1	1	1		2	1	2		2	1	3		1	1	4		3	1	5		4	1	6
2	1	1		4	1	2		3	1	3		4	1	4		5	1	5		5	1	6
4	2	2		1	2	1		1	2	1		2	2	1		2	2	3		2	2	2
3	2	3		3	2	3		4	2	2		5	2	6		4	2	6		1	2	4
				5	2	6		5	2	5										3	2	5

Routing tables as broadcast next (table RA to RA field):

Net	x	RA		Net	x	RA		Net	x	RA		Net	x	RA		Net	x	RA		Net	x	RA
RA 1				**RA 2**				**RA 3**				**RA 4**				**RA 5**				**RA 6**		
1	1	1		2	1	2		2	1	3		1	1	4		3	1	5		4	1	6
2	1	1		4	1	2		3	1	3		4	1	4		5	1	5		5	1	6
4	2	1		1	2	2		1	2	3		2	2	4		2	2	5		2	2	6
3	2	1		3	2	2		4	2	3		5	2	4		4	2	5		1	2	6
				5	2	2		5	2	3										3	2	6

Note that x is incremented on receipt. The algorithm can be blindly followed to complete the tables or it may be noted that only the paths to the missing nets from RA 1, RA 4 and RA 5 are needed.

Completed tables:

Net	x	RA		Net	x	RA		Net	x	RA		Net	x	RA		Net	x	RA		Net	x	RA
RA 1				**RA 2**				**RA 3**				**RA 4**				**RA 5**				**RA 6**		
1	1	1		2	1	2		2	1	3		1	1	4		3	1	5		4	1	6
2	1	1		4	1	2		3	1	3		4	1	4		5	1	5		5	1	6
4	2	2		1	2	1		1	2	1		2	2	1		2	2	3		2	2	2
3	2	3		3	2	3		4	2	2		5	2	6		4	2	6		1	2	4
5	3	2		5	2	6		5	2	5		3	3	1		1	3	3		3	2	5

Figure 8.14 RIP example

packet has reached its destination net because its own address is in the entry for Net 1. RA 1 then sends the message directly to the DA on Net 1.

In the absence of any changes to the network RIP will give an optimum solution to the routing problem (as defined by the system administrator when setting the distance metric for each network). To take account of network changes the routing tables are sent every 30 s and a destination is declared as unreachable (i.e. the distance is set to 16) if not updated within 180 s. However, RIP can take some time to respond to network changes, hence the maximum distance is set at 15 and RIP is not suitable for routing based on real time measures such as loading, varying delays, etc. Another disadvantage of RIP is that there are no alternative routes. Newer dynamic routing protocols, such as OSPF (Open Shortest Path First), address these issues.

A disadvantage with all dynamic routing is the overhead associated with exchanging routing information. There is also a hazard with dynamic routing: namely 'livelock'. This can occur if the routing tables become inconsistent, which can happen because information about changes to the network takes time to propagate. This may mean that a packet meant for DA C is sent from router A via router B, whilst B sends it via A; hence the packet loops between A and B. The packet is moving (unlike in a 'deadlock' situation) but it does not get delivered. It will eventually be discarded when its Time To Live (TTL) value expires.

8.4 Circuit switching

The Public Switched Telephone Network (PSTN) is most definitely a WAN. Traditionally, this is a topic covered in telecommunications rather than data communications. However, as explained in chapter 10, there is convergence between the telecommunication and data communication industries, so the topic is briefly considered here.

The PSTN is optimized for speech, which is an analogue signal. Originally therefore, the PSTN provided analogue lines. However, digital lines provide better performance in the presence of noise and Time Division Multiplexing (TDM) can easily be applied to digital signals to make better use of links, so operating agencies converted the PSTN to a digital system. Once this was achieved it was natural to use these digital links for transporting data and, indeed, to view speech as just another form of data. The data rates of these links were determined by what was needed for speech. There are several stages to convert an analogue speech signal into a serial stream of bits:

• **Band limit** the analogue signal. The frequency range of an analogue speech signal for telephony is from 300 Hz to 3400 Hz, so a filter with a −3 dB frequency of 3400 Hz limits the maximum input signal frequency.

• **Sample** the band limited analogue signal. The sampling theorem [STR] states that the sampling rate must be greater than twice the maximum signal frequency (this is why the signal must be bandlimited). A sampling frequency of 8 kHz was chosen to leave a 600 Hz guard band between 3400 Hz and half the sampling frequency.

- **Quantize** the samples to the nearest digital level. This is the stage when the signal is converted from analogue to digital. The definition of an analogue signal is that it is a continuous signal which can take any amplitude level within a specified range, whilst a digital signal is one selected from a discrete set of possible events. In this case the events are amplitude levels, e.g. speech in telephony has 255 discrete levels as standard. The sampled analogue level is 'rounded' to the nearest of these levels, the rounding errors causing quantization noise.
- **Digitize** the selected level, e.g. for speech, as there are 256 possible permutations of 8 bits, each level can be converted to an eight bit word. Quantization and digitization, although treated as two processes here, are usually performed in one step in an Analogue to Digital Converter (ADC).
- Convert from **parallel to serial** data.

Summarizing for speech: 8000 samples are taken per second and each sample is converted into an 8 bit word. The output data rate is therefore 64 kbps. This is the base rate for digital telecommunication links. BT offers these lines (or multiples of them) for leasing as KiloStream lines. At the receiver, the corresponding processes are carried out in 'Last In, First Out' order:

- Convert from **serial to parallel**.
- Convert from a digital word to a discrete amplitude level using a Digital to Analogue Converter (DAC).
- Use a **filter** with a −3 dB frequency of 3400 Hz on the DAC output to remove frequency components caused by the sampling process.

Ignoring any effects of the channel, the receiver output is an analogue signal that only differs from the original by the quantization noise. This noise can be reduced to any required level by increasing the number of bits used by the ADC (i.e. increasing the resolution). Eight bits is sufficient for speech in telecommunications, whilst 16 bit resolution is used in hi-fi. The coding process outlined above is called Pulse Code Modulation (PCM).

These 64 kbps speech channels can be multiplexed using Time Division Multiplexing (TDM), where a byte is taken in turn from each of 30 channels. Thus each of the 30 channels has access to the full bandwidth of the communication link for the time it takes to transmit one byte (i.e. for one time slot). Two extra channels are required: one to carry signalling information for call set-up, etc. and the other for frame alignment purposes to ensure that the bytes are distributed to the correct channels at the receiver. Thus the output data rate of a 30 channel PCM multiplexer is 32×64 kbps = 2.048 Mbps. This is the next level in the hierarchy of digital data rates. BT offers these lines (or multiples of them) as MegaStream lines.

These leased lines can be used to set up a private WAN, for example using X.25 or TCP/IP. As leased lines they provide an end-to-end digital link. The PSTN, on the other hand, still has an analogue link from the subscriber's home or office to the local exchange where the signals are converted into digital. The signals are then transmitted and switched in digital form until they reach the destination local exchange. Unfortunately, the analogue link for the local loop means that modems must be used to send data over the PSTN, which reduces its suitability for data.

The Integrated Services Digital Network (ISDN, or Narrowband ISDN to distinguish it from the Broadband ISDN discussed in chapter 10) is the logical next step in improving on the digital PSTN, by providing a digital link from the local exchange to the subscriber's premises. The link provides either a Primary Rate Access (PRA), which is the same as 30 channel PCM (BT calls this service ISDN30), or a Basic Rate Access (BRA), which provides two 64 kbps channels (BT calls this ISDN2). The primary service is suitable for large organizations whilst the basic service is suitable for small companies or private users. The aggregate data rate for the primary service is 2.048 Mbps whilst the user has access to 30 bearer (or B) channels and one signalling (or D) channel, all at 64 kbps. Hence this service is also called 30B + D and the total data rate available to the user is 1.984 Mbps. The basic service provides 2 B channels, both at 64 kbps, plus a 16 kbps D channel. Hence this service is also known as 2B + D and it provides 144 kbps for the user at an aggregate rate (including protocol overhead) of 192 kbps. The basic service can be provided over an existing two wire, twisted pair connection in the local loop, although a Network Termination Unit (NTU) is needed at the customer's premises. For more details see [STA] or [HAL]. Note that an ISDN phone must include an ADC and DAC, as the whole point of ISDN is that it provides an end-to-end digital link.

The idea behind ISDN is that speech is just another form of data service, as is fax (group IV fax machines are designed to operate over 64 kbps lines, see chapter 1), file transfer, etc., hence the term 'Integrated Services'. ISDN provides a dial-up, end-to-end digital connection suitable for many data communication applications. If the line is used heavily then it may be worthwhile to lease it whilst keeping the ISDN connection as a back-up.

The new hierarchy of digital links to support current and future services, including both narrowband and broadband ISDN, is called the Synchronous Digital Hierarchy (SDH). It replaces the Plesiochronous Digital Hierarchy (PDH) [MAD], and can be considered as a natural extension to the base 64 kbps channel and 30 channel PCM, as at every stage of the hierarchy easy access can be obtained to any 64 kbps channel. The lowest level of provision in the SDH is the STM-1 (Synchronous Transport Module - level 1) with a bit rate of 155.52 Mbps. The STM-1 frame contains 2430 time slots, each of which is a byte. Hence the frame rate is 8 kHz and each byte provides a 64 kbps channel. The STM-1 has a 'payload' which carries Virtual Containers (VCs). For example, 63 VCs, each holding a 30 channel PCM signal, could be packed into an STM-

1. The SDH also has the advantage that the protocol standard is open ended, e.g. provision of higher rate services depends on the available technology rather than having to wait until new standards are ratified. Each level of the hierarchy can be multiplexed together, using TDM, to generate the next level, e.g. four STM-1s can be combined into an STM-4 with a data rate of 622.08 Mbps, four of these can be combined into an STM-16 with a data rate of 2488.32 Mbps, etc.

Exercises

(1)   State three different modes of switching in data communications.

(2)   State another term for (i) virtual circuit; (ii) datagram.

(3)   Ten computers, all from different manufacturers and with different protocols, are to be fully interconnected. Determine how many different suites of interface programs have to be written if: (i) no common standards exist; (ii) the seven layer RM is used.

(4)   What do the acronyms ISO and OSI stand for?

(5)   Justify why standards should be open.

(6)   State the seven layers of the seven layer RM.

(7)   What is the consequence of having datagram and virtual circuit networks in the seven layer RM?

(8)   Give one X.25 protocol for each of the network service layers of the seven layer RM.

(9)   Which protocols cover the connection and operation of a PAD and what are they collectively called?

(10) What are the functions of the PTI of the X.25 protocol?

(11) Describe the client-server model of network applications.

(12) Compare and contrast the protocols TCP, UDP and IP.

(13) Is RARP normally required for a terminal with a hard disk?

(14) Assign the routing protocols RIP and OSPF and the address resolution protocols ARP and RARP to particular layers in the TCP/IP protocol stack. Also, explain any difficulty with these assignments.

(15) Which class of network does a host with an IP address of 143.56.18.0 belong to?

(16) Ignoring special IP addresses, determine the maximum number of networks which could be connected to the Internet.

(17) (a) Use Telnet to access a Telnet server;
(b) Use Archie to find a file and anonymous FTP to retrieve it;
(c) Find and retrieve a file in Gopher space;
(d) Use a Web browser to find and retrieve a file.

(18) Use the Internet to find out about:
(a) WAIS;
(b) the routing protocol OSPF.
Present your findings in a roughly 300 word report and include relevant URL and RFC references.

(19) Compare and contrast the seven layer RM with TCP/IP in terms of open standards and layering.

(20) Discuss the importance of layering for network architectures.

(21) Compare the fortunes of the two network management protocols: CMIP and SNMP. Use the Internet and trade, research and professional body journals as references. Quote the references used and briefly comment on the usefulness of the different reference sources.

(22) What is a socket in TCP/IP?

(23) Do TCP and IP refer to bytes or packets in their sequence identification number fields?

(24) Assign routers and gateways to appropriate layers in the seven layer RM.

(25) State how livelock could occur in a network.

(26) Compare and contrast dynamic and static routing methods.

(27) Determine the final routing tables for the internet of figure 8.13, if router RA 2 is removed and RIP is used. Use the same assumptions as in chapter 8.

(28) For each of the major functions of a network protocol, listed in the X.25 summary, state the appropriate TCP/IP protocol (out of TCP, IP or ICMP) which covers the function.

(29) List examples of networking applications and give the names of the seven layer RM and TCP/IP applications that support these services.

(30) What is the most significant difference between the ISDN and the digital PSTN?

(31) State the stages involved in converting an analogue signal to a serial bit stream.

(32) State the difference between a KiloStream link and a 64 kbps digital speech channel.

(33) State the names of different services which can be provided over a 2.048 Mbps link.

(34) Write your own summary of what you have learnt in this chapter.

9 Local Area Networks

Local Area Networks (LANs) were originally a way of sharing a resource, such as a printer or modem, amongst several workstations. The solution chosen was to provide a common medium between the workstations and the server, e.g. the printer server. Only one station can use the medium at any one time but it provides a high speed channel, e.g. 10 Mbps in some versions of Ethernet. The alternative way of doing this would have been to use a company's digital PABX (Private Automatic Branch eXchange) to switch the data over telephone lines. However, although switching means many channels can be simultaneously supported, the data rates available then (typically 64 kbps) were too low to offer a satisfactory solution.

The common medium can be a coaxial or fibre optic cable, a twisted pair, a particular radio frequency band for wireless LANs, etc. An important aim of LAN protocols is that each station or node on the network has an equal chance of gaining access to the common medium; hence LANs use peer-to-peer protocols (i.e. equal ranking) rather than master-slave protocols. The LAN protocols that govern access to the medium are termed Medium Access Control (MAC) protocols.

LANs provide a convenient way for workstations to be connected to form a network. They have developed beyond their original application, e.g. the working practices of many companies now rely on the corporate network to enable information to be rapidly exchanged and distributed. Thus a typical LAN application is E-mail, as discussed in chapter 8 on WANs, although they are still used to share laser printers, etc. Chapter 8 considered internets, i.e. networks of networks, whilst this chapter focuses on the networks themselves.

9.1 LAN topologies

Topology is about defining networks in terms of their connectivity. Thus a **ring**, for example, is where the output from node A (see figure 9.1) is connected to the input of node B, the output from node B is connected to the input of node C, and the output from node C is connected back to the input of node A. Topologically this is a ring, regardless of whether it is physically laid out on the floor as a circle, a triangle or whatever. Thus each node on a ring acts as a regenerator and the data flows one way around the ring. An example of a LAN using a ring topology is Token Ring.

Other topologies which are important in LANs include a **bus**, which is where the channel has a defined end or termination (see figure 9.1). A coaxial cable can be used as a **passive bus**, with matched loads terminating the cable at either end to prevent reflections (see chapter 4). In this case each node is attached to

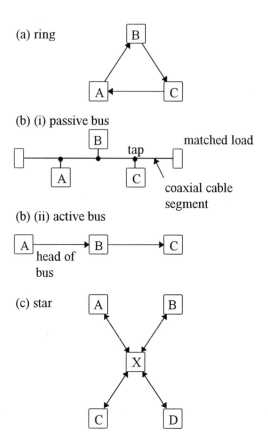

Figure 9.1 LAN topologies

the cable by a 'tap', so called because it taps into the cable. Between the passive tap and the rest of the interface circuits of the node is the transceiver (transmitter/receiver). This monitors or receives signals on the cable through a high impedance to avoid changing the cable's characteristic impedance. It transmits through a low impedance driver to launch the signal in both directions down the cable. This means that the signal is broadcast over the common medium and every other node attached to the bus can receive the signal. Hence a wireless LAN is topologically like a passive bus. Examples of passive bus LANs are two versions of Ethernet: 10Base5 and 10Base2.

Alternatively, an **active bus** can be made by connecting the output from node A to the input of node B and the output from node B to the input of node C. In this case node A is the head of the bus and node C is the termination. Obviously two buses are need to provide bi-directional communication. An example of a network using this topology is DQDB (Dual Bus Distributed Queue), actually a MAN (Metropolitan Area Network) rather than a LAN, see chapter 10.

A **star** topology (see figure 9.1) implies a central active node. Using a digital PABX for data is an example of such a LAN, as is 10BaseT (yet another version of Ethernet, see section 9.4.2).

9.2 LAN standards

The IEEE (Institute of Electrical and Electronics Engineers, a US professional body) is the most important organization for defining LAN and MAN standards. The relevant standards all start with 'IEEE 802.' and many have been taken up by the international standards bodies ISO and IEC (whose corresponding joint standards start with 'ISO/IEC 8802-'). Figure 9.2 shows the relationship between some of these LAN/MAN standards and the seven layer RM.

<table>
<tr><td colspan="6"></td><td>LAN/MAN
layers</td><td>7 layer RM</td></tr>
<tr><td colspan="5">802.2</td><td>LLC</td><td rowspan="2">2 – data link
layer</td></tr>
<tr><td>802.3
CSMA
/CD</td><td>802.4
Token
Bus</td><td>802.5
Token
Ring</td><td>802.6
DQDB</td><td>802.7
Slotted
Ring</td><td>MAC</td></tr>
<tr><td>802.3</td><td>802.4</td><td>802.5</td><td>802.6</td><td>802.7</td><td>physical</td><td>1 – physical
layer</td></tr>
</table>

802.2 Logical Link Control (LLC) protocol
802.3 LANs using the CSMA/CD MAC protocol (loosely called Ethernet)
802.4 Token Bus, a bus using token passing as the MAC protocol
802.5 Token Ring, a ring using token passing as the MAC protocol
802.6 DQDB, the IEEE MAN standard (see chapter 10)
802.7 Slotted Ring access method

Figure 9.2 LAN standards

Clearly, the interface between the Logical Link Control (LLC) protocol and the layer above corresponds to that between a point-to-point data link layer protocol, such as LAP-B, and a network layer protocol, such as X.25. Thus the function of the LLC sub layer is to provide extra facilities not provided by the MAC sub layers (see section 9.3).

Loosely, the terms IEEE 802.3, CSMA/CD (Carrier Sense Multiple Access with Collision Detection) and Ethernet are taken to mean the same thing. However, strictly, Ethernet refers to the original LAN developed by the Xerox Corporation [MET] with support from Intel and Digital Equipment Corporation (DEC). This was the basis for the first IEEE 802.3 standard (10Base5) but it is not wholly compatible with it. Common usage is followed in this book, namely to refer to the IEEE 802.3 series of LANs as Ethernet.

The Token Bus has not been taken up by many users. Briefly, it uses a similar MAC protocol to Token Ring but on a bus topology. It does this by setting up a logical ring on a passive bus (although a different bus standard to Ethernet). Referring to figure 9.1 and considering the passive bus: although physically any node can communicate directly with any other node, the protocol is set up so that node A only sends packets to node B, node B only sends packets to node C, and node C only sends packets to node A. Hence a ring protocol can be used to govern access to a bus. The advantages of this are:

- a passive bus is inherently more reliable than a ring, since a break anywhere in a ring will stop it working, whilst if a node fails in a high impedance state it will not disturb the rest of a bus;
- as explained later, the Token Ring protocol guarantees to deliver the data within a certain time, which is not the case for Ethernet.

Manufacturing industry was supposed to be a prime application area for Token Bus. Network reliability and robustness are critical for manufacturing, which perhaps explains the above design choices. Unfortunately, the protocol required to set up and maintain the logical ring was probably too complicated, allowing nodes to be removed or inserted at will with the ring automatically reconfiguring.

As discussed in chapter 8, the seven layer RM is not a network architecture, but it does allow a network architecture to be created by selecting different seven layer RM standards. Such network architectures are called 'functional profiles' or 'functional stacks'. A functional stack ensures inter-operability by specifying the particular seven layer RM standards to be used and, if necessary, by specifying which options must be supported. One functional stack is TOP, the Technical and Office Protocol, which is based on Ethernet and whose development was led by Boeing. Another is MAP, the Manufacturing Office Protocol, based on Token Bus and whose development was led by General Motors. These functional stacks have now come together and are looked after by the MAP/TOP users' group.

The next section covers the LLC protocol; then follow the Ethernet and Token Ring LANs, which together account for over 75% of all LANs installed.

9.3 Logical Link Control protocol

The Logical Link Control (LLC) protocol provides three types of service [ISO/IEC 8802.2]. Type 1 is a basic, unacknowledged, datagram service that minimizes the protocol overhead by leaving error correction and packet sequencing to higher level protocols. The type 2 service establishes a virtual circuit link between users before transferring data and the type 3 provides an acknowledged datagram service. The DSAP and SSAP (see figure 9.3) identify the next highest protocol, allowing different protocol stacks to be run over the same network. The control byte has a similar format and function as HDLC's control byte, see chapter 7.

As explained below, the MAC protocols provide a Frame Check Sequence for error detection and some means of recognizing the start and end of a frame. Hence, the LLC and MAC protocols together provide the same facilities as HDLC.

Length in bytes   1   1   1 or 2

DSAP	SSAP	Control	data

DSAP Destination Service Access Point   SSAP Source Service Access Point

Figure 9.3 LLC protocol format

9.4 Ethernet

Ethernet refers to a family of LANs which all use the Carrier Sense Multiple Access with Collision Detection (CSMA/CD) MAC protocol. The acronym is a handy mnemonic for remembering how the protocol works. The use of the CSMA/CD protocol implies data packets are being broadcast, i.e. every node can communicate directly with any other node, so this protocol is suitable for a passive bus or wireless LAN.

In CSMA/CD each transceiver monitors (senses) the cable. If a transceiver has a frame to transmit it must wait until any data on the bus has passed, wait a little longer to allow a brief interframe delay, and then transmit. The node has gained exclusive access to the shared medium once all other nodes recognize that the bus is busy. This is the Carrier Sense Multiple Access part of the MAC protocol.

Unfortunately, more than one waiting node can decide that the bus is free and start to transmit a data packet, in the same way as two people might start talking at the same time after a pause. If this happens there will be a data 'collision' in which the packets corrupt each other so their information is lost. The transmitting nodes detect this because they continuously compare what they are transmitting with the signal on the line. Having detected a collision, a transmitting node will transmit a 4 byte jamming signal (to ensure that other transmitting nodes will recognize that an error has occurred) and then stop and wait a randomly selected time interval before starting the Carrier Sense Multiple Access stage again. This is the Collision Detection part of the MAC protocol.

If a collision occurs again to the same node it goes through the same process except the maximum waiting time is increased. The first time a collision occurs the node randomly chooses to wait either 0 or 1 'collision domains' of 512 bit periods (see section 9.4.1), hence there is a 50% chance of a collision occurring again for two nodes contending for access. The second time it chooses either 0, 1, 2 or 3 collision domains, hence there is a 25% chance of a collision occurring, etc. This is the truncated binary exponential backoff algorithm, as the number of choices is doubled after each consecutive collision, until there are 1024 choices after ten attempts. After that no further increase in the maximum waiting time is made and the node finally gives up after the fifteenth attempt [ISO/IEC 8802.3].

Three Ethernet LANs are considered together, namely: 10Base5, 10Base2 and 10BaseT. The general format for describing Ethernet LANs is *cModex* where

- *c* refers to the data rate in Mbps;
- *Mode* refers to the mode of modulation, e.g. 'Base' means that the signal is not modulated and 'Broad' means that the signal is modulated on to a carrier wave (see chapter 3);
- *x* either refers to the maximum length of a cable segment in units of 100 m (to the nearest 100 m), thus the maximum cable segment length for 10Base5 is 500 m whilst for 10Base2 it is actually 185 m;
- or, if *x* is a character string, T refers to the use of twisted pair and F refers to the use of fibre optic cable.

Some other versions of Ethernet are 10BaseF, 10Broad36, 1Base5, and most importantly 100BaseT which brings a big increase in capacity. Such high speed LANs are considered separately in section 9.7. For a discussion of the different versions of Ethernet see [SMY].

In order to detect that a collision has occurred the signal from a remote node must have sufficient amplitude, in comparison to the locally generated signal, to cause the signal at the local node to be outside specified tolerances. Thus, the maximum allowed signal attenuation is essentially what limits the maximum length of an Ethernet cable segment.

An important part of the CSMA/CD protocol not yet mentioned is that a collision must be detected before a transmitter has finished sending the packet (for a discussion of this requirement see [STA]). This means that a frame must be padded out to a minimum length if there is only a small amount of data, see figure 9.4.

The preamble is transmitted first. Because they send data in packets, LANs must use the synchronous mode of communication. The preamble enables the receiving node's clock extraction circuit to lock on to the transmitter clock. The SFD then enables the receiver to achieve frame synchronization by detecting the final 11 instead of the previous 10 bit patterns.

length in bytes

7	1	6	6	2	$46 \le \ell \le 1500$	4
Preamble	SFD	DA	SA	Length	data	PAD	FCS

Preamble	used for synchronization, each byte – 1010 1010
SFD	Start Frame Delimiter – 1010 1011
DA	Destination Address SA Source Address
Length	Length of data field data LLC PDU
FCS	Frame Check Sequence PAD extra bytes

Figure 9.4 CSMA/CD frame format (leftmost bit transmitted first)

The DA and SA are each 6 bytes long and use the same address format as Token Ring. If the first bit is a 1 then the packet is addressed to a group of cards (either multicast to a restricted group or, if the DA is all 1s, broadcast to every receiver). If the first bit is a 0 then the packet is addressed to a particular card. Every Ethernet or Token Ring Network Interface Card (NIC) or adapter produced must have a unique address, the first three bytes being the manufacturer's code (which starts with the msb = 0). These are the physical device addresses which are ultimately used to deliver packets to the correct destination. An address resolution process, between addresses used for routing packets and the physical device addresses, is described in chapter 8.

The length field gives the length of the actual data. If this is less than 46 bytes then extra padding bytes are added in the PAD field. The maximum length of the data is 1500 bytes.

The FCS is a 4 byte CRC as discussed in chapter 7.

A receiver will only accept a frame as valid if it passes the following tests:

• It is longer than the minimum length (a frame that is too short indicates that it has been involved in a collision).
• The frame is properly aligned on a byte boundary.
• The error detection algorithm gives the expected result.

9.4.1 Ethernet physical layer

Some specifications for 10Base5 and 10Base2 are now described:

The characteristic impedance of the cable is 50 Ω. 10Base5 cable has a greater diameter (10 mm) than that used for 10Base2 (5 mm), hence alternative names for these LANs are 'thick' and 'thin' Ethernet. A larger diameter results in a lower attenuation per unit length, hence the maximum length of a cable segment is 500 m for 10Base5 but only 185 m for 10Base2.

The maximum number of transceivers per cable segment is 100 on 10Base5 and 30 on 10Base2.

The transceiver spacing between taps must be a multiple of 2.5 m on 10Base5. Hence bands are marked on the cable at 2.5 m intervals to assist in correctly locating the taps. This is to ensure that reflections from discontinuities (caused by the taps) in the cable's characteristic impedance do not build up to create a 'ghost' signal which would result in a collision. The minimum transceiver distance for 10Base2 is 0.5 m but there are no further restrictions on spacing. For 10Base5 a tap is physically inserted into the cable to make contact with the central conductor. For 10Base2 the tap is made using a BNC 'T' piece.

A Network Interface Card (NIC) is commonly used to connect a workstation to a LAN. For 10Base2 this generally includes the transceiver, whilst for 10Base5 an external transceiver is required. An external transceiver is connected to a NIC by a maximum of 50 m of cable using the 15-way Attachment User Interface (AUI). Thus the typical interface for a 10Base5 NIC is AUI and for a 10Base2 NIC it is a BNC connector.

A 10Base2 cable segment can be made of lengths of cable joined by BNC 'T' pieces. The third connector on each 'T' piece is connected to a BNC connector on the NIC. The spare ends at either end of the segment must be capped with 50 Ω BNC terminations. The best way to find out how networks are connected is to look at one; the second best way is to study a catalogue of networking equipment.

The Manchester line code is used for the lower data rate ($\leq$ 10 Mbps), baseband versions of Ethernet. This guarantees a clock transition in the middle of each data bit but at the cost of doubling the signal bandwidth. It transmits two code bits (i.e. two signalling events) for one data bit. A data 0 is transmitted as 10 and a data 1 is transmitted as 01 [STA]. Using bipolar signalling ensures that there is no d.c. power in the transmitted signal, as clearly the average transmitted signal amplitude will be zero.

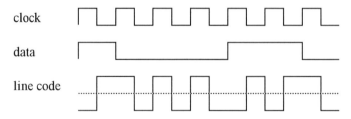

Figure 9.5 Manchester line code

A maximum of four repeaters is allowed from one end to the other of an Ethernet LAN. Essentially, a repeater is two transceivers connected back to back, one transceiver connected to one segment and the other to another. A repeater is thus used to connect LAN segments at the physical layer.

An Ethernet repeater links two segments by regenerating the signal from one segment and sending it over the next segment. In regeneration a digital signal is recovered from a noisy and distorted received signal. The digital signal is then transmitted over the next link, in the same way as it was over the first link. If there are no errors the new transmitted signal is the same as the original transmitted signal. The signal has been 'regenerated' and any noise or distortion has been removed. An Ethernet repeater is actually a regenerator. Strictly, with a repeater the received signal is simply boosted (i.e. amplified) before being retransmitted, which does not remove noise or distortion. Clearly, after a few stages noise will tend to 'swamp' the signal. Analogue signals must use a repeater, which is why analogue signals cannot be sent over such long distances as digital signals which use a regenerator.

The maximum end-to-end length for a 10Base5 Ethernet from node A to node B is therefore

Node A, 50 m AUI interface	50 m
4 repeaters, each 2 × 50 m AUI interface	400 m
5 segments, each 500 m	2500 m
Node B, 50 m AUI interface	50 m
Total:	3000 m

Note that of the five segments used, two segments may only be used as link segments, i.e. can only be used for repeaters [SMY]. The remaining three segments can support other nodes and are termed active segments.

Taking 10Base5 as an example, the minimum length frame = 576 bits, including the preamble, and the data rate = 10 Mbps; thus the minimum holding time H_{min} = 57.6 μs. In the worst case, a node A at one end of the LAN will determine that the bus is free and start to transmit its data, see figure 9.6.

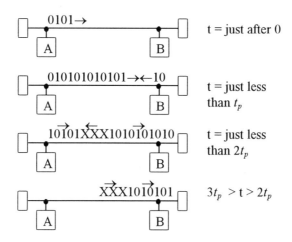

XXX Jamming sequence

Figure 9.6 Worst case for collisions in Ethernet

Just before this signal arrives at node B at the other end of the LAN this too will decide that the bus is free and start to transmit. The time taken for A's signal to arrive at B is the propagation delay across the network t_p. A collision will occur almost instantly at node B and so B will cease transmitting its data and transmit the 4 byte jamming sequence.

This jamming signal will propagate back across the LAN, eventually reaching node A after a further time t_p. When node A detects the collision it too will cease transmitting its message and transmit the jamming signal.

Thus the minimum holding time H_{min} must be longer than $2t_p$ for the CSMA/CD protocol, in order for a node to be able to detect a collision before it has finished transmitting the packet. Given that the velocity of propagation V_p is $\geq 2.31 \times 10^8$ m/s (it varies according to the type of cable), the theoretical maximum end-to-end length ℓ_{max} of an Ethernet LAN is

$$\ell_{max} = \frac{V_p \times H}{2} = 6653 \text{ m} \tag{9.1}$$

As found before, the maximum length according to the installation rules is 3000 m for 10Base5. This means that the maximum propagation delay $t_p = 13.0$ μs and hence the factor $a = t_p / H \leq 0.226$, confirming that this is a LAN (see chapter 7).

From figure 9.6, if a node has transmitted for $2t_p$ ($\equiv 260$ bits) without a collision it has seized control of the bus. This value is the theoretical 'collision domain'; the specified collision domain being 512 bits.

9.4.2 10BaseT

This is a version of Ethernet which supports a data rate of 10 Mbps over Unshielded Twisted Pair (UTP cable with RJ45 connectors). At this data rate taps cannot be used on UTP cable, so instead a central 'hub' is used with two twisted pairs (i.e. a 4W connection with one pair for transmit and one for receive) running a maximum of 100 m from the hub to a workstation, see figure 9.7. Thus the central hub is connected by spokes to each workstation. The hub is active as it regenerates a workstation's signal and broadcasts it to every other node on the same bus. Clearly, this is a star network but it still needs a bus MAC protocol (i.e. topologically it is a star but logically it is a bus).

This cabling scheme is compatible with structured cabling, where a small room can house the hub; other rooms or desks on the same floor being provided with a 4W connection to the hub. This is the 'horizontal' wiring sub-system. The hubs on different floors are connected together by the 'backbone' cabling sub-system [EIA 568, JAI, TYL]. Providing every room with a connection point is called 'flood' wiring and is how new buildings should be wired, with cables at least to category 5 standard to support 100 Mbps data rates. One reason for structured cabling is that the decision on which type of LAN to install can be made later. In the section on Token Ring it will be shown that this is normally installed with a central hub connected by two twisted pair cables to each workstation, i.e. physically there need be no difference between the cabling for 10BaseT and Token Ring (or indeed for ISDN), as RJ45 connectors can be used for all these networks. Other reasons for structured cabling are discussed in section 9.5 on Token Ring.

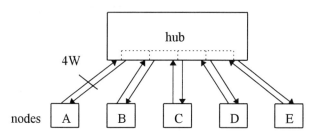

Figure 9.7 10BaseT hub

It is however rather wasteful for the central hub for 10BaseT to broadcast packets on to all other nodes when usually the packet need only go to one node. An Etherswitch can read a packet's DA and switch it to that node. This means that multiple 10 Mbps connections can be set up between pairs of nodes by the switch. Assuming that the switch is non-blocking (i.e. has sufficient internal cross-points) a connection can be made between any pair of free links. Depending on the application this can greatly increase the data throughput of the LAN. Unfortunately, for a client-server application with just one server it will be of no benefit. Note that there are no standards for Etherswitches and some switches act to divide an Ethernet into smaller segments rather than establish dedicated paths.

It is quite common to have different versions of Ethernet in the same organization. They may be connected in different ways. Bridges (see section 9.8) connect LANs at the MAC sub layer whilst routers (see chapter 8) connect networks at the network layer. To summarize briefly different ways of accessing or connecting networks at the physical layer:

- As well as an RJ45 connector, hubs generally also have a BNC or AUI connector (or both) to allow a 10BaseT network to access a 10Base2 or 10Base5 network.
- A multiport repeater works as a repeater but to multiple bus segments simultaneously.
- Repeaters can be used to connect different types of Ethernet, assuming that they all operate at the same data rate.
- A fan-out allows several nodes to share the same transceiver by using multiple AUI connections.

Hence quite complicated Ethernet networks can be set up but, for obvious reasons, a connection which would complete a loop in such a network must be avoided.

9.5 Token Ring

Token Ring was adopted and further developed by IBM [BUX]. The IEEE 802.5 standard [ISO/IEC 8802.5] specifies Shielded Twisted Pair (STP) with a characteristic impedance of 150 Ω and IBM Cabling System hermaphrodite connectors (i.e. the plugs and sockets are identical). The maximum number of nodes is 250. Also available are versions using either Unshielded Twisted Pair (UTP) or STP, with RJ45 connectors. UTP is more prone to interference so the maximum number of nodes is limited to 72. All types of cabling can support data rates of 4 Mbps or 16 Mbps.

The management of the wiring for a ring is more difficult than for a bus and the reliability is more critical. If the ring is made by linking directly from one node to the next then changing a node may mean tracing out the underfloor wiring, which in most buildings is not a simple matter. A Token Ring network is therefore usually set up with a central hub (sometimes called a Multistation Access Unit, MSAU or MAU – which should not be confused with a MAU on an Ethernet, see glossary). This has two twisted pair cables on the spokes going to each node, one for transmit and one for receive. Thus each node is attached by a 4W cable to a port on the hub, the cable and node together forming a 'lobe'. The ring still exists but is completed inside the hub, see figure 9.8. The hub interface circuits automatically bypass a lobe if the attached node is not switched on or a fault is detected. The maximum distance between nodes is specified in terms of parameters such as attenuation, delay, etc. rather than length but a maximum lobe length of 100 m is a reasonable estimate for a 4 Mbps network wired with the IBM Cabling System and a passive hub [GÖH]. Hubs can be connected in a ring to increase the number of nodes attached, as in figure 9.8, or, alternatively, the hubs can be arranged as a star from a central hub. As with Ethernet, Token Ring LANs can be extended by using repeaters, bridges (see section 9.8) or routers (see chapter 8).

The advantage of using hubs is that wiring changes can be managed better and the ring is fault tolerant. Topologically, using hubs, the cabling can be connected as a star whilst physically the network remains a ring. Structured cabling means planning and managing the wiring, generally using a hierarchical scheme with hubs and flood wiring [JAI, TYL], whilst to leave open the choice between Token Ring, 10BaseT, and ISDN, UTP cable with RJ45 connectors needs to be specified.

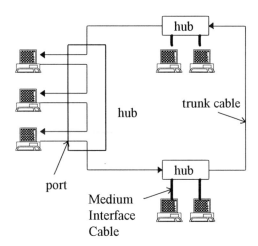

Figure 9.8 Token Ring hubs

The line code used for Token Ring is Differential Manchester. As with the Manchester line code, this guarantees a clock transition in the middle of each data bit but at the cost of doubling the signal bandwidth. The actual coding is different, however, in that a data 0 always starts with a transition whilst there is no starting transition for a data 1. Hence the name 'differential', as the transmitted signal depends on the previous signal level. Again, bipolar signalling ensures that there is no d.c. power in the transmitted signal.

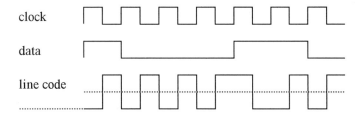

Figure 9.9 Differential Manchester line code

9.5.1 Token Ring MAC protocol

In a Token Ring LAN, the output of one node is connected to the input of its neighbouring downstream node, the output of that node is connected to its neighbour, and so on until the ring is completed. Messages only go one way around the ring so, for one node to talk to another across the ring, it is necessary for the intervening nodes to pass on the message. The intervening nodes thus act as regenerators. The idea of a token is to avoid collisions. For example, on a railway without a signalling system a token may be used to govern access to a stretch of single track. A train is not allowed to proceed unless it has the token. With only one token there should only ever be one train at a time on the track and so a collision should not occur.

In Token Ring terms a token is a control frame with a bit set to identify it as a token. A node must wait until it receives the token on its upstream link before it can transmit. Once it has received the token it starts the 'Timer, Holding Token' (THT), which limits the time the node is allowed to start transmitting a frame. This prevents one node from monopolizing the ring. The maximum data length is not specified in terms of bytes, rather the time required to transmit a frame may be no greater than the token holding period.

Whilst it has the token a node may transmit information frames. These are put on the downstream link and circulate all round the ring before arriving back on the upstream link, as it is the responsibility of the source to remove the frames from the ring. The source can send another information frame as it removes the first one. After it has transmitted all of its frames or finishes a frame after the THT times out, whichever occurs soonest, the node must release the token to its downstream neighbour, so that it can send information in its turn.

Clearly, since the information frame has been all round the ring it will have been read by the destination as it copied it, bit for bit, on to the next link (apart from changing a few bits to acknowledge reception).

The operation of the Token Ring MAC protocol can be explained in more detail by referring to the frame format of figure 9.10. This shows a non-routing frame; routing in Token Ring is discussed in section 9.8.

The Starting Delimiter and Ending Delimiter define the frame boundaries. The DA and SA have the same format as in Ethernet, see section 9.4. The FCS is a 4 byte CRC as discussed in chapter 7. The maximum length of the data is not specified but is limited by the THT, a typical maximum is 5000 bytes.

Enlarging upon the discussion above, the destination will change the A and C bits in the Frame Status byte before forwarding them on to the next link and a token frame is identified by having the T bit in the Access Control byte = 0. The other bits in the Access Control byte are for the monitor node and for the operation of a priority scheme.

Active monitor
One node on the ring, the active monitor, is responsible for monitoring the operation of the ring. All nodes are capable of assuming this role. Control procedures ensure that there is always one, and only one, active monitor in the ring. The functions of the active monitor include:
• Ensuring that frames do not continuously circulate around the ring. The M bit in the Access Control byte is set to 0 when a frame is transmitted. When the frame passes the monitor the M bit is set to 1. Hence, if a frame is received by

the monitor with the M bit already at 1 the frame is removed, as it has not been taken off the ring by its source, and a new token is issued by the monitor.

• The active monitor provides the timing for all other nodes in the ring.

• If an information frame is being transmitted the source is responsible for transmitting the data on its downstream node and removing the same data from its upstream node. However, if a token is being repeated around the ring then this does not apply. The 24 bit token will circulate around the ring until a node has a message to send. This means that the minimum delay around the ring must be 24 bit periods to avoid the start of the token frame from overwriting its end. This delay is provided by a 24 bit register in the active monitor.

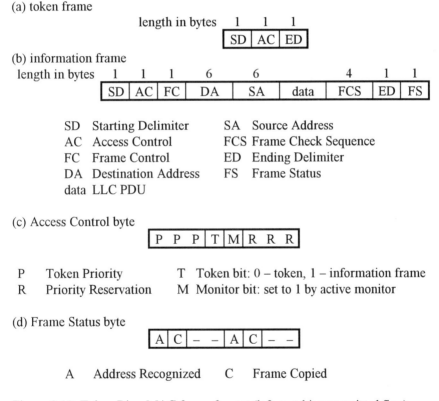

(a) token frame

length in bytes   1   1   1

| SD | AC | ED |

(b) information frame

length in bytes   1   1   1   6   6   4   1   1

| SD | AC | FC | DA | SA | data | FCS | ED | FS |

SD Starting Delimiter   SA Source Address
AC Access Control   FCS Frame Check Sequence
FC Frame Control   ED Ending Delimiter
DA Destination Address   FS Frame Status
data LLC PDU

(c) Access Control byte

| P | P | P | T | M | R | R | R |

P Token Priority   T Token bit: 0 – token, 1 – information frame
R Priority Reservation   M Monitor bit: set to 1 by active monitor

(d) Frame Status byte

| A | C | – | – | A | C | – | – |

A Address Recognized   C Frame Copied

Figure 9.10 Token Ring MAC frame format (leftmost bit transmitted first)

Priority
A mechanism operates to ensure that high priority frames are transmitted before low priority frames. Whilst waiting for a token, a node compares the priority level of its waiting frame with the priority level given by the Priority Reservation bits in the Access Control byte of all passing frames. If its waiting frame has a higher priority then it updates the Priority Reservation bits to the higher

level. The lowest priority level is 000 and the msb is at the left, e.g. 110 is higher than 011.

When the node holding the token generates a new token it sets the Token Priority bits to the same level as given by the Priority Reservation bits of the last frame it received. A node receiving the token is only allowed to seize it if it has a message with a priority level at least equal to that in the Token Priority field. This guarantees that the first downstream node with a high priority message seizes the token before upstream nodes with lower priority messages.

The mechanism works like a ratchet to increase the Priority Reservation bits to the level of the highest priority message waiting to be transmitted. A further mechanism ensures that the node which raised the priority level is responsible for lowering it, once the high priority frames have been transmitted.

9.6 Ethernet and Token Ring compared

A difference between Token Ring and Ethernet is that the Token Ring MAC protocol is deterministic, i.e. an upper bound can be set on the time taken to transmit a packet. At first consideration, this might be taken as implying that Token Ring is better for safety critical applications. However, in a safety critical application all aspects of a network must be considered. Since there is always some chance that equipment will fail and a message be lost then no network can be considered to be non-deterministic. So, although the Token Ring protocol is deterministic a Token Ring network is not. In fact, because Ethernet was designed for simplicity [MET] and because a faulty node will usually fail in such a way as not to affect the rest of the bus, Ethernet is often chosen for safety critical applications.

A second difference between Token Ring and Ethernet is how they behave under overload conditions. Token Ring will work flat out delivering as many messages as it can whilst, because of all the collisions occurring, the throughput of an Ethernet may decrease as the load increases. Hence, for applications which must continue working under abnormal or overload conditions, Token Ring is probably a better choice than Ethernet.

As an approximate guide, for a 10Base2 Ethernet installation the peak data throughput is typically 7 Mbps, whilst under normal traffic conditions a typical load would be 15%, with 1% of packets deferred because the bus is busy and 0.03% suffering collisions.

If a LAN is becoming too heavily loaded then it can be split into two, or more, smaller LANs. These can be connected using bridges (see section 9.8), so that to the user it appears that nothing has changed. The split needs to be chosen sensibly, e.g. along departmental lines, so that only a small fraction of the traffic needs to be sent over a bridge. Ideally, splitting a LAN in two would result in each of the daughter LANs having half the traffic load of the parent.

A third difference between Token Ring and Ethernet is that Token Ring has a priority scheme. Again this might help in an overload situation to keep some critical application running.

9.7 High speed LANs

There are high speed LANs derived from both Token Ring and Ethernet. FDDI (Fibre Distributed Data Interface) is a 100 Mbps LAN with a MAC protocol based on Token Ring. This LAN is described below. A proposal for Fast Ethernet is 100BaseT which uses CSMA/CD as a MAC protocol run over twisted pairs. There is also 100BaseVG – AnyLAN, which uses a new access method: Demand Priority Protocol (DPP). FDDI is the most advanced in terms of standards.

9.7.1 FDDI

FDDI has a dual, counter-rotating, ring topology for resilience, with two classes of nodes or stations, see figure 9.11: Dual Attachment Stations (DAS), which attach to both rings, and Single Attachment Stations (SAS), which only attach to one ring.

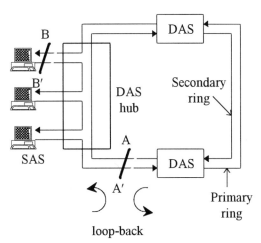

Figure 9.11 FDDI dual ring

The ports connecting the nodes to the ring will bypass the connection if a fault occurs. For example, assuming there is a break A-A' then the network will heal itself so that every node is still connected, as the ports either side of the break provide a loop-back path. But note that there is now only one ring, i.e. the overall network capacity is halved. On the other hand, if there is a break B-B′ then the SAS node will be cut off, but the rest of the network will operate as before. Note that SAS nodes must be connected to a hub. Hence SAS nodes are less critical nodes that have no redundant link. The ring supports 1000 access ports, e.g. a maximum of 500 DAS nodes can be connected. The overall length of the ring is limited to 100 km. The MAC sub layer standard is [ISO 9314-2], from the original ANSI X3 standards committee proposal [BED].

The initial interconnection medium standard kept costs down by specifying multimode fibre with LEDs (see chapter 6), at a wavelength of 1300 nm and with a velocity of propagation of 2×10^8 m/s. For multimode fibre the maximum distance between nodes is 2 km. Other media are available, e.g. single mode fibre with up to 60 km between nodes and, for short distances of up to 100 m over twisted pair, a variant called TPDDI can be used. The various transmission media can be mixed on the same network.

FDDI covers the geographical area of a Metropolitan Area Network (MAN) and there are a few changes to the Token Ring MAC protocol to take account of this, as follows:

The Token is released early, immediately after the last information frame the node transmits, rather than waiting for the frame to circulate around the ring. Note that this has implications for the Token Ring priority process. Since the propagation delay (t_p) around the ring can be up to 0.5 ms, which corresponds to 50 kbits, early token release is necessary to allow multiple frames on the ring to make more effective use of the LAN. Note that early token release is an option with Token Ring.

FDDI provides some support for isochronous data, using a priority scheme based on that of Token Bus. A Target Token Rotation Time (TTRT) is defined for the network, which takes account of the size of the network and the requested amount of time-critical, isochronous traffic. Note that the TTRT is only a target, as the actual time can exceed this. When a token arrives at a node, the node transmits its agreed amount of isochronous data and then any anisochronous data, until either the TTRT algorithm determines that it must release the token or it has no more data to transmit. If the token arrives late at a node then the node can only transmit its isochronous information frames before releasing the token. This ensures that the isochronous data is sent every time the token goes around the network, with any spare capacity available for anisochronous data.

What we have termed 'isochronous' data is sometimes referred to as 'synchronous' data and similarly with 'anisochronous' and 'asynchronous'. We do not use synchronous and asynchronous in this way because synchronous already has two other well established meanings in communications: namely that the transmitter and receiver clocks are locked together (see chapter 7) or that concurrent processes are locked together by having to exchange messages.

Another change to the Token Ring protocol is the line code, as using Differential Manchester would double the required bandwidth to 200 MHz. A

4B/5B code was chosen because it is bandwidth efficient. With a 4B/5B code 4 data bits are channel coded to produce a 5 bit signal. Hence the signalling rate down the line is $5/4 \times 100$ Mbps = 125 Mbps (strictly 125 Mbaud since signalling events per second are being measured, see chapter 3). As there are 32 possible permutations of 5 bit line code words to choose from, the 16 permutations of 4 bit data words are assigned a line code word with a maximum of 2 consecutive zeros. Since no code word starts with two consecutive zeros this means the maximum number of consecutive zeros is three.

After the 4B/5B coding, fibre systems use the NRZI line code, as with HDLC (see chapter 7) except here inverting on 1 rather than 0. The bandwidth is 125 MHz and the combination of 4B/5B and NRZI coding ensures that there are never more than 3 consecutive bits in the data without a clock transition, which simplifies clock recovery. For TPDDI a three level code is used which reduces the required bandwidth to 62.5 MHz. The code is often called NRZI-3 as it is a development of NRZI with three amplitude levels, +1, −1 and 0. Transitions occur for a data 1 and are the same polarity until either +1 or −1 is reached when the polarity of the transitions is reversed [JAI].

The MAC protocol format for non-routing frames is shown in figure 9.12. Note that since the priority is not provided by the Access Control byte of Token Ring there is no Access Control byte. The maximum length of a frame is 4500 bytes. This includes 4 symbols for the preamble, hence the maximum length of the data is 4478 bytes or 8956×5 bit symbols [JAI].

(a) token frame

length in 5 bit symbols   16   2   2   2

preamble	SD	FC	ED

(b) information frame

length in 5 bit symbols

    16   2   2   12   12   ≤8956   8   1   3

preamble	SD	FC	DA	SA	data	FCS	ED	FS

SD   Starting Delimiter   SA   Source Address
FC   Frame Control   FCS Frame Check Sequence
DA   Destination Address   ED   Ending Delimiter (N.B. different length in token)
data   FS   Frame Status

(c) Frame Control byte

C	1	F	F	Z	Z	Z	Z

C   Class of service – 0 anisochronous, 1 isochronous
F   Type of frame – MAC (i.e. network data) or Information
Z   Control bits

Figure 9.12 FDDI MAC frame format (leftmost bit transmitted first)

With a minimum frame of 22 symbols the minimum holding time H_{min} for FDDI = 0.88 μs. Hence, for the maximum propagation delay, the parameter $a = t_p/H_{min} = 568$, making FDDI a WAN (see chapter 7).

Of the high speed LANs:
- FDDI is a natural upgrade path for a Token Ring network.
- Fast Ethernet will provide a natural upgrade for Ethernet LANs.
- 100BaseVG – AnyLAN is designed as an upgrade path for both, as it supports both Ethernet and Token Ring frames. VG stands for Voice Grade as it is designed to use four twisted pairs of voice grade quality cables. It uses 5B/6B channel coding on each pair (similar to FDDI's 4B/5B line code), transmitting 120 Mbps of which 5/6, i.e. 100 Mbps, is available for the MAC protocol. It can also use two pairs of STP or two fibre optic cables.

However, there are alternative options which are explored in the next chapter on fast packet switching.

9.8 Bridges

Bridges operate at the MAC sub layer in layer 2 of the seven layer RM. They are used to connect LANs together so that the bridged LAN appears as one LAN to the user, see figure 9.13. They 'filter' packets, only passing packets on to the other LAN if required. Hence bridges can be used to split an overloaded LAN into two or more LANs to reduce the load. The filtering also has a LAN management function, in that only valid frames are forwarded and intelligent bridges can bar access to a LAN by unauthorized users. Because they operate at the MAC sub layer they support all protocol stacks used on the bridged LAN. The bridge interface to a LAN is called a port. Multiport bridges can bridge between more than two LANs.

Bridges also allow a bridged LAN to extend beyond the physical limitations of distance or number of attached nodes of a single LAN. Indeed a WAN can be created by using pairs of half bridges, linked by a long distance channel. A half bridge is therefore also called a remote bridge, see figure 9.13.

In order to only transmit packets when necessary a bridge must have a table of the MAC addresses of the nodes attached to the LANs on either side of it. A learning bridge can build this table up automatically. This is possible because every MAC PDU contains the SA as well as the DA. Hence if a frame arrives on port 1 from LAN 1 with a SA of *a*, then *a* must be on LAN 1. Subsequently, any frame addressed to node *a* which arrives on port 1 is not forwarded, whilst frames with this DA which arrive on port 2 from LAN 2 are forwarded. Hence the table is built up as each node transmits. If the bridge does not know the destination it will forward the packet. Table entries are deleted if not confirmed within a certain time to allow the bridge to keep its table up to date.

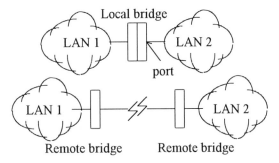

Figure 9.13 Local and remote bridges

Bridges are generally used to connect the same type of LAN, e.g. source routing bridges are used for Token Ring or FDDI LANs, and Spanning Tree Algorithm (STA) bridges for Ethernets. However, because the MAC addressing for Token Ring and Ethernet is compatible, special bridges do exist for connecting a Token Ring to an Ethernet.

As to be expected from the name, with source routing the SA defines the route, whilst STA bridges are transparent to the other network nodes, i.e. the bridges find the route. However, in order to find a route with source routing a spanning tree must be set up, so STA bridges are discussed first.

9.8.1 Spanning Tree Algorithm bridges

The first task is to define a tree topology, as shown in figure 9.14. This is really an upside down tree with the root at the top, connected by branches to the leaves at the bottom. It is a binary tree as each parent node has two children. There are no loops, which is a necessary property of a topology for Ethernet LANs.

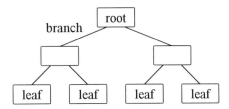

Figure 9.14 Tree topology

Figure 9.15 shows an irregular topology, as might be created as a network organically grows, with the nodes being bridges and the links or arcs being LANs. This network has loops so it is unsuitable as it stands for Ethernet.

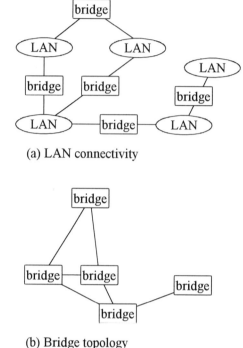

(a) LAN connectivity

(b) Bridge topology

Figure 9.15 Irregular bridge topology

One possible spanning tree of this irregular network is shown in figure 9.16. A spanning tree has the properties
- There are no loops.
- Every node is attached to the tree.
- Adding any unused link from the irregular topology creates a loop.
- Deleting any link from the spanning tree isolates at least one node.
A spanning tree is a suitable topology for Ethernet.

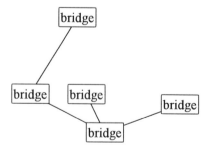

Figure 9.16 A spanning tree topology of figure 9.15 (b)

The essential function of spanning tree bridges is that they will automatically configure themselves to create a spanning tree topology by putting some links into a standby mode. This is carried out by periodically exchanging Bridge Protocol Data Units (BPDUs) and following the Spanning Tree Algorithm (STA), as laid down in the IEEE 802.1 (D) standard on MAC bridges [ISO/IEC 10038]. Hence, if any active link fails the network can reconfigure itself using all available links, active or standby.

The BPDUs are addressed to the MAC group address of the bridges on the network. Each bridge has a unique identifier determined by its MAC address and priority level, and each port on a bridge has a unique identifier. Each LAN has a path cost, e.g. determined by its data rate, etc. The STA is explained below by means of an example, for a more detailed explanation see [HAL] and [STA].

Spanning Tree Algorithm

Starting with the network of figure 9.15 (a), redrawn as in figure 9.17 (a) and assuming the path cost is 1 for each LAN (i.e. the STA will seek a spanning tree based on minimizing the number of hops to the destination).

- The bridge with the lowest identifier is chosen as the 'root bridge' (B1 in this case).
- Each bridge except the root bridge determines its 'root port', by comparing BPDUs originating from the root bridge as they arrive on different ports. The root port is the one with the lowest path cost to the root bridge. Each bridge calculates a port's path cost by adding on the path cost of the link on which the BPDU arrived to the path cost in the BPDU. It then transmits the updated BPDU from its other ports. In case the path costs are the same the port with the lowest identifier is chosen as the root port. The BPDUs start with path cost = 0 from the root bridge.
- The root ports and all ports of the root bridge are active, i.e. set to the forwarding state. The network is now in the state shown in figure 9.17 (b).
- Root ports attach a bridge to the spanning tree, whilst the other bridge ports can be used to attach LANs to the bridge, to extend the spanning tree. For example, LANs attached to the root bridge are directly connected to the root of the spanning tree by the root bridge ports. Ports used to connect LANs in this way are called 'designated ports'.
- The bridge with the lowest cost path from its root port is chosen to connect a LAN to the spanning tree. Again, in case of equal costs the bridge with the lowest identifier is chosen. It becomes the 'designated bridge' and the port becomes the designated port for that LAN. Clearly, there can only be one designated port per LAN and a designated port cannot be a root port.
- All unused ports are set to the blocking state, i.e. are on standby. All root ports and all designated ports are in the forwarding state. Thus a bridge receives BPDUs on its root port and transmits them from its designated ports. The

network is now in the state shown in figure 9.17 (c), i.e. the bridges have set up the spanning tree of figure 9.16.

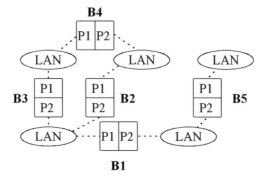

(a) Initial state, key: B*n* – Bridge *n*, P*m* – Port *m*

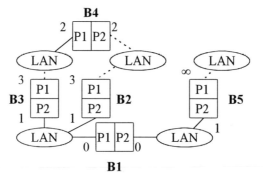

(b) B1 is chosen as the root bridge. Path costs from B1 are shown. On each bridge, the port with the lowest path cost is the root port; if ports tie then the lowest port identifier is chosen. Root ports shown by solid lines.

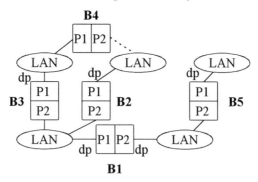

(c) Spanning Tree (solid lines). Designated ports (dp) chosen.

Figure 9.17 Spanning Tree Algorithm

9.8.2 Source routing bridges

Although this is designed for any type of LAN it is generally used for Token Ring or FDDI, so the description below is based on a Token Ring implementation. The standard is specified in an addendum to the IEEE 802.5 standard. For more information see [HAL] and [STA].

The source must include routing information in the data field. Basically, this consists of a series of route designators, each containing a pair of LAN and bridge identifiers. As it regenerates a packet, each bridge inspects it to see if its identifier is in the routing information field. If it is, it forwards the packet to the required LAN and updates the Access Control byte as if it were the DA.

Whether routing information is in the data field is determined by the first bit of the source address. The first bit of the MAC address of a node is always 0, according to the standard MAC addressing scheme for 802. LANs, so this bit is redundant and can be set to a 1 if routing is needed. If the DA is on the same LAN as the SA (or the final bridge) routing is not needed; this case is identified by the first bit of the DA being set to 0.

The algorithm to set up the route is in three stages:

• When a node has a frame to transmit to a new DA, for which it does not know the route, it causes a spanning tree to be set up across the whole network. It then sends a 'Spanning Tree Explorer' frame, copies of which will propagate to all nodes but terminate when they reach the leaf nodes. The spanning tree is then dismantled, having ensured that each LAN gets only one copy of the frame. A frame will have reached the required DA, informing it that the SA is requesting a route.

• The DA then responds by returning an 'All Routes Explorer' frame. Each bridge which gets one of these frames adds its bridge id, and the net id of the LAN attached to the port it received the frame on, to the routing field. It then broadcasts the updated frame from its other ports. Since the spanning tree has been dismantled it may be that some frames are going around loops. The bridge therefore inspects the routing information field before transmitting the frame to a LAN, discarding it if the frame has already been to that LAN.

• The SA will get versions of the all-routes broadcast frame from all possible routes. It then inspects the routing field to determine the best route to send the frame. This route is entered into the SA's routing table and used for all frames sent to that DA.

9.8.3 STA and source routing compared

With transparent routing, e.g. STA bridges, the bridges collectively decide the route that frames will take, whilst for source routing it is the SA that decides. Hence source routing bridges do not have routing tables, as they only need to act on the instructions contained in the routing information field. On the other hand every node in a source routing bridged LAN must have routing tables, whilst only the bridges in a STA bridged LAN need routing tables.

With source routing all links remain active, whilst with STA bridges links causing loops will be placed on standby; thus not all the available bandwidth will be used. Source routing can be used for any LAN if the routing information field is specified, currently that only applies to Token Ring and FDDI.

There is a trade-off between bridge overhead when forwarding frames (source routing best) and transmission overhead associated with finding a route (STA best).

There are also Source Routing Transparent (SRT) bridges, which use source routing if the incoming packet contains routing information and transparent routing if it does not.

Exercises

(1)   State what CSMA/CD stands for.

(2)   State what MAC and LLC stand for and where they fit in the seven layer Reference Model.

(3)   List the sequence of events that occur when an Ethernet transceiver transmits a message, which is involved in a collision, and then successfully retransmits.

(4)   State why Ethernet repeaters must not be connected to form a ring.

(5)   State the collision domain and minimum frame length in bits for 10Base5 Ethernet. Explain why the collision domain must be less than the minimum frame length.

(6)   Calculate the maximum time before a collision would be detected in a maximum length 10Base5 LAN, given that the velocity of propagation is 2.31×10^8 m/s. Hence find the maximum number of bits transmitted before a collision is detected.

(7)   State how many frames can be on a Token Ring network at any one time.

(8)   Describe how the active monitor in a Token Ring network ensures that no frame can continuously circulate around the ring.

(9)   Describe the priority mechanism of Token Ring.

(10) Complete the following table by inserting 'ring', 'bus' or 'star' as appropriate

	10Base2	10BaseT	Token Ring	Token Bus
Logical operation				
Physical operation				
Cabling topology				

(11) Compare how Ethernet and Token Ring ensure that no node can permanently seize the LAN.

(12) State differences which may be important to a user between Token Ring and Ethernet.

(13) State whether Token Ring or Ethernet would be most suitable for the following applications: (i) a lightly loaded, safety critical application; (ii) a system which must continue to work under overload conditions; (iii) an application where a few workstations occasionally need to send large files; (iv) an application where many workstations frequently send small files.

(14) State what 'deterministic' means in the context of MAC protocols.

(15) What are the implications for Token Ring's priority mechanism if the token is released early?

(16) What is the data rate for 100BaseVG – AnyLAN?

(17) Classify the Manchester and Differential Manchester linecodes in terms of xB/yB, as in the 4B/5B code for FDDI.

(18) (a) Give reasons for using a bridge. (b) Describe how a bridge can automatically determine a table of the active nodes on its attached LANs.

(19) Discuss the differences between bridges, routers, gateways and repeaters, with particular reference to the seven layer Reference Model.

(20) State how a 1Base5 and a 10Base2 network could be linked together.

(21) Why is FDDI a natural upgrade path for Token Ring?

(22) In figure 9.17 (a) swap the bridge identifiers B1 and B4 and determine the new spanning tree.

(23) Write your own summary of what you have learnt in this chapter.

10 Fast Packet Switching

LANs such as Ethernet and Token Ring provide a high speed connection compared to WANs such as X.25; they allow workstations to communicate at high speed with little delay, creating a seamless environment where the end users are unaware of the supporting network. The challenge is to extend this seamless environment by providing high speed connections over a wide area, i.e. over WANs and MANs. Fast packet switching is the generic name for new high speed WAN and MAN services and is the topic of this chapter. The protocols considered are: frame relay, which is an access protocol for a WAN; ATM (Asynchronous Transfer Mode), which is a cell relay based WAN protocol; and DQDB (Distributed Queue Dual Bus) which is a MAN protocol. They are not mutually exclusive, indeed both Frame Relay and DQDB can be used to access an ATM network. However, before looking at these protocols we need to consider the topic of congestion, as it is crucial to the design of WANs and WAN protocols.

10.1 Congestion

A network becomes congested when a node receives more data on its inputs than it can handle. The data may be from many Source Addresses (SA) and be addressed to many Destination Addresses (DA). These SA and DA may be remote from the node experiencing congestion. The new concept for networks today (e.g. cell relay and frame relay) is to ease congestion by discarding low priority data. Flow control to reduce the incoming data to resolve the problem is obviously essential; indeed, without flow control, the congestion would rapidly get worse due to attempts by the DA to have the discarded data retransmitted. The ability to discard low priority data is necessary because high speed networks need to respond rapidly to congestion conditions and cannot wait for flow control measures to take effect. Low priority data is identified by particular bits in the protocol header, e.g. in frame relay the Discard Eligibility (DE) bit is set to identify frames that the network has not guaranteed to deliver.

Congestion control is sometimes confused with flow control but, although related, they are different concepts. Flow control is used across a virtual circuit to ensure that the SA sends data no faster than the slowest node or link can normally deal with. Congestion control, on the other hand, is used over a whole network when a node becomes overloaded. This may happen when data from several SAs converges on one node, even though individually the SAs may be behaving well in terms of flow control.

There are three main types of congestion control: implicit, forward explicit and backward (or backward explicit).

• In implicit congestion control the DA assumes that the reason why data is missing is that congestion has occurred. It then signals back to the SA to slow down transmission. Clearly, any virtual circuit can implement implicit congestion control; TCP/IP uses it solely.

• With forward explicit congestion control the congested node explicitly signals to the DA that congestion has occurred. The DA then signals back to the SA as with implicit congestion control.

• The final option is backward congestion control, where the congested node signals directly to the SA to slow down (note that backward congestion control is explicit). This is the most complex solution, as it requires network nodes to be able to identify the SA of messages, but it is also the most direct and secure method (secure: because it can throttle back the data flow at the point where the data enters the network, i.e. independently of the SA).

Frame relay can use all three types of congestion control.

10.2 Frame relay

Frame relay, like X.25, is an access protocol to a packet switched WAN. As explained in chapter 8 for X.25, the core network may use a different protocol but, as the core and access protocols must provide a consistent set of functions, it is convenient to consider the core protocol to be the same as the access protocol. For example, referring to congestion (see above), frame relay can implement all three types of congestion control, which enables it to be used with different core networks which may only support one option. Frame relay is ideal for 'bursty' traffic at data rates up to 34/45 Mbps. A typical application would be to provide a seamless interface between several LANs by using a common WAN. Frame relay standards are CCITT I.122, Q.922 and Q.933.

   The major difference between frame relay and X.25 is that frame relay only provides error detection, not error correction, which is consistent with how it deals with congestion. Frames with errors are simply dropped, the protocol relying on the end-to-end protocols (layers 3 and 4 of the seven layer RM) to recover missing frames by initiating ARQ. In X.25, each incoming packet is checked by each node in the network at layer 2 of the X.25 protocol stack (using the LAP-B protocol), ARQ being initiated by the network node if required; this process being repeated at layer 3 (using the X.25 protocol itself) at the destination to recover any missing packets. Eliminating error correction at layer 2 has been made possible by improvements in line performance; compare a link via modems over an analogue line with a BER of, say, 1×10^{-3} with an optical fibre link having a BER of typically 1×10^{-8}. X.25 can improve the error rate over the analogue line to 1×10^{-6} with its link-by-link error correction scheme but the improvement is not required for the digital link [DET]. Clearly, for networks with lines suffering high error rates, a protocol such as X.25 may still be required but, for high performance networks, a 'stripped-down', fast protocol is provided by frame relay – improving network latency by reducing protocol overhead.

Another difference between the two access protocols is that X.25 is a protocol stack covering layers 1 through 3 of the seven layer RM whilst frame relay is thought of as a layer 2 protocol. However, although switching at layer 2 (like a LAN bridge) it still provides the routing function of a layer 3 protocol (as well as other layer 3 functions such as flow control).

Figure 10.1 shows the structure of a frame relay frame. The flag and means of generating the Frame Check Sequence (FCS) using a Cyclic Redundancy Check are as described for HDLC (see chapter 7). The data field is ≤ 4096 bytes long as in X.25. DLCI is the Data Link Connection Identifier which identifies the virtual circuit across the network node interface (in X.25 the virtual circuit identifier is carried in the layer 3 protocol header). X.25 could withhold an acknowledgement for flow control but there is no control byte with frame relay – hence there are no acknowledgements – so frame relay must have explicit means of flow control: it can implement both forward and backward explicit congestion control (using the FECN and BECN, the Forward and Backward Explicit Congestion Notification bits) as well as implicit congestion control. The DE, or Discard Eligibility bit, is used to mark frames which can be 'dropped' if congestion occurs.

When a frame relay network is set up, a minimum information rate and a peak information arrival rate are agreed between the network provider and the user [PRE], as well as a Committed Information Rate (CIR), which is the average data rate under normal conditions. The ratio between the peak and the average rates gives a measure of the 'burstiness' of the data source, which varies from 1 for isochronous data to over a 1000 for LAN data. Frames which would bring the information rate above the peak rate are not accepted by the network. When spare bandwidth is available the data rate is incremented, at regular time intervals, until the peak rate is reached. Conversely, if congestion occurs, the data rate is decremented until the minimum rate is reached or the congestion clears. The network provider thus guarantees a minimum service but the user can expect, under normal conditions, a better service. This is possible because of the statistical gain expected from having many users (i.e. not all users are expected to simultaneously use the network at the peak rate).

byte	bit							
	7	6	5	4	3	2	1	0
1	Flag (01111110)							
2	0	CR	DLCI (high)					
3	1	DE	BE CN	FE CN	DLCI (low)			
4	Data ($\ell \leq 4096$ bits)							
etc.	...							
	...							
	Data							
	Frame Check Sequence (high)							
	Frame Check Sequence (low)							
	Flag (01111110)							

CR   Command/Response
DLCI   Data Link Connection Identifier
DE   Discard Eligibility
BECN   Backward Explicit Congestion Notification
FECN   Forward Explicit Congestion Notification

Figure 10.1 Frame relay frame, bit 7 of top byte transmitted first

In terms of the seven layer RM, the frame relay protocol switches at layer 2, covers both layer 2 and 3 but with some omissions, and requires suitable layer 3 and 4 protocols to compensate for these omissions. The advantage of frame relay is that its variable frame length provides a convenient interface with existing LANs and WANs (e.g. Ethernet, X.25, etc.). Frame relay is seen as a LAN interconnection solution, as a WAN for anisochronous data, and as both a means of accessing an ATM network (which operates at data rates from 34 Mbps up) and a migration path to ATM.

10.3 ATM

Asynchronous Transfer Mode is a connection oriented, cell relay protocol; a cell always having the same length, e.g. an ATM cell consists of 48 bytes for data and a 5 byte header, see figure 10.2. A data length of 48 bytes is an unsatisfactory compromise between 64 bytes and 32 bytes! The data communications industry preferred 64 bytes, as it would increase the protocol efficiency; the telephony industry preferred 32 bytes, as it would decrease the holding time (the time that a PDU occupies a channel) [JEF]. The term 'relay' is also used in frame relay: in both frame and cell relay error correction is not provided on a link-by-link basis, instead faulty cells or frames are discarded when detected.

This is consistent with how these networks deal with congestion: a network node simply discarding low priority cells or frames when it experiences congestion.

Header 1 (5 bytes)	Data 1 (48 bytes)	Header 2 (5 bytes)

...   ...

Figure 10.2 ATM cells

One advantage of cell relay over frame relay is that it is well suited for mixing isochronous data (voice/video) with anisochronous data. Isochronous data has tight real time limits, so with frame relay it might be necessary to abort a long frame whereas with ATM the worst case would be to wait for the end of a 53 byte cell. The 'Asynchronous' in ATM refers to the temporary assignment of channels to time slots, rather than the permanent assignment as found with TDM systems (such as 30 channel PCM); it is clearly a synchronous protocol in terms of having the receiver clock locked to the transmitter clock. Although time slots are not permanently assigned, ATM can carry isochronous data because cells can be reserved to be available at regular time intervals; anisochronous data can then use whatever channel capacity remains, enabling ATM to support 'bandwidth on demand'. It is the ability to mix different kinds of data services which enables ATM to achieve economies of scale and hence allow bandwidth on demand to be economically provided. Because of this, ATM has been chosen as the protocol to support B-ISDN (Broadband-ISDN), which is an ideal network concept [POP] in that it is capable of supporting all foreseeable services, i.e. it is the logical progression of the ISDN concept, taking account of higher data rate services, such as HDTV (High Definition TV), etc. However, whether ATM will be used for all these services will depend on its cost versus performance characteristic. The ATM forum, consisting of representatives from the computer and communication industries, has been formed to accelerate the standards development process [QUI]. For a list of some ATM standards see [POP].

The ATM protocol stack, as shown below in figure 10.3 [POP, QUI], is different from the seven layer RM:

Layers	*Sub-layers*
Higher layers	
ATM Adaption Layer (AAL):	Convergent Sub-Layer (CS) Segmentation And Reassembly sub-layer (SAR)
ATM layer	
Physical layer:	Transmission Convergence sub-layer (TC) Physical Medium Dependent sub-layer (PMD)

Figure 10.3 ATM protocol stack

10.3.1 Physical layer

The physical layer [POP] consists of the Transmission Convergence (TC) sub-layer (where the ATM cells are assembled into a form suitable for transmission over the physical medium) and the PMD (Physical Medium Dependent sub-layer) itself. One of the chosen physical media is the SDH (Synchronous Digital Hierarchy), where the ATM cells are loaded in a VC-4 (Virtual Container-4) and carried in a STM-1 (Synchronous Transport Module-1) frame. This defines the data rate limits for the TC sub-layer for this particular ATM service, i.e. the payload data rate is 149.760 Mbps whilst the gross transmission rate is 155.520 Mbps. Note that the frame rate for an STM-1 frame is 125 μs, so each byte carries a 64 kbps data stream. Another TC sub-layer option is based on these rates, but it transports the data as a bit stream at a maximum data rate of 149.760 Mbps. It therefore needs to increase the gross rate to 155.520 Mbps, which it does by inserting an extra cell after every 26 data cells and by inserting idle cells in any unused data cells. ATM can also run on the PDH (Plesio-chronous Digital Hierarchy) and IBM have led the way for a 25.6 Mbps service based on the physical layer of the Token Ring LAN.

10.3.2 ATM layer

The ATM layer [BAL, JEF, POP, QUI] consists of the ATM protocol itself. This deals with the point-to-point transfer of cells over the network and the routing of cells over virtual circuits (actually called virtual connections in ATM documentation) by fast, hardware-based switching in the network nodes. There are two types of virtual connections: Permanent Virtual Connections (PVCs), which are established at network configuration time, and Switched Virtual Connections (SVCs), which are set up temporarily as required (i.e. dynamic-ally). The ATM cell has a means of detecting errors; but only if they occur in the header. Hence, we can consider the header separately from the data, as in figure 10.4.

(a) User-Network Interface

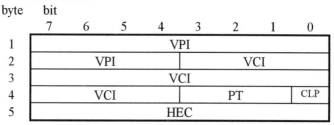

(b) Network-Node Interface

GFC   Generic Flow Control (4 bits)
VPI   Virtual Path Identifier (8 or 12 bits)
VCI   Virtual Channel Identifier (16 bits)
PT   Payload Type (3 bits)
CLP   Cell Loss Priority bit
HEC   Header Error Check (8 bits)

Figure 10.4 ATM header, bit 7 of top byte transmitted first

The Header Error Check (HEC) is an eight bit CRC (Cyclic Redundancy Check) with generator polynomial $x^8 + x^2 + x + 1$, see chapter 7. This is used not only to detect faulty cells but also to achieve cell synchronization, as a known sequence (which defines the cell boundary) is generated when an error-free header is checked. Eight bits are used to check 40 data bits, which is a far higher proportion than in the CRC check in HDLC, so the CRC can also be used to correct single bit errors in the header. The data field is not checked for errors by the ATM protocol but it can be checked by higher layer protocols if required. There is a two bit Payload Type (PT) field, which indicates whether the cell contains control or user data, and a Cell Loss Priority (CLP) bit, which determines the cell's priority (as discussed in the section on congestion, low priority cells are candidates for deletion at any node where congestion occurs).

The Virtual Path Identifier (VPI) and Virtual Channel Identifier (VCI) make up the address which indicates the next link over which the cell is to be sent (together they are referred to as the VPI:VCI value). Connections may be bundled together in the same path, so they have the same VPI, in which case they are all switched together at the path level, or individual channels may be switched at the channel level, see figure 10.5. The VCI is 16 bits long whilst the VPI is 12 bits between network nodes, i.e. at the Network Node Interface (NNI), or 8 bits long over the link between the user and the network, i.e. at the User Network Interface (UNI). The other 4 bits of the UNI are the Generic Flow Control bits, whose use has not been finalized yet. Both the VPI and VCI may be changed by a network node, ready for the next node to act on [POP]. The ATM switch contains an address translation table: the VPI:VCI value is used to address this table and locate the appropriate entry, enabling the output port and any new VPI:VCI value to be read out. Incidentally, security is enhanced because of this indirect relationship between the VPI:VCI and the call destination and source.

Avoid confusing the VCI with a virtual circuit: it is the combination of VPI and VCI which is unique and it is likely that the VCI will be different at different points in the network; but cells following the same virtual circuit will have the same VPI:VCI at the same point in the network.

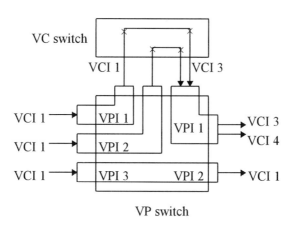

Figure 10.5 Multiplexing virtual channels in ATM

Because nodes are dealing with constant length cells and all the decisions are made on the basis of a 5 byte header, it is possible to do the switching in hardware. The mode of routing can be virtual cut-through, i.e. as soon as the header has been received the cell can be forwarded. These factors enable ATM switching to be fast. ATM signalling is based on the ISDN protocol LAP-D, a Signalling Virtual Channel Identifier (SVCI) being set up for call set up and clear down, etc. As ATM can be carried over both the SDH and the PDH it is fully compatible with KiloStream and MegaStream data rates, enabling current services such as narrowband ISDN and the connectionless SMDS (Switched Multimegabit Data Service) to be supported.

ATM needs to police the rate of arrival of data from a user. It does this with a so-called 'leaky bucket' [GAL], which basically ensures that cells which would push the average data rate above an agreed value are not accepted or are marked as eligible for deletion (using the CLP bit). Whenever a cell arrives the bucket is incremented (the leaky bucket is a virtual buffer, as the cells themselves are not actually buffered). If the bucket is not empty, it is decremented at the agreed average cell transmission rate (i.e. the bucket leaks at a constant rate, which is where the physical analogy breaks down). Cells which cause the bucket to overflow can be discarded immediately or can be marked by setting the CLP bit. This is an example of a traffic control process, which aims to avoid congestion occurring as far as possible; as opposed to a congestion control process, which deals with congestion once it has occurred.

Agreed performance characteristics are negotiated for ATM links in the same way as for frame relay, e.g. a CBR or ABR (Committed or Available Bit Rate) service can be requested. The CBR service guarantees an average data rate under normal conditions whilst any spare bandwidth is shared out amongst all the ABR channels.

10.3.3 ATM Adaption Layer (AAL)

The function of this layer [BAL, JEF, QUI] is to provide an interface between the higher layers and the common ATM layer, i.e. to provide for different service requirements. Five types of AAL are provided (note that ATM is basically a connection-oriented service, so all types except where specifically mentioned are virtual circuit services):

- AAL1 – a constant bit rate service for audio/video;
- AAL2 – a variable bit rate service for audio/video;
- AAL3/4 – a service for other types of data with a CRC on the data in each cell; includes an option for a connectionless-oriented service (increasingly, this service will be supplanted by AAL5);
- AAL5 – also known as SEAL (Simple and Efficient Adaption Layer) for data;
- AALX – a null type, enabling the user to implement their own AAL.

Only AAL1 provides a constant bit rate service (inherently providing timing information), supporting, for example, standard speech circuits. AAL2 explicitly provides timing information between the source and data; an application for AAL2 would be transmitting compressed video in raw form. AAL3/4 started out as the two types AAL3 and AAL4, both designed with CRC error detection for the data of individual cells; the difference between them was that AAL4 was for a connectionless service but, since otherwise they were similar, they were combined. The CRC check on the data of each cell is now thought to be too much of an overhead; AAL5 evolved in response to this concern and makes the full 48 bytes of the data field available for data (frame relay generally uses AAL5).

The segmentation and reassembly of user data into 48 byte segments is carried out by the SAR (Segmentation And Reassembly) sub-layer. The other AAL sub-layer is called the Convergent Sub-layer (CS). The functions of these sub-layers depend on the class of service. They cope with problems such as lost cells, variations in delay between incoming cells, errors, etc. For example, for AAL5 the user data has a block error check added and is then padded to a multiple of 48 bytes in the CS sub-layer, which adds little overhead, before being segmented in the SAR sub-layer. By contrast, for the AAL3/4 service the user data is first segmented to a maximum length of 64 kbytes and a header and trailer added by the CS sub-layer (making up the CS Protocol Data Unit) before having more system information added at the SAR sub-layer (making up the SAR-PDU) [QUI].

Although the queuing delay at a switch is low, it does introduce a variation in the rate of arrival of cells at the destination, a cause of Cell Delay Variation (CDV). For speech and similar time critical calls, this variation will cause jitter [JEF]. One approach to reduce this is to use a Synchronous Residual Time Stamp (SRTS) provided by AAL1. This marks the cell stream with an offset against a common network wide clock. Unfortunately, not all networks provide a common clock (e.g. it is not currently planned for public networks in Europe) and even for those that do this idea will not work if a call is routed to a different clock domain. An alternative approach is to provide sufficient buffering at the destination and use flow control techniques to keep the buffer approximately half full. This variation is why 'asynchronous' appears with good reason in the title ATM. It is an issue which has not been fully resolved.

10.3.4 ATM conclusion

Compared to a protocol like HDLC, ATM has done away with the need for a flag to achieve cell synchronization (by clever use of its Header Error Check) and has also sacrificed reliability for speed (ATM has no control byte so there can be no ARQ). All this and a fixed cell length gives low network latency and fast switching. The 155.520 Mbps data rate based on the SDH is fast and immediately extendible when higher data rate services come on line. ATM provides the means for implementing a high capacity network to support all currently foreseen types of service; it is a suitable means of implementing the B-ISDN concept.

10.4 ATM and LAN emulation

LAN emulation [SEE] masks an ATM network from clients on a LAN, allowing existing Ethernet or Token Ring applications (running under TCP/IP, Novell NetWare, etc.) to run over an ATM network without the need to change anything on the LAN. LAN emulation would generally use AAL5. For the purpose of LAN emulation, the principal differences between ATM and LANs are:
1. ATM is connection-oriented whereas LANs are connectionless;
2. LANs have broadcast and multicast facilities;
3. LANs use MAC addressing.

At the LAN/ATM interface, therefore, address resolution between the 48 bit MAC address and the 28 bit ATM address must be carried out and the LAN packet buffered whilst a link is established over the ATM network. LAN emulation is performed (in software) at the MAC layer, hence it supports both routing and bridging.

The LAN emulation software (or driver) is called the LAN Emulation Client (LEC), see figure 10.6. If it has data to transmit it first checks if it already has a connection to the destination LEC; if not it queries a LAN Emulation Server (LES). If the LES knows the ATM address of the destination LEC it will return it; if not it forwards the request to the Broadcast/Unknown Server (BUS). The BUS then broadcasts a message asking the DA to reply; if successful this allows a connection to be set up between the LEC and the newly validated address. (If the LEC has a broadcast or multicast message to transmit it forwards it directly to the BUS).

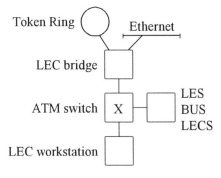

Figure 10.6 LAN emulation

The appropriate LES and BUS addresses are determined during the LEC initialization process, when a connection is established to a LAN Emulation Configuration Server (LECS) which returns the required ATM addresses and LAN types (LAN emulation supports both Ethernet and Token Ring, allowing clients on different types of LANs to communicate). A LEC has to request permission from a LES to join its LAN.

A LEC can be a work-station, file server, bridge, router, etc. If the LEC is a LAN bridge it can represent many LAN clients and will maintain an address table with the MAC addresses of all known attached clients. It may happen that a destination address is unknown (since although it may be on a LAN attached to a LAN bridge LEC it may not have made itself known by sending a message). Packets with unknown addresses are broadcast, in the hope that the destination will reply and the address become validated.

ATM high-speed switching can provide a high capacity backbone for LANs, as well as a high capacity link to individual work stations. To ease a possible future upgrade to ATM, new installations should be star wired using structured cabling [SYN]. Twisted pair cable, which must be capable of supporting 155 Mbps data rates, or fibre optic cable may be used. If the right decisions are taken today it will be possible to replace existing LAN hubs (FDDI, Ethernet or Token Ring) with ATM switches, when needed, to provide an immediate increase in performance and functionality.

10.5 DQDB

The Distributed Queue Dual Bus is the Medium Access Control (MAC) protocol chosen by the IEEE as part of their Metropolitan Area Network (MAN) standard IEEE 802.6. It was originally developed by the University of Western Australia and Telecom Australia. A MAN is based on the philosophy of a LAN, i.e. there is a shared medium over which any station can communicate directly with any other station (which contrasts with the use of a switch, as in ATM, to interconnect stations). The distinguishing features of MANs compared to LANs are:

- coverage of a larger geographic area;
- the ability to handle isochronous data, such as speech;
- high data throughput to support high speed data services;
- intended for use by public network operators.

Unfortunately, the requirement to cover a larger area means that the dominant LAN protocols, Ethernet and Token Ring, are unsuitable.

An unbridged Ethernet has a physically determined upper bound on its maximum length, as the CSMA/CD protocol relies on a collision to a frame being detected before the transmission of the frame has ended (see chapter 9). With Token Ring the protocol would work over longer lengths; however, the time taken for a frame to circulate all the way around the ring would be excessive (Token Ring is an example of a stop-and-wait protocol, which becomes inefficient when the propagation delay becomes significant). Token Ring is the basis of the FDDI protocol (see chapter 9), which does cover longer lengths (the maximum ring perimeter for FDDI is 100 km), but FDDI is better considered as an extended LAN (an ELAN) rather than a MAN, as its isochronous data handling is primitive. FDDI2 with improved performance for isochronous data has been proposed, but has been overtaken by ATM.

10.5.1 Physical layer

If a MAN is to be used by public network operators it must run on existing digital transmission links, i.e. it must be able to use the physical media of the PDH (Plesiochronous Digital Hierarchy) and the SDH (Synchronous Digital Hierarchy).

At the physical layer DQDB is carried on a contra-directional pair of buses (the dual bus part of the protocol) connected as in figure 10.7. A frame generator at the head of each bus generates a frame every 125 μs, consisting of a header followed by a number of empty slots for data. Each byte therefore supports a 64 kbps data stream. The number of bytes is not defined in the standard as it depends on the data rate of the bus; typically, in Europe, DQDB will initially run at 34 Mbps and 139 Mbps, i.e. the 3rd and 4th order TDM rates in the PDH. The 139 Mbps bus may be set up as a backbone MAN Switching System (MSS), see figure 10.8 (where the backbone is set up as a looped bus, see below), and the 34 Mbps bus could then be used as a Customer Access Network (CAN), gaining access to the backbone at an Edge Gateway (EG) [DET2]. Note that the 125 μs frame period is the same as for 30 channel PCM and for ATM, therefore DQDB can support existing KiloStream and MegaStream services as well as providing a means of accessing an ATM network.

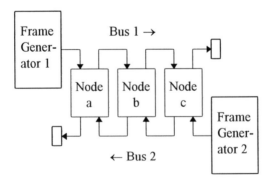

Figure 10.7 Dual bus

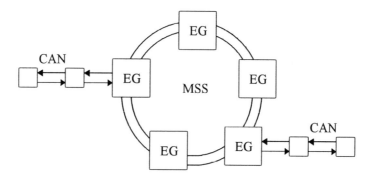

MSS   MAN Switching System at 139 Mbps
EG   Edge Gateway
CAN   Customer Access Network at 34 Mbps

Figure 10.8 MAN Switching System

Typically, a DQDB network is configured as a looped bus, with both frame generators in the same node, see figure 10.9 [DET2]. All nodes have the ability to generate frames so a looped bus can heal itself after a break to form an open bus. FDDI can also heal itself after a break; however, with DQDB the healed bus has the same functionality as in the looped bus configuration whilst, with FDDI, healing results in the primary and secondary rings being combined into one ring.

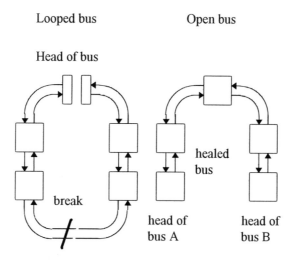

Figure 10.9 Self-healing dual bus

10.5.2 MAC layer

DQDB can carry isochronous data using a Pre-Arbitrated (PA) access method (although this option might not be used in public networks). The head of the bus sends a sufficient number of PA slots to satisfy the demands of all the nodes with isochronous data. Bytes in these slots are reserved for particular stations to use, the station having previously set up this virtual circuit.

Anisochronous data is segmented into 53 byte cells consisting of 48 bytes for the data and a 5 byte header, as for ATM. The distributed queue part of the protocol refers to the way empty slots are assigned on a first come, first served basis for this data, using the Queued-Arbitrated (QA) access method. An unsophisticated way to arrange this would be to use a central queuing mechanism; however, as can be gathered from the name 'distributed queue', the queuing is carried out by all nodes carrying out the same algorithm [DET2, HAL].

The header of a QA slot contains two bits, see figure 10.10: 'Busy', which is set if the slot is not empty, and 'Request', which is set by a node to reserve its place in the queue.

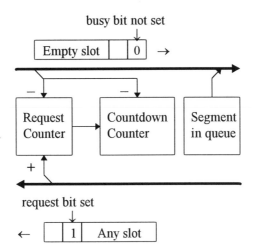

Figure 10.10 Distributed queue

When a node wants to transmit, it first determines in which direction the destination lies, i.e. to which bus it must gain access. It then waits until it can signal a request, which it does by setting the first free Request bit of a slot header on the *other* bus. As this slot with the Request bit set passes along the other bus, each node increments its Request Counter. Because the other bus has been used, effectively these nodes are upstream to the node wishing to transmit. The value of the Request Counter, at the time when a node wishes to transmit, marks the node's place in the queue (it wishes to transmit now, but other nodes downstream of it have already requested permission to transmit; it must therefore wait its turn). The node places its message segment in a buffer and transfers the value of the Request Counter to a Countdown Counter. Each empty slot that passes going downstream will be used by one of the waiting down-stream nodes, so the node's place in the queue will move forward; to mark this the Countdown Counter is decremented (as is the Request Counter). When the Countdown Counter reaches zero the node has reached the front of the queue and its message segment can be written into the next empty slot.

This process occurs in both directions, so two sets of counters, etc., are needed for each priority level, of which there are three. Lower priority requests do not cause the Request Counters for higher priority levels to be incremented, which means that higher priority cells are not held up by lower priority cells.

Under light load conditions the delay is small (as with CSMA/CD) whilst under heavy load conditions the bus utilization approaches 100% (as with Token Ring). The bus bandwidth is efficiently and fairly distributed (almost fairly: there is still a residual 'fairness' problem in DQDB, as under equal demand conditions nodes nearer the head of the bus can achieve higher data throughputs as a result of bus propagation delays [AKY]).

The DQDB cell structure [ISO/IEC 8802-6] is very similar to an ATM cell, with a 5 byte header and a 48 byte data field. The first byte in the header, see figure 10.11, is the Access Control Field (ACF): the first bit to be transmitted is the Busy bit, followed by the Type bit. Then follow three bits reserved for future use. The final three bits in the ACF are the three Request bits R2 ... R0, one for each priority level (R2 has the highest priority). This is followed by the 20 bits of the Virtual Channel Identifier, i.e. the address field. The Header Check Sequence is a CRC on the header alone as in ATM.

byte   bit

	7	6	5	4	3	2	1	0
1	B	T	Reserved			R2	R1	R0
2	VCI							
3	VCI							
4	VCI			Payload		Reserved		
5	HCS							

B	Busy bit
T	Type (0 for QA, 1 and B = 1 for PA)
R2...R0	Request bits for priority levels 2...0
VCI	Virtual Channel Identifier
HCS	Header Check Sequence
Payload	00 for user data (other values reserved)

Figure 10.11 DQDB header, bit 7 of top byte transmitted first

10.6 Conclusion

We started this book with a clear distinction between telephony and data communications. A decade or so ago telecommunications traffic was predominantly speech. The network was therefore optimised for speech, with circuit switching over analogue lines. Data was transmitted over these lines using modems. When people wanted to set up the first LANs they found the data rates offered by telecommunications companies to be too low for their purposes. They therefore developed their own solutions, based on the concept of a shared, high speed medium rather than switched, low speed lines. However, to improve the manageability of LANs, the physical layout came to be star-wired with a central hub (10BaseT and Token Ring) although the LAN still operated as a shared medium. When users wanted still more bandwidth the solution was to offer switching hubs (Etherswitch). The balance between speech traffic and data traffic was changing all this time towards data; and telecommunications companies were changing from an analogue network to a digital network because of the advantages of digital transmission for speech (improved speech quality – especially over long distances – and the ease of multiplexing channels together). The telephony and data communication industries were clearly converging. The first investigations into how the demands of both industries could be satisfied led to ISDN, where speech was considered as just another form of data. Meanwhile, the demand of users for yet more bandwidth meant that (narrowband) ISDN could not satisfy their requirements and this led to B-ISDN. The various forms of fast packet switching considered in this chapter support B-ISDN, allowing both low speed data (e.g. speech) and high speed data (potentially there is no upper limit to the data rate) to be carried over the same WAN or MAN. It may well be that, in the future, LANs will become redundant and fast packet switching will reach right to the users' workstations (e.g. IBM's ATM service at 25.6 Mbps). We will then have reached the situation just before the introduction of the first, shared media LANs: all traffic being carried over switches; but we will have progressed because now the traffic will be carried as packets (or cells) and be suitable for computer data as well as speech. The data communications industry, which split off from the telecommunications industry with the introduction of the first LANs, will have converged as an equal partner with the telecommunications industry. The question today is: who will be the dominant partners in the new industry?

Exercises

(1) State whether implicit congestion control is forward or backward.

(2) Explain what is meant by the term 'access protocol'.

(3)   Why must frame relay support all three types of congestion control?

(4)   Discuss in your own words why frame relay is considered a layer 2 protocol whilst X.25 operates at both layer 2 and layer 3, although both are network access protocols.

(5)   What do frame relay and cell relay have in common?

(6)   State how a network node can determine which frame relay packets or ATM cells are to be discarded if congestion occurs.

(7)   For a 64 kbps data stream, determine and comment on the cell packetization delay and protocol efficiency for:
    (i)   an ATM cell;
    (ii)   an ATM header with 64 byte data, as preferred by the data communications industry;
    (iii)   an ATM header with 32 byte data, as preferred by the telephony industry.

(8)   Which AAL class would be used for the following applications:
    (i)   a 64 kbps digital speech channel;
    (ii)   a 64 kbps videophone channel (combining a colour TV image with speech in the same 64 kbps channel).

(9)   Identify three causes of delay in a frame relay or cell relay network, and an additional cause of delay in an X.25 network.

(10) Explain what the term 'asynchronous' means in ATM.

(11) State what DQDB stands for and briefly explain what the terms refer to.

(12) Explain the operation of DQDB's queuing mechanism.

(13) State different ways of accessing an ATM network.

(14) For a 5000 km link operating at 155 Mbps, determine the amount of data which will have entered the link by the time a flow control message from the DA reaches the SA. Assume that the velocity of propagation is 2×10^8 m/s. Comment on the implications of your result for congestion and traffic control.

(15) Compare and contrast the use of FDDI and DQDB for a MAN.

(16) Using the Internet and trade, research and professional body journals as references, find out the latest information for an ATM network on:

(i)   the use of the GFC bits in an ATM header;
(ii) how jitter is to be managed;
(iii) signalling for setting up a SVC.

Quote references used and briefly comment on the usefulness of the different reference sources.

(17) Using the Internet and trade, research and professional body journals as references, write approximately 250 words to explain how ATM is carried over SONET (Synchronous Optical NETwork), a US physical medium standard.

Quote references used and briefly comment on the usefulness of the different reference sources.

(18) Write your own summary of what you have learnt in this chapter.

Appendix A: Greek alphabet

uppercase	lower case	name
A	α	alpha
B	β	beta
Γ	γ	gamma
Δ	δ	delta
E	ε	epsilon
Z	ζ	zeta
H	η	eta
Θ	θ	theta
I	ι	iota
K	κ	kappa
Λ	λ	lambda
M	μ	mu
N	ν	nu
Ξ	ξ	xi
O	ο	omicron
Π	π	pi
P	ρ	rho
Σ	σ	sigma
T	τ	tau
Y	υ	upsilon
Φ	φ	phi
X	χ	chi
Ψ	ψ	psi
Ω	ω	omega

Appendix B: units

Engineering notation

In communications it is common practice to use engineering notation for numbers; this is similar to the standard scientific notation except the exponent is a multiple of 3. For example, the number 167,253,892.5 is written as 1.673×10^8 to four significant figures in scientific notation, i.e. as a number multiplied by a factor comprising the base (or radix) 10 raised to the exponent (or power) 8. However, in engineering notation the exponent would be taken as the next lower multiple of 3, and the same number would be written as 167.3×10^6.

The advantage of engineering notation is that there are standard unit prefixes which enable numbers to be concisely written down; e.g. if the number 167.3×10^6 referred to a resistance it could be written down as 167.3 MΩ. These standard unit prefixes are given below:

prefix	symbol	factor
tera	T	10^{12}
giga	G	10^9
mega	M	10^6
kilo	k	10^3
milli	m	10^{-3}
micro	μ	10^{-6}
nano	η	10^{-9}
pico	p	10^{-12}
femto	f	10^{-15}
atto	a	10^{-18}

Rationalized MKS system

Turning now to units themselves, in chapter 5 (section 5.1) the reader may have wondered why μ_o is *defined* as $4\pi \times 10^{-7}$ H/m whilst the value for ε_o is found experimentally e.g. from equation 5.1

$$c = \frac{1}{\sqrt{(\mu_o \varepsilon_o)}}$$

The reason is that the value for μ_o occurs in the formula defining the ampere. One ampere is that constant current which, if maintained in two straight conductors of infinite length, negligible cross section area, and placed one metre apart in a vacuum, will produce of force of 2×10^{-7} N per metre between the conductors. The force (see [BLE]) between the conductors is

$$F = \frac{\mu_o i_1 i_2 \ell}{2\pi d}$$

where i_1 and i_2 are the currents in the wires, ℓ is the length of that part of the wires being considered and d is the distance between them. Therefore $\mu_o = 4\pi \times 10^{-7}$ H/m. In this steady state case the currents in the wires produce magnetic fields whose interaction gives rise to the force between the wires; no electric fields are generated.

Only the units of length, mass, time and one electrical quantity need to be defined in order to have the base units from which all other electrical units can be derived. Defining the permeability of free space as $\mu_o = 4\pi \times 10^{-7}$ is shown above to be equivalent to defining the ampere. The factor of 4π is needed to rationalize the system of units (i.e. to arrange things so that 4π occurs in problems with spherical symmetry, 2π in problems with circular symmetry and no π with rectangular problems).

Defining the other base units: it was mentioned in chapter 5 that the unit of length is defined in terms of the speed of light, specifically the metre was defined in 1983 as the length of the path travelled by light in a vacuum during a time interval of 1/299 792 458 of a second. The base unit of time, the second, was defined in 1967 as the duration of 9 192 631 770 periods of the radiation of a particular transition of a caesium-133 atom. And the kilogram was defined in 1889 as the mass of a certain platinum-iridium cylinder kept at Sèvres. This system of units is called the rationalized MKS system, after its base units of the metre, kilogram and second. It is the basis of the official SI (*Système International d'Unités*) system of units. The common base units of the SI system are the metre, kilogram, second, ampere, kelvin (K, unit of temperature) and candela (cd, unit of luminous intensity). Other units are derived from these. For example, the unit of energy or work done (E) is the joule (J). Now the kinetic energy of a body is

$$E = \frac{1}{2}mv^2 \quad \text{J}$$

where m is the mass of the body (in kg) and v is its velocity (in m/s), hence the joule is equivalent to kg $\times$ m^2 $\times$ s^{-2}. Similarly, the unit of power (P) is the watt (W) and since power is the rate at which work is done (or energy consumed) then

$$P = E / t \quad \text{W}$$

hence the watt is equivalent to a J $\times$ s^{-1} or a kg $\times$ m^2 $\times$ s^{-3}. Writing units in terms of the base units can help in deciding whether an equation is correct or not, as if the units on either side of the equation are not the same the equation must be incorrect (on the other hand, if the units do balance the equation can still be incorrect). This is the basis of dimensional analysis, where equations are analysed in terms of length L, mass M, time T and charge Q (however, personally, I work in terms of the units m, kg, s and C as the fewer substitutions the less the chance of errors occurring). The most common SI units for electrical engineering are given below (note the full name of the units starts with lowercase even if the abbreviation starts with a capital letter):

quantity (and symbol)	unit name	unit	unit equivalent
capacitance (C)	farad	F	$J^{-1} \times C^2$, or $m^{-2} \times kg^{-1} \times s^2 \times C^2$
charge (Q)	coulomb	C	
conductance (G)	siemens	S	Ω^{-1}, or $m^{-2} \times kg^{-1} \times s \times C^2$
current (I)	ampere	A	$s^{-1} \times C$
energy (E)	joule	J	$m^2 \times kg \times s^{-2}$
frequency (f)	hertz	Hz	s^{-1}
force (F)	newton	N	$m \times kg \times s^{-2}$
inductance (L)	henry	H	$J \times s^2 \times C^{-2}$, or $m^2 \times kg \times C^{-2}$
mass (m)	kilogram	kg	
length (ℓ)	metre (US meter)	m	
potential difference (V)	volt	V	$J \times C^{-1}$, or $m^2 \times kg \times s^{-2} \times C^{-1}$
power (P)	watt	W	$J \times s^{-1}$, or $m^2 \times kg \times s^{-3}$
resistance (R)	ohms	Ω	$J \times s \times C^{-2}$, or $m^2 \times kg \times s^{-1} \times C^{-2}$
time (t)	second	s	

Exercise on appendix B: units

(1) Check that the units for the following equations balance:

(i)   Ohm's law: $V = I \times R$;

(ii) power $P = I \times V$;

(iii) power $P = I^2 \times R$;

(iv) energy $E = \dfrac{1}{2}CV^2$

(v)   energy $E = \dfrac{1}{2}LI^2$

Appendix C: decibel

A common engineering expression for the ratio of two powers is the decibel (dB), named after Alexander Graham Bell (1847-1922). The original unit was the bel but this was too large, so the decibel came into general use (deci is used as a unit prefix for a factor of $1/10$ – as in decimetre).

Bell was a Scottish born American inventor and teacher of the deaf, whose most famous invention is the telephone (1876). The words first spoken by telephone were to his assistant: 'Watson, come here; I want you'.

The decibel is a logarithmic unit. Some logarithms (logs) to base 10 (i.e. common logs) are given below, from which it can be seen that the logarithm is the exponent to which the base (in this case 10) is raised to yield the number.

base 10 raised to an exponent	number (or anti-log)	logarithm	logarithm evaluated
10^0	1	$\log_{10}(1)$	0
10^1	10	$\log_{10}(10)$	1
10^2	100	$\log_{10}(100)$	2
10^3	1000	$\log_{10}(1000)$	3

The advantages of logarithms are that multiplication and division can be done by the addition and subtraction of the logs of the numbers, and that a large range of numbers is compressed into a smaller range when dealing with the logs. Hence the range from 1..1000 can be expressed logarithmically as a range from 0..3 and multiplying 10×100 can be done by *adding* the log of 10 (i.e. 1) to the log of 100 (i.e. 2) to get the answer 3 and then taking the anti-log (i.e. 1000). (The anti-log is simply the inverse operation of taking a logarithm, i.e. the anti-log of 3 is $10^3 = 1000$.)

By definition, for a power ratio P_o/P_i – of output power P_o to input power P_i – the value in dB is

$$10 \log_{10}(\frac{P_o}{P_i}) \quad \text{dB}$$

Hence we can construct the following table. Note that common power ratios are referred to by the approximate gain in dB (e.g. a gain of $1/2$ corresponds to -3 dB). Also note that:

- a ratio does not have any units, dB simply states the form in which the ratio is presented;
- an increase by a factor of 2 (e.g. from 1 to 2, 2 to 4, etc.) corresponds to an increase of 3 dB;

- a decrease in power (i.e. the output power is some fraction of the input power, as in 1/10) is indicated by a minus decibel figure. This indicates loss in the system, i.e. a negative gain is equivalent to a loss or attenuation.

power ratio (P_o/P_i)	gain to 3 sig. fig.	approx. gain
1	0.00 dB	
2	3.01 dB	3 dB
4	6.02 dB	6 dB
8	9.03 dB	9 dB
10	10.00 dB	
100	20.00 dB	
1/2	−3.01 dB	−3 dB
1/10	−10.00 dB	

Variations on the dB:

(i) The decibel for amplitude ratios
The decibel is a power ratio. However, if (and only if) the input and output impedances of a system are the same, then alternative expressions are

$$10\log_{10}(\frac{P_o}{P_i}) = 20\log_{10}\left(\frac{V_o}{V_i}\right) = 20\log_{10}(\frac{I_o}{I_i}) \ \ \text{dB}$$

where V_o/V_i is the voltage ratio and I_o/I_i is the current ratio. Proof: for a voltage ratio with input resistance R_i and output resistance R_o,

$$P_i = V_i^2 / R_i \quad \text{and} \quad P_o = V_o^2 / R_o$$

$$\text{hence} \quad \frac{P_o}{P_i} = \frac{V_o^2}{R_o} \times \frac{R_i}{V_i^2} = \left(\frac{V_o}{V_i}\right)^2 \quad \text{if} \quad R_o = R_i$$

$$\text{and} \quad 10\log_{10}\left(\frac{V_o}{V_i}\right)^2 = 20\log_{10}\left(\frac{V_o}{V_i}\right)$$

(ii) The dBm

The dBm is a unit of power as it considers the output power relative to 1 mW. Hence, given the ratio in dB and knowing that this is relative to 1 mW, the output power can be calculated; e.g. 20 dBm is +20 dB gain on 1 mW, i.e. 100 mW.

(iii) The dBW

As for the dBm, except it considers the power relative to 1 W, i.e. 1 dBW = 1 dBm + 30 dB.

(iv) Natural logarithms

The natural logarithm of a number is the exponent to which the base e (2.71828 to six significant figures) is raised to yield the number. Thus the natural logarithm of 2 (written as $\log_e(2)$ or $\ln(2)$) is 0.693. Natural logs of power ratios have a unit called the neper, corresponding to the bel as used for common logs of power ratios. The neper is used in chapter 4 to find the attenuation of a transmission line.

e is, like π, an irrational number (i.e. not expressible as the ratio of two whole numbers and hence its decimal expansion goes on forever without repeating); it is called the natural number because it turns up in many areas of maths, e.g. £1000 invested at 7% per year compound interest for 5 years is worth $£1000 \times e^{0.07 \times 5} = £1419$ at the end of the 5 years.

Exercises on appendix C: decibel

(Knowledge of the following standard formulae is assumed: a) Ohm's law: $V = I \times R$; b) Power $W = I \times V = I^2 \times R = V^2 / R$.)

(1)   Find the gain in dB for the following simple ratios:
a) $P_o/P_i = 1/2$; b) $V_o/V_i = 4$; c) $V_o/V_i = 1/100$; d) $P_o/P_i = 1/100$.

(2)   Find the power ratios for the following gains in dB:
a) −20 dB; b) −6 dB; c) +3 dB; d) +20 dB.

(3)   Determine the voltage and power ratios for a gain of −3 dB. Check your answer by showing that

$$\frac{P_o}{P_i} = \left(\frac{V_o}{V_i}\right)^2$$

(4)   The gain of 1 km of cable is −6 dB. Determine:
a) the attenuation (N.B. not the gain) of 1 km of cable in dB;
b) the attenuation of 3 km of cable in dB.

(5)   An operational amplifier is connected as a voltage follower (i.e. as a buffer amplifier with a voltage gain of 1×). The input resistance is 1 MΩ and the output resistance is 10 Ω. Determine the overall gain of the op-amp in dB.

(6)   A circuit introduces a power loss of +20 dB and has input and output impedance of 75 Ω. Determine the voltage gain, both in dB and as a ratio.

(7)   The output power of a circuit is −6 dBm and the output resistance is 50 Ω. Determine the output power in watts and the voltage levels in volts.

(8)   The output power of a system is 100 mW. Determine the power in dBm and dBW.

(9)   An long transmission line has an attenuation of 0.3 neper/km. If 10 V is applied at the input to the cable what is the voltage after 5 km?

Appendix D: ASCII code table

$b_6b_5b_4 \rightarrow$ $b_3b_2b_1b_0$ $\downarrow$	000	001	010	011	100	101	110	111
0000	*NUL*	*DLE*	*SP*	0	@	P	`	p
0001	*SOH*	*DC1*	!	1	A	Q	a	q
0010	*STX*	*DC2*	"	2	B	R	b	r
0011	*ETX*	*DC3*	#	3	C	S	c	s
0100	*EOT*	*DC4*	$	4	D	T	d	t
0101	*ENQ*	*NAK*	%	5	E	U	e	u
0110	*ACK*	*SYN*	&	6	F	V	f	v
0111	*BEL*	*ETB*	'	7	G	W	g	w
1000	*BS*	*CAN*	(	8	H	X	h	x
1001	*HT*	*EM*	)	9	I	Y	i	y
1010	*LF*	*SUB*	*	:	J	Z	j	z
1011	*VT*	*ESC*	+	;	K	[	k	{
1100	*FF*	*FS*	,	<	L	\	l		
1101	*CR*	*GS*	-	=	M	]	m	}
1110	*SO*	*RS*	.	>	N	^	n	~
1111	*SI*	*US*	/	?	O	_	o	*DEL*

Example: character uppercase 'Y' is ASCII 1011001_2 or 59_{16}. When a byte is used for an ASCII character the msb (bit position 7) is set to 0. Hence 'Y' becomes

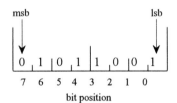

Note the symmetry in the code, in that bit position 5 (the shift key) is the difference between upper and lower case letters. Also note that the first 32 codes are control characters, used in communications or formatting. The definitions of these characters and of the *SP* and *DEL* characters are given below:

NUL	Null, or all zeros	DC1	Device Control 1
SOH	Start Of Heading	DC2	Device Control 2
STX	Start of Text	DC3	Device Control 3
ETX	End of Text	DC4	Device Control 4
EOT	End Of Transmission	NAK	Negative Acknowledge
ENQ	Enquiry	SYN	Synchronous idle
ACK	Acknowledge	ETB	End of Text Block
BEL	Bell or alarm	CAN	Cancel
BS	Backspace	EM	End of Medium
HT	Horizontal Tab	SUB	Substitute
LF	Line Feed	ESC	Escape
VT	Vertical Tab	·FS	File Separator
FF	Form Feed	GS	Group Separator
CR	Carriage Return	RS	Record Separator
SO	Shift Out	US	Unit Separator
SI	Shift In	SP	Space
DLE	Data Link Escape	DEL	Delete

Exercises on appendix D: ASCII code table

(1)   Convert the following characters to ASCII, giving the result in binary:
a) E; b) e; c) H; d) p; e) l.

(2)   Determine the characters coded with the following ASCII binary strings
(the leftmost bit is the msb):
a) 1010010; b) 0110101; c) 1110010; d) 01100010; e) 01111111.

(3)   Decode the following message sent using 7 bit ASCII (leftmost bit is msb):
100100011001011100101111111110110001100010

Answers

Answers to chapter 1

(1) and (2) See glossary.

(3)

Types of data	isochronous	anisochronous
Text		yes
Numerical data		yes
Graphical data		yes
Voice	yes	
Video	yes	

(6) ASCII and EBCDIC are the two principal codes today, also acceptable are Morse code and the Baudot code.

(7) $\cdot \cdot \cdot \cdot \quad \cdot \quad \cdot - \cdot \cdot \quad \cdot - \cdot \cdot \quad - - -$

(8) 111 dot lengths. N.B. there is no character gap at the end of the message and the word gap is four more dot lengths than the character gap.

(10) Yes.

(11) Both even and odd parity will detect all odd numbers of bit errors, but not even numbers of bit errors.

(12) 11011000

(13) (i) 'h'; (ii) error detected, therefore unable to say which character was transmitted.

(14) (i) 'j'; (ii) error detected, therefore unable to say which character was transmitted.

(15) (a) Probability of no errors $= P(0) = (1-p)^n = 0.9990$

(b) (i) Probability m errors $= P(m) = p^m (1-p)^{n-m} \dfrac{n!}{(n-m)!}$; (ii) $P(1) = 0.0009990$; (iii) from the answer to part (a) the probability of any error is $P(\text{error}) = 1 - P(0) = 0.001$, hence single bit errors account for 99.9% of all errors.

(16) $P = 0.1$ hence $I = \log_2 10 = 3.322$ bits.

(17) $P = 1/26$ hence $I = \log_2 26 = 4.700$ bits.

(18) $H = 4.18$ bits. From the answer to question (17), purely in terms of the letters of the alphabet, the redundancy is $\dfrac{(4.7 - 4.18)}{4.7} \times 100 = 11.1\%$

(19) The messages must be equiprobable.

(20) Huffman coding and the Lempel-Ziv algorithm.

(21) The source entropy is $H = 2.368$ bits. There is no uniquely correct answer for the code; however, using the Huffman coding scheme as suggested in this chapter gives the result below with average code word length $\overline{L} = 2.390$ bits.

267

F	D	H	B	G	E	C	A
1	010	0000	0001	0010	0011	0110	0111

(22) There are 2000 × 1500 pixels ≡ 3 Mbits in the black and white fax. In the grey scale image, each pixel can be coded with 4 bits hence there are 12 Mbits of information.

Answers to chapter 2

(1)   3.1 kHz.

(2)   Cost can be assumed to be approximately proportional to bandwidth, so the smaller the bandwidth the better. The 3.1 kHz bandwidth of the analogue telephone channel is adequate for understanding speech. A greater bandwidth would introduce more noise without leading to much increase in the speech signal power, degrading the signal-to-noise ratio.

(3) $v(t) = 3 + \dfrac{12}{\pi}\left(\sin(2\pi 250t) + \dfrac{1}{3}\sin(6\pi 250t) + \dfrac{1}{5}\sin(10\pi 250t) + ...\right)$

(4)   The power of the 9th harmonic $P_9 = \dfrac{(4V_o)^2}{2R(\pi 9)^2} = \dfrac{0.0100 \times V_o^2}{R} \equiv 1\% \times P_o$;

hence, adding the result for the fundamental and all terms up to and including the 7th harmonic, $P = 96\% \times P_o$.

(5)   Gibb's phenomenon.

(6)   (i) A V; (ii) 0 V; (iii) A V; (iv) $\dfrac{2A\tau}{T}$ V.

(7)   (i) odd; (ii) even; (iii) even; (iv) even.

(8)   (i) By inspection $v(t) = A + A\sin\left(\dfrac{2\pi t}{T}\right)$; but derive the answer using the Fourier Series and the orthogonal property of sine functions.

(ii) An even function has only cosine terms, thus

$$v(t) = \dfrac{8A}{\pi^2}\left(\cos\left(\dfrac{2\pi t}{T}\right) + \dfrac{1}{9}\cos\left(\dfrac{6\pi t}{T}\right) + \dfrac{1}{25}\cos\left(\dfrac{10\pi t}{T}\right) + ...\right)$$

Note that the triangular waveform is a closer approximation to a sine wave than is a square wave; and this is reflected in the frequency spectrum in that the harmonics are lower in amplitude than for a square wave.

(iii) We have already worked out the d.c. term and noted that it is an even function in questions (6) and (7), thus

$$v(t) = A + \dfrac{4A}{\pi}\left(\cos(\omega t) - \dfrac{1}{3}\cos(3\omega t) + \dfrac{1}{5}\cos(5\omega t) + ...\right) \text{ where } \omega = \dfrac{2\pi}{T}$$

(iv) $v(t) = \dfrac{2A\tau}{T} + \dfrac{4A\tau}{T}\displaystyle\sum_{n=1}^{\infty}\dfrac{\sin\left(\dfrac{n\omega\tau}{2}\right)}{\left(\dfrac{n\omega\tau}{2}\right)}\cos(n\omega t)$ where $\omega = \dfrac{2\pi}{T}$

This is a spectrum with harmonics at frequencies n/T Hz (i.e. both even and odd harmonics), with their amplitudes weighted by a $\sin(x)/x$ function. Note the amplitude of a harmonic will be zero for $\sin(x) = 0$, i.e. for $f = n/\tau$ (except for the d.c. term). This general equation for a pulse can save working out the Fourier Series from first principles, e.g. the answer to part (iii) can be derived from it.

(9) Using the result for question (8) part (iv) after shifting the waveform in time to make it an even function, which does not affect the amplitude spectrum:

$$V(f) = 0.75 + 1.5\sum_{n=1}^{\infty}\dfrac{\sin\left(\dfrac{n\pi}{4}\right)}{\left(\dfrac{n\pi}{4}\right)}\cos(n2\pi 50 t)$$

$$= 0.75 + 1.350\cos(\omega t) + 0.9549\cos(2\omega t) + \ldots$$

$$\ldots \; 0.4502\cos(3\omega t) + 0\cos(4\omega t) + \ldots \text{ where } \omega = 2\pi 50$$

(10) (i) DFT and FFT; (ii) Fourier Transform (only).

(11) To prove this see a mathematics book, e.g. [KRE].

(14) (i) A lpf with a cut-off of 20 kHz in series with a hpf with a cut-off of 10 kHz results in a bandpass from 10 kHz to 20 kHz (note the lpf and hpf pass bands overlap); (ii) A lpf with a cut-off of 10 kHz in parallel with a hpf with a cut-off of 20 kHz results in a bandstop from 10 kHz to 20 kHz (note the lpf and hpf pass bands do not overlap and an adder is necessary to combine the outputs from the two filters).

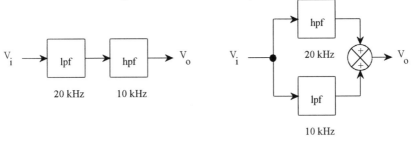

        (i) bpf   (ii) bsf

(15) Theoretically this makes a hpf with a cut-off of 5 kHz but, as stated in the question, in practice this is a rather dubious circuit.

(16) Only the 3rd and 5th harmonics will be received.

(17) (i) $\tau = RC = 1 \times 10^{-3}$; (ii) $f_o = \dfrac{1}{2\pi RC} = 159.2$ Hz; (iii) $t_r = \dfrac{0.35}{f_o} = 2.199$ ms.

(18) $\left|\dfrac{V_o}{V_i}\right| = \sqrt{\dfrac{1}{\left(1+(\omega CR)^2\right)}} = \sqrt{\dfrac{1}{5}}$ (for $\omega = \dfrac{2}{CR}$) $= 0.4472 \equiv -6.990$ dB.

(19) (i) $\left|\dfrac{V_o}{V_i}\right| = \sqrt{\dfrac{1}{\left(1+(\omega CR)^2\right)}} = \sqrt{\dfrac{1}{10}}$ (for $\omega = \dfrac{3}{CR}$) $= 0.3162 \equiv -10$ dB.

(ii) $\angle\left(\dfrac{V_o}{V_i}\right) = -\tan^{-1}(\omega CR) = -\tan^{-1}(3) = -71.57°$.

(20) A hpf with a cut-off frequency of $f_o = 159.2$ Hz.

(i) $\left|\dfrac{V_o}{V_i}\right| = \dfrac{\omega CR}{\sqrt{1+(\omega CR)^2}} = \dfrac{3}{\sqrt{10}}$ (for $\omega = \dfrac{3}{CR}$) $= 0.9487 \equiv -0.4576$ dB.

(ii) $\angle\left(\dfrac{V_o}{V_i}\right) = \tan^{-1}\left(\dfrac{1}{\omega CR}\right) = \tan^{-1}\left(\dfrac{1}{3}\right) = 18.43°$.

Note that the phase of the hpf is exactly 90° ahead of the phase of the lpf.

(21) (i) −6 dB;

(ii) $\left|\dfrac{V_o}{V_i}\right| = \dfrac{1}{\left(1+(\omega_o CR)^2\right)} = \dfrac{1}{\sqrt{2}}$ and $CR = 15.92 \times 10^{-6} \rightarrow \omega_o = 40{,}430$ rad / s

(22) (i) Attenuation = order $\times$ (2 decades $\times$ 20 dB / dec) $= 120$ dB;

(ii) rise time $t_r = \dfrac{0.5}{B} = 50$ μs.

(23) A linear phase characteristic, which gives a constant delay versus frequency characteristic.

(24) A first order lpf attenuates less than a higher order filter, hence the amplitude of the high frequency terms will be greater in a first order filter. It is these high frequency terms which determine the slope of the pulse, hence the rise time is less with a first order filter.

Answers to chapter 3

(1) All received signals must be between −15 V and −3 V or +3 V and +15 V. Data 1 is a negative voltage and an ON control signal is positive.

(2) SG is to establish a common reference voltage (in this case 0 V) and provide a return path for unbalanced circuits. RTS and CTS switch the modem to transmit mode in HDX operation. DCD warns the DTE that a carrier signal has been detected by the modem in receive mode, i.e. data will be arriving on the RXD line.

(3) To connect two DTEs together via their RS-232 interfaces, without the need to go through modems.

(5) To return the line to the idle state, ready for the next start transition.

(6) Redundancy is $3/11 = 0.2727$. Efficiency is $1 - \text{redundancy} = 0.7272$.

(7) Asynchronous protocol 01100001011, invert for RS-232.

(8) The analogue PSTN has a limited frequency range, from 300 to 3,400 Hz. Since it is unable to pass frequency components outside this range, some parts of the spectrum of a digital data signal would not be recovered at the receiver (especially any d.c. or low frequency component).

(10) The data (assumed to be NRZ data) is ANDed with a clock to produce RZ data, which then clocks a D-type configured as a divide by two circuit. The output of the divide-by-two is then used to drive the PSK modulator of figure 3.17. The output signal is a DPSK signal as required.

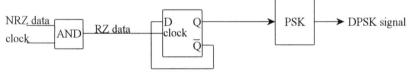

(11) They use different carrier frequencies and are therefore incompatible.

(12) Generally different carrier frequencies are used for the forward and reverse channel.

(13) The Hayes command set is a set of instructions for modems which can be issued from the terminal keyboard. ATD 207958 autodials the number 207958.

(14) Error correction allows reliable data transfer over noisy dial-up telephone lines. Data compression increases data throughput and therefore reduces the cost of dial-up calls.

(15) See glossary.

(16) $C = 2B\log_2 M = 2 \times 3,100 \times \log_2 (12 + 4) = 24,800$ bps.

(17) $C = B\log_2 ((S/N) + 1) = 3,100 \times \log_2 (1001) = 30,898$ bps.

(18) There are 16 states. Hence the baud rate is $9,600/16 = 600$ baud.

(19) $C = 2B\log_2 M = 2 \times 2000 \times \log_2 32 = 20,000$ kbps.

(20) The channel bandwidth determines the baud rate; hence to increase the data rate requires more bits per baud, as in multi-state signalling.

(21) From figure 3.22: 01 10 00 10

(22) 1 1 0 1

(23) Note that, using 2 input XOR gates, the diagram is symmetrical about a horizontal axis, e.g. the sequence of possible output bits from node D mirrors the sequence from node A. This is a problem if an error causes both nodes A and D to have a cumulative path difference of 1.

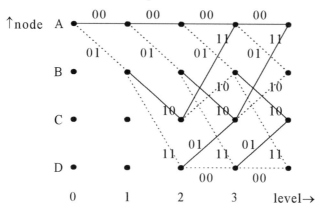

Answers to chapter 4

(1) a) Unipolar – one signal level is at earth potential; b) Bipolar – signal levels symmetrical about earth potential; c) Differential – two wire connection with equal and opposite, bipolar signal levels in the two wires; d) as c).

(2) Common mode noise is reduced and earth-borne noise avoided.

(3) a) Six differential circuits need 12 wires; b) seven wires (six signal and one common return) are needed for six unipolar circuits.

(4) a) 'Lossless' line (if high frequency); b) 'distortionless' line; c) digital line using ADC at transmitter and DAC at receiver; d) use equaliser at receiver.

(5) a) Characteristic impedance does not vary with line length (this is the whole point of it being a characteristic impedance!); b) does not vary with signal amplitude; c) generally varies with frequency.

(6) a) 120 Ω; b) diameter = 0.469 mm.

(7) A line for high bit rate transmission needs to be correctly terminated to avoid reflections that could interfere with signals on the line. At low data rates the line has had time to settle to a steady state before the next signal is transmitted. For high bit rates $2t_p \geq t_r$ (with minimum bit period $T = t_r$).

(10) Frequency $f > 637$ kHz from $\omega L > 10 \times R$, similarly $f > 1.59$ kHz from the rule $\omega C > 10 \times G$; hence above $f = 637$ kHz this cable can be treated as lossless. a) Characteristic impedance is 100 Ω. b) Velocity of propagation is 2×10^5 km/s = 2×10^8 m/s.

(11) From $LG = RC$ the required L_d = 0.2 H/km. A lumped inductance = 2 × $(L_d - L)$ = 0.399 H can be added to the cable every 2 km. a) Characteristic impedance is 2 kΩ. b) Velocity of propagation is 10 × 10³ km/s = 10 × 10⁶ m/s. c) Resonant frequency is 1.59 kHz. d) Attenuation is 0.869 dB/km.

(13) a) A distortionless channel is necessary for analogue signals. Therefore, at low frequencies a distortionless transmission line or alternative technique (e.g. use of an equaliser or ADC/DAC) is required. The distortionless line works with passive components; this may be an advantage compared to use of an equaliser, which may need an amplifier, or ADC/DAC technique. b) The lumped inductances are a severe limitation for digital transmission as they restrict the channel bandwidth; they need to be removed.

(14) From $LG = RC$ required L_d = 50 mH/km. From $L_c = L_d d / n$ then

$$L_c = \left(50 \times 10^{-3}\right) d / 1000 \qquad (1)$$

From $\omega_o = \dfrac{2}{\sqrt{(L_c C d / n)}}$ then $L_c \times d = 9.006$ $\qquad (2)$

Solving (1) and (2) gives L_c = 21.2 mH and d = 424 m.

(16) Voltage reflection coefficient is − 1/3. The reflected voltage is − 4 V.

(17) Current reflection coefficient is + 1/3. The reflected current is + 40 mA.

(18) Characteristic impedance is 50 Ω. a) With a terminating resistor greater than the characteristic impedance there will be a reflected voltage pulse of positive amplitude, the voltage reflection coefficient is 1/3 hence the amplitude of the reflected pulse is + 1.67 V and the pulse seen at the load is + 6.67 V. The reflected pulse will be dissipated by the source impedance. b) With a matched load there is no reflection and the voltage seen at the load is + 5 V. c) With a terminating resistor less than the characteristic impedance there will be a reflected voltage pulse of negative amplitude, the voltage reflection coefficient is − 2/3 hence the amplitude of the reflected pulse is − 3.33 V and the pulse seen at the load is + 1.67 V. The reflected pulse will be dissipated by the source impedance.

(19) a) From 75 Ω to 50 Ω the voltage attenuation factor is 0.423. The impedances at the input and output are different so we cannot use 20 × log(V_o / V_i), instead we must calculate the input and output powers: P_i = V_i^2 / 75 and P_o = $(V_i \times 0.423)^2$ / 50. Hence the gain is − 5.72 dB. b) From 50 Ω to 75 Ω the voltage attenuation factor is 0.634. Hence $P_i = V_i^2$ / 50 and P_o = $(V_i \times 0.634)^2$ / 75 and the gain is − 5.72 dB also.

(20) (i) $\rho = -1/2$, hence Z_o = 81 Ω (nominally 75Ω); (ii) V_p = 2 × 10⁸ m/s; (iii) the pulse reflected from the load is − 1 V hence at the source also $\rho = -$ 1/2 and Z_s = 27 Ω; (iv) From $Z_o = \sqrt{\dfrac{L}{C}}$ and $V_p = \sqrt{\dfrac{1}{LC}}$ then C = 61.7 pF/m and L = 0.405 μH/m.

Answers to chapter 5

(1)   1190 m.

(2)   Relative permittivity = 1.22 and $V_p = 2 \times 10^8$.

(3)   2.26 V.

(5)   5.77 MHz.

(6)   86.6 km.

(7)   Electrical lengths: (i) 1.5 m; (ii) 15,000 m. Physical lengths: (i) 1.425 m; (ii) 14,250 m.

(8)   Narrowband as 3.1 kHz/1 MHz = $3.1 \times 10^{-3} < 10\%$.

(9)   (i) 120 stations; (ii) from d.c. to 4.5 kHz (actually from 100 Hz), hence appreciably colouring the sound.

(10) From (7): to enable sensible antenna lengths to be used, as you could hardly have a portable radio with a 15,000 m antenna! From (8): to enable narrowband antennas to be used, as they are easier to implement. From (9): to enable multiple stations to share the frequency spectrum; only one station is possible in one area with baseband transmission.

(12) 136 ×

(13) 20 dBW.

(14) 4.15×10^{-15} W or −144 dBW. Note that the noise power is independent of the resistor value.

(15) EIRP = 13 dBW, free-space path loss = 193.1 dB, receiver antenna gain = 27.3 dB, required receiver SNR = 20 dB. The maximum noise power (N) is found from $13 - 193.1 - N + 27.3 = 20$ dB. Hence $N = - 172.8$ dBW. Substituting equation 5.17 gives $T_{sys} = 190$ K, hence maximum $T_r = 90$ K.

(16) (i) Mirror diameter = 12 mm (approximately 1/2 inch) and surface accuracy = 40 nm; the accuracy is to optical standards but the mirror diameter is small. (ii) Dish diameter = 9 km and surface accuracy = 3 cm.

Answers to chapter 6

(5)   (i) Monomode, SCS fibre with a laser diode light source; (ii) LED light source with a step index multimode, plastic fibre.

(6)   (i) Attenuation 0.0631; (ii) pulse spreading = 1.07 µs; (iii) maximum data rate = 933 kbps.

(7)   (i) Numerical aperture = 0.245; (ii) acceptance angle = 14.2°; (iii) critical angle = 80.7°; (iv) maximum pulse spreading allowed = 0.488 µs, hence maximum cable length = 7.23 km.

(9)   At the centre of the core: (i) the acceptance angle = 14.1°; (ii) the critical angle = 80.6°.

(10) Receiver sensitivity = − 35 dBm.

(11) Receiver sensitivity = − 36.4 dBm.

(12)

cable→ optical source↓	monomode	graded index	step index
LED	No	Possibly	Yes
Laser Diode	Yes	Possibly	No

(13) (i) Eliminated using monomode fibre; (ii) eliminated at one wavelength using graded index fibre; (iii) minimized for a step index, multimode fibre by having a large critical angle.

Answers to chapter 7

(3) Polling is where the master device asks a slave if it has any data to send, implicitly giving permission for the slave to send the data to the master; Selecting is where the master identifies a slave to receive data from the master.

(4) The DLE character is used to achieve data transparency (by inserting a DLE character before every valid control character and every simulation of the DLE character by the data) and to define control codes not included in the standard character set.

(5)

Master	Slave
←SYN SYN ENQ	←SYN SYN ACK
←SYN SYN STX ... data ... ETX BCC	←SYN SYN NAK
←SYN SYN STX ... data ... ETX BCC	←SYN SYN ACK
←SYN SYN EOT	←SYN SYN EOT

(6) (1)100 0101   (1)100 0011   (0)100 0110   (1)100 0100   ((0)000 0100)

(7) The row and column in error are indicated by ×. Hence the 1 received which is common to both the row and column in error should be a 0.

✓	×	✓	✓	✓
0	1	1	0	✓
0	0	1	0	✓
0	0	0	0	✓
0	1	1	0	✓
0	0	0	0	✓
1	→0	0	1	×
0	0	1	1	✓

(8) Detected – yes, corrected – no.

(9) Compare and contrast does not mean make a list; however, summarizing:

	Basic Mode	IBM 3270	HDLC
char. or bit oriented	char.	char.	bit
transparent	no	yes	yes
char. set	ASCII	EBCDIC	any
check algorithm	vert. and hor. parity	CRC	CRC
ARQ process	stop-and-wait	stop-and-wait	continuous
transmission mode	HDX	HDX	FDX

(13) Bit stuffing and stripping.

(14) FDX rather than HDX mode of operation.

(15) Detected by a CRC, corrected by ARQ using the control byte.

(16)

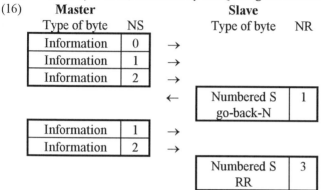

Master			**Slave**	
Type of byte	NS		Type of byte	NR
Information	0	→		
Information	1	→		
Information	2	→		
		←	Numbered S go-back-N	1
Information	1	→		
Information	2	→		
			Numbered S RR	3

(18) LAP-B, LAP-D, LAP-M, SDLC.

(19) Check sequence in hex is DC.

(20) (i) 3; (ii) 5. A Hamming distance of two is required for parity.

(21) For $m = 16$, $c = 5$ gives $2^5 > m + c + 1$ whilst $c = 4$ gives $2^4 < m + c + 1$. Hence minimum number of check bits is 5.

(22) 3 check bits required, $c_1 = 0$, $c_2 = 1$, $c_3 = 0$. Message is therefore 1010010.

(23) Source data is $d_4 \ldots d_1 = 1010$.

(24) The transmitted sequence is 2483496.

(25) (a) The remainder is 010, see below. The transmitted frame is therefore 11001010. As shown below (b), this has a remainder 000 when divided by the same generator polynomial.

(25) (a)	(25) (b)	(26)
11010	11010	01011
1001) 11001000	100) 11001010	100) 01011010
1001	1001	0000
1011	1011	1011
1001	1001	1001
0100	0100	0100
0000	0000	0000
1000	1001	1111
1001	1001	1001
0010	0000	1100
0000	0000	1001
r = 010	r = 000	r = 101

(26) The remainder is not zero, see above, therefore the error has been detected.

(27) The transmitted frame sequence is 11001010 which has even parity. The x^0 bit $= 1$ in the generator polynomial generates this.

(28) (a) The received sequence is 01100101. As shown below this results in zero remainder. Hence the name 'cyclic', as a valid frame will give zero

remainder if cycled any number of bits. (b) Any whole number which is multiplied by the generator polynomial will clearly give zero remainder when divided by the same generator polynomial.

$$
\begin{array}{r}
0\ 1\ 1\ 0\ 1 \\
\hline
1\ 0\ 0\ 1\ )\ 0\ 1\ 1\ 0\ 0\ 1\ 0\ 1 \\
0\ 0\ 0\ 0 \\
\hline
1\ 1\ 0\ 0 \\
1\ 0\ 0\ 1 \\
\hline
1\ 0\ 1\ 1 \\
1\ 0\ 0\ 1 \\
\hline
0\ 1\ 0\ 0 \\
0\ 0\ 0\ 0 \\
\hline
1\ 0\ 0\ 1 \\
1\ 0\ 0\ 1 \\
\hline
r=\ \ \ 0\ 0\ 0
\end{array}
$$

(30) $\dfrac{W}{\left(1+\dfrac{2t_p}{H}\right)}$

(31) $t_p = 50\ \mu s$, $H = 10\ \mu s$. Hence (i) $U = 9.09\%$; (ii) $U = 63.6\%$.

(32) $p = 0.01$ and $(1-p)^n = 0.366$. Hence (i) $U = 3.33\%$; (ii) $U = 23.3\%$.

Answers to chapter 8
(1) Packet, circuit and message switching.
(2) (i) connection oriented; (ii) connectionless.
(3) (i) 90, as each manufacturer must write 9 programs; (ii) 10.
(4) See glossary.
(6) See figure 8.5.
(7) Different network layers require different transport layers to compensate.
(8) See figure 8.4.
(9) X.3, X.28 and X.29, collectively called 'triple X'.
(10) Flow control and retransmission of missing packets.
(13) No.
(14) Routing and addressing are network layer functions. All these protocols should therefore be network layer protocols. However, the routing protocols use UDP, a transport layer protocol, and it is contradictory to have a hierarchy where a lower layer uses an upper layer.
(15) Class B.
(16) $2^7 + 2^{14} + 2^{21} = 2\ 113\ 664$ networks.
(22) A socket is the combination of the IP host address and the TCP application port number.
(23) IP's identification field refers to frames, TCP's sequence number to bytes.

(24) Routers are layer 3, a minimum gateway would be layers 1 - 4 but a gateway could be from 1 - 7.

(25) If the routing tables become inconsistent.

(27)

RA 1			RA 3			RA 4			RA 5			RA 6		
Ne	x	RA	Ne	x	RA	Ne	x	RA	Ne	x	RA	Ne	x	RA
1	1	1	2	1	3	1	1	4	3	1	5	4	1	6
2	1	1	3	1	3	4	1	4	5	1	5	5	1	6
3	2	3	1	2	1	2	2	1	2	2	3	1	2	4
4	2	4	5	2	5	5	2	6	4	2	6	3	2	5
5	3	3	4	3	1	3	3	1	1	3	3	2	3	4

(28) Control of the connection: TCP; Addressing: IP and TCP sockets; Segmentation: TCP; Flow control: TCP; Multiplexing: TCP allows multiple virtual connections between same hosts; Acknowledgement of data: TCP; Distinguishing between end-user information and control messages: IP; Identification and reporting of error conditions: ICMP;

(29)

Service	RM application	TCP/IP application
E-mail	MOTIS	SMTP
file transfer	FTAM	FTP
remote log in	JTM	Telnet
virtual terminal	VT	Telnet (NVT)
network management	CMIP	SNMP

(30) An ISDN link is digital to the desk top.

(32) A KiloStream link is a leased line.

(33) MegaStream, 30 channel PCM, ISDN primary service (30B+D, ISDN30).

Answers to chapter 9

(2) The LLC is the top part of layer 2, the MAC the bottom part.

(4) A packet would continuously circulate, stopping nodes accessing the bus.

(5) Collision domain is 512 bits, minimum length frame is 576 bits; ensuring that a collision is detected before transmission has been completed.

(6) Maximum length $\ell = 3000$ m. Hence maximum time $t_{max} = 2\ell/V_p = 26.0$ μs. Hence maximum number of bits = 10 Mbps $\times t_{max} = 260$ bits.

(7) One and two are both correct answers. A frame is released as the previous information frame arrives back at the source. Hence parts of two frames can be on the ring. If the early token release option is chosen (see FDDI in section 9.7) then multiple frames can be on the ring.

(10)	10Base2	10BaseT	Token Ring	Token Bus
Logical operation	bus	bus	ring	ring
Physical operation	bus	star	ring	bus
Cabling topology	bus	star	normally star, can be a ring	bus

(11) In Token Ring each node has a 'Timer, Holding Token' which causes the node to release the token when it times out. In Ethernet, after transmission of a frame has finished every node waiting to transmit has an equal chance of gaining access to the bus. The maximum length of the data is 1500 bytes in Ethernet whilst in Token Ring it is limited by the THT.

(12) Token Ring has a priority system and continues to work at full capacity under overload conditions. Ethernet works well for large packets sent at relatively infrequent intervals. It was designed for reliability and simplicity, which enabled it to be made at lower cost, which helped it to achieve volume sales, which allowed lower prices, etc.

(13) Ethernet (i) and (iii), Token Ring (ii) and (iv).

(14) An upper bound can be set on the delay in receiving a message.

(15) The token priority cannot be set to the value of the priority reservation bits in the AC byte if the token is released before an information frame returns.

(16) 100 Mbps.

(17) Both are examples of 1B/2B codes.

(18) (a) To split an overloaded LAN. To build a WAN using LANs. To implement network management. To extend the physical reach or number of nodes on a network. (b) An important part of the learning process is forgetting!

(19) Repeaters operate at the physical layer, bridges at the MAC sub layer in the data link layer, routers at the network layer. Gateways operate at the minimum at layer 4, the transport layer, but can operate at all layers.

(20) Bridge or router but not with a repeater, as the data rates are different.

(21) It has a higher data rate (100 Mbps compared to 16 Mbps). It uses essentially the same MAC protocol, so source routing bridges can be used as with Token Ring networks.

(22) Root bridge is B1, designated ports are dp, other ports attached by solid lines are root ports. Spanning Tree shown by solid lines.

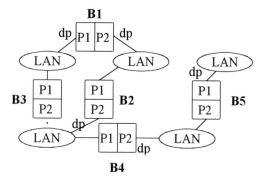

Answers to chapter 10

(1) Implicit congestion control must be forward and vice versa, backward congestion control must be explicit.

(2) An access protocol allows a WAN to be accessed, but the core of the WAN (the telecommunications 'cloud') can use a different protocol.

(3) Because frame relay is an access protocol, the core protocol may be different and not support all types of congestion control. Therefore frame relay must support all three types to be compatible with the core network.

(5) They do not support ARQ on a link by link basis, they police user data, if congestion occurs they drop cells or frames which are in excess of agreed data rates.

(6) If the Discard Eligibility bit is set in a frame relay header or the Cell Loss Priority bit is set in ATM cell header.

(7)

Data length (bytes)	Packetization delay	Protocol efficiency
48	6 ms	90.6 %
64	8 ms	92.8 %
32	4 ms	86.5%

(8) (i) AAL1; (ii) AAL2

(9) Packetization, queuing, routing (or switching), and propagation delay are common to all three networks. In addition, X.25 packets can experience delay due to the ARQ process.

(10) The term basically means that time slots are not dedicated to a particular circuit. This has the consequence that, due to variable transmission times caused by queues at network nodes, the data can have a considerable variation in time of arrival (jitter) compared to the estimated time of arrival. Unpredictable arrival of data is actually a characteristic of an asynchronous communication link, so the term is apt.

(11) Distributed Queue Dual Bus. The queue is distributed over all nodes in the MAN and the bus topology is a contra-directional pair of buses.

(13) Frame relay, LAN emulation and DQDB are covered explicitly in this chapter.

(14) 484 kbytes.

Answers to appendix C

(1) a) −3 dB b) +12 dB c) −40 dB b) −20 dB

(2) a) 1/100 b) 1/4 c) 2 d) 100

(3) Voltage ratio = 0.7079, power ratio = 0.5012 and 0.7079 = $\sqrt{0.5011}$ as required. (Actually 1/2 power ratio corresponds to $1/\sqrt{2}$ voltage ratio).

(4) a) +6 dB b) +18 dB

(5) $P_i = \dfrac{V_i^2}{10^6}$; $P_o = \dfrac{V_o^2}{10}$; $V_i = V_o$; therefore $\dfrac{P_o}{P_i} = 10^5$ or 50 dB

(6) Voltage loss is also +20 dB since the input and output resistances are the same, hence the gain is −20 dB. As a voltage ratio this is 1/10.

(7) Output power is 250 μW and voltage is 0.112 V.

(8) +20 dBm or −10 dBW.

(9) $10e^{-0.3 \times 5} = 2.23$ V.

Answers to appendix D

(1) a) 1000101 b) 1100101 c) 1001000 d) 1110000 e) 1101100

(2) a) R b) 5 c) r d) b (N.B. msb set to 0 for 8 bit ASCII) e) DEL – Delete character

(3) 1001000 1100101 1100101 1111111 1101100 01100010 decodes as H e e *DEL* l p, i.e. 'Help'.

References

Bibliography
Distance learning or Computer Based Learning courses: [MAD] [CAL]
Text books for parts I and II, which the student may wish to refer to for a
second opinion: [BLA] [FRI] [GRE] [HAL] [HEL] [MIL] [O'R] [STA] [TOM]
Text books for part III: [HAL] [STA]
Books giving practical experiments: [EHR] [HUG]

References by chapter
1 [CHE] [HAY] [HUF] [KRE] [PUG] [SHA]
2 [CON] [HOR] [IFE] [KRE] [STR] [TUF]
3 [CON] [HAL] [HAY] [SHA] [TEX] [VIT]
4 [GLA] [TEX]
5 [BLE] [EHR] [FEY] [GLA] [GRI] [JOR] [WHE]
6 [EHR] [GHA] [JAI] [SEN]
7 [ISO/IEC 3309] [ISO/IEC 4335] [PET] [STA]
8 [CAR] [HAL] [ISO/IEC 8208] [MAD] [RFC 1058] [RFC 1723] [STA] [STE] [STR]
9 [BED] [BUX] [EIA 568] [GÖH] [HAL] [ISO 9314-2] [ISO/IEC 10038][ISO/IEC
   8802.2] [ISO/IEC 8802.3][ISO/IEC 8802.5] [JAI] [MET] [SMY] [STA] [TYL]
10 [AKY] [BAL] [DET] [DET2] [GAL] [HAL] [ISO/IEC 8802-6][JEF] [POP]
   [PRE] [QUI] [SEE] [SYN]

References in alphabetical order
[AKY] Akyilidiz IF, Liebeherr J, Tantawi AN: 'DQDB$^{+/-}$: A Fair and Waste-free
   Media Access Protocol for Dual Bus Metropolitan Networks', IEEE Transactions on
   Communications, Vol. 41, No. 12, Dec 1993, pp. 1805-1815.
[AZI] Asimov I: *Asimov's Biographical Encyclopedia of Science and Technology*, David
   and Charles, 1991.
[BAL] Baldwin C: 'ATM : The Frontier of Networking', Chipcom Application Report,
   Chipcom Corporation, 1993.
[BED] Bedford M: 'Lore of the Lan', Computer Shopper, April 1992, pp. Networking
   323-328.
[BLA] Blake R: *Basic electronic communication*, West Publishing Co., 1993.
[BLE] Bleaney BI and Bleaney B: *Electricity and Magnetism*, 3rd Ed., Oxford
   University Press, 1976.
[BUX] Bux W, Closs F, Janson PA, Kümmerle K, Müller HR, Rothauser EH: 'A
   Local-Area Communication Network based on a reliable Token-Ring System', Proc.
   IFIP International Symposium on Local Computer Networks, Florence 1982, pp. 69-82,
   North-Holland, ed. Ravasio PC, et al, 1982.
[CAL] Engineering CAL*Group*: 'Data Communications Modules', CBL Technology
   Ltd., Derwent Business Centre, Clarke Street, Derby DE1 2BU, UK.
   http://www.shef.ac.uk/uni/projects/calg/datacoms.html
[CAR] Cartwright D: 'Pathfinders', LAN magazine, April 1995, pp. 52-62.
[CHE] Chester AS: 'Did Morse get it right? A statistical background to the code',
   Wireless World, Aug. 1983, pp. 62-64.
[CON] Connor FR: *Signals*, 2nd. Ed., Edward Arnold, 1982.

[DET]   Dettmer R: 'Frame relay: the networker express', IEE Review, Nov/Dec 1992, pp. 381-385.

[DET2] Dettmer R: 'MAN about town', IEE Review, Mar 1992, pp. 91-95.

[EHR]   Ehrlich R: *Turning the world inside out: and 174 other simple physics demonstrations*, Princeton University Press, 1990.

[EIA 568] EIA/TIA 568, Commercial Building Telecommunications Wiring Standard.

[FEY]   Feynman RP: *QED: the strange theory of light and matter*, Penguin books, 1990.

[FRI]   Friend GE: *Understanding Data Communications*, 2nd Ed., Howard Sams, 1988.

[GAL]   Gallagher I and Wardlaw M: 'Asynchronous Transfer Mode', BT Information Exchange, Issue 11, 1/94, 6.3 Switching.

[GHA]   Ghassemlooy Z, Wilson B: 'Principles of Optical Fibre Communications', Sheffield Hallam University, School of Engineering Information Technology, short course book in two parts, 1991.

[GLA]   Glazier, EVD and Lamont HRL: *Transmission and Propagation*, the services textbook of radio vol.5, HMSO, 1958.

[GÖH]   Göhring H-G, Kauffels F-J: *Token Ring: Principles, Perspectives and Strategies*, Addison-Wesley, 1992.

[GRE]   Green DC: *Transmission principles for technicians*, 2nd Ed., Longman, 1995.

[GRI]   Griffiths J: *Radio wave propagation and antennas*, Prentice Hall International, 1987.

[HAL]   Halsall F: *Data communications, computer networks and open systems*, 4th Ed., Addison-Wesley, 1996.

[HAY]   Haykin S: *Communication Systems*, 3rd Ed., John Wiley & Sons, 1994.

[HEL]   Held G: *Understanding Data Communications*, 4th Ed., Sams Publishing, 1994.

[HOR]   Horowitz P, Hill W: *The Art of Electronics*, 2nd Ed., Cambridge U.P., 1989.

[HUF]   Huffman DA: 'A Method for the Construction of Minimum-Redundancy Codes', Proc. IRE, Vol. 40, No. 9, pp. 1098-1101, Sept. 1952.

[HUG]   Hughes L: 'Introduction to Data Communications: A Practical Approach', Whale Lake Press, PO Box 631, Station M, Halifax, Nova Scotia, Canada.

[IFE]   Ifeachor EC, Jervis BW: *Digital Signal Processing: a practical approach*, Addison-Wesley, 1993.

[ISO 9314-2] BS EN 29314-2: 1993, Information processing systems – Fibre Distributed Data Interface (FDDI) – Part 2: Token Ring Media Access Control (MAC).

[ISO/IEC 10038] BS ISO/IEC 10038 : 1993, Information technology – Telecommunications and information exchange between systems – Local area networks – Media access control (MAC) bridges.

[ISO/IEC 3309] BS ISO/IEC 3309 : 1993 (E), Information Technology – Telecommunications and information exchange between systems – High-level data link control (HDLC) procedures – Frame structure.

[ISO/IEC 4335] BS ISO/IEC 4335 . 1993 (E), Information Technology – Telecommunications and information exchange between systems – High-level data link control (HDLC) procedures – Elements of procedures.

[ISO/IEC 8208] BS ISO/IEC 8208 : 1990 (E), Information Technology – Data Communications – X.25 Packet Layer Protocol for Data Terminal Equipment.

[ISO/IEC 8802.2]BS ISO/IEC 8802-2 : 1994, Information technology – Telecommunications and information exchange between systems – Local and metropolitan area
networks. Specific requirements. Part 2. Logical link control.

[ISO/IEC 8802.3]BS ISO/IEC 8802.3 : 1993 (E), Information technology – local and
metropolitan area networks. Part 3. carrier sense multiple access with collision
detection (CSMA/CD) access method and physical layer specification.

[ISO/IEC 8802.5]BS ISO/IEC 8802-5 : 1992 (E), Information technology – Local and
metropolitan areas networks. Part 5. Token ring access method and physical layer
specifications.

[ISO/IEC 8802-6]   BS ISO/IEC 8802-6 : 1994, Information technology – Telecommunications and information exchange between systems – Local and metropolitan area
networks – Specific requirements. Part 6. Distributed Queue Dual Bus (DQDB) access
method and physical layer specifications.

[JAI]   Jain R: *FDDI Handbook: High-Speed Networking Using Fiber and Other
Media*, Addison-Wesley, 1994.

[JEF] Jeffrey M: 'Asynchronous transfer mode: the ultimate broadband solution?',
Electronics & Communication Engineering Journal, June 1994, pp. 143-151.

[JOR]   Jordan EC: *Electromagnetic waves and radiating systems*, 2nd Ed., Prentice
Hall Inc., 1968.

[KRE]   Kreyszig E: *Advanced Engineering Mathematics*, 7th Ed., John Wiley Inc,
1994.

[MAD]   Madin R, Norcliffe A and Simmonds A: 'Data Communications: full text', the
book of the video-based course, PAVIC Publications, The Adsetts Centre, Sheffield
Hallam University, Pond Street, Sheffield S1 1WB, UK.

[MET]   Metcalfe RM, Boggs DR: 'Ethernet: Distributed Packet Switching for Local
Computer Networks', Comm. ACM (USA), Vol. 19, No. 7, July '76, pp. 395-404.

[MIL]   Miller MA: *Introduction to Digital and Data Communications*, West, 1992.

[O'R]   O'Reilly JJ: *Telecommunication Principles*, Van Nostrand Reinhold (UK),
1984.

[PET]   Petersen WW and Brown DT: 'Cyclic Codes for Error Detection', proc. IRE,
Jan. 1961, pp. 228-235.

[POP]   Popple G and Glen P: 'Specification of the broadband user-network interface',
Electronics & Communications Engineering Journal, Vol. 6, No. 2, April 1994, pp.
105-112.

[PRE]   Preston D: 'Frame Relay in Theory and Practice', British Telecommunications
Engineering, Vol. 13, Part 2, July 1994, pp.133-137.

[PUG]   Pugh A: 'Facsimile today', Electronics & Communication Engineering Journal,
October 1991, pp. 223-231.

[QUI]   Quinnell RA: 'ATM networking, EDN – special report', EDN, March 3, 1994,
pp. 67-84.

[RFC 1058]   'Routing Information Protocol', updated by RFC 1723 'RIP Version 2,
Carrying Additional Information'.

[SEE]   Seeley A: 'Fast Track', PCLAN, March 95, pp. 25-32.

[SEN]   Senior JM: *Optical Fiber Communications: Principles and Practice*, 2nd Ed.,
Prentice Hall, 1992.

[SHA]   Shannon CE: 'A Mathematical Theory of Communication', Bell System
Technical Journal, Vol. XXVII, No. 3, July 1948, pp. 379-423 and October 1948, pp.
23-656. Reprinted in: Shannon CE, Weaver W: 'The Mathematical Theory of
Communication', University of Illinois, 1949.

[SMY] Smythe C: 'ISO 8802/3 local-area networks', Electronics & Communication Engineering Journal, Vol. 5, No. 1, Feb. 93, pp. 25-33.

[STA] Stallings W: *Data and Computer Communications*, 4th Ed., Macmillan Inc., 1993.

[STE] Stevens WR: *TCP/IP Illustrated, Volume 1: The Protocols*, Addison-Wesley, 1994.

[STR] Stremler FG: *Introduction to communication systems*, 3rd Ed., Addison-Wesley, 1990.

[SYN] SynOptics Technology White Paper: 'The Road to ATM Networking', SynOptics.

[TEX] Texas Instruments: 'Data Transmission Circuits: Line Circuits', Data Book, Vol. 1, section 4, 1995/1996.

[TOM] Tomasi W, Alisouskas V: *Telecommunications: voice/data with fiber optic applications*, Prentice Hall International, Inc., 1988.

[TUF] Tufte ER: 'The Visual Display of Quantitative Information', Graphics Press, Box 430, Cheshire, Connecticut, USA, 1983.

[TYL] Tyler G: 'Offices of bricks, mortar – and cable', Management Services, June 1992, pp. 32-34.

[VIT] Viterbi AJ: 'Error Bounds for Convolutional Codes and an Asymptotically Optimum Decoding Algorithm', IEEE Trans. on Information Theory, Vol. IT-13, No. 2, pp. 260-269, 1967.

[WHE] Whelan PM and Hodgson M J: *Essential principles of physics*, 2nd Ed., John Murray, 1989.

Glossary

To save space in the glossary, items are often just referenced by their mnemonic, i.e. if there is no entry under the full name try using the first letters of each word in the query.

100BaseT - fast Ethernet.

100BaseVG - **AnyLAN** - a high speed LAN based on voice grade cables.

10Base2 - an IEEE 802.3 LAN standard, see Thin Ethernet.

10Base5 - an IEEE 802.3 LAN standard, see Thick Ethernet.

10BaseT - an IEEE 802.3 LAN standard based on UTP.

23B + D - the North American and Japanese version of ISDN Primary Rate Access.

2B + D - ISDN Basic Rate Access.

30B + D - the European standard ISDN Primary Rate Access.

802.1 ... 802.6 - see IEEE 802.1 ... 802.6

μ (Greek mu) - abbreviation of 'micro', used in units to denote millionths (10^{-6}).

Ω - see Ohm.

AAL - ATM Adaption Layer protocol.

ACIA - see UART.

ACK - in bisync, the control character indicating an acknowledgement.

Acknowledgement - a message or signal which informs a transmitting device that the receiver has either successfully (positive acknowledgement - ACK) or unsuccessfully (negative acknowledgement - NACK) received data. This enables errors to be corrected by retransmitting unsuccessfully received data.

Acoustic Coupler - portable modem device which transmits data using a telephone handset.

Active - a device or component which can increase signal power, which a device wholly consisting of passive components cannot do.

Adapter - see NIC.

ADC - Analogue to Digital Converter.

Address - typically used to identify different devices, either in a polling/selecting environment or in a local area network.

Address field - part of a frame or packet used to identify the source or destination address; e.g. in an HDLC frame the eight bits representing the identity of the slave station.

ALU - see CPU.

AM - see Amplitude Modulation.

AMI - Alternate Mark Inversion, a pseudo-ternary line code.

Amplitude - the strength or volume of a signal. The value in volts or amps of a waveform.

Amplitude Modulation (AM) - transmission of information by varying the amplitude of a sine wave.

Analogue signal - a continuous (smoothly changing) signal that can take any amplitude level within a given range. The electrical signal is an analogue of some other form of signal; e.g. voice, where the electrical voltage varies in direct proportion to the sound. As opposed to digital.

Analogue transmission - transmission which encodes data on to a tone in the audible frequency range for transmission along analogue speech circuits. Or more generally, where the transmitted signal is proportional to the original signal. As opposed to digital.

Angle modulation - a general term for both frequency and phase modulation, as in both cases the angle of a sine wave carrier is modulated.

Anisochronous - not real time data. As standard computer data applications, e.g. file transfer, E-mail, etc. As opposed to isochronous.

ANSI - American National Standards Institute.

Application layer - layer 7, the highest layer of the seven layer RM; it provides the end user with access to the network.

ARQ - see automatic repeat request.

ASCII - American Standard Code for Information Interchange. The ANSI 7-bit character code, with an 8th bit for parity checking. See also International Alphabet No. 5.

ASIC - Application Specific Integrated Circuit.

ASK - Amplitude Shift Keying. Another name for amplitude modulation with a digital signal as the information source, where digital states are represented by different amplitudes of the carrier.

Asynchronous - communications where the unit of transfer is a single character and no clock signal is supplied to the receiver from the transmitter. Alternatively, in computer terminology at a higher functional layer, when inter-process messages are not acknowledged - with the result that processes are not kept in step with each other. As opposed to synchronous.

Asynchronous Transfer Mode (ATM) - set of communication facilities allowing direct access to 64 kbps data streams (or multiples of) for drop and insert. A form of cell relay, supports B-ISDN.

AT&T - American Telephone & Telegraph. Major world-wide telecommunication company and operating agency.

ATM - see Asynchronous Transfer Mode. Or Automatic Teller Machine, machine providing common banking services.

Attenuation - loss of signal power during transmission.

Automatic Repeat reQuest (ARQ) - an error correction method where the receiving device detects an error in data transmission and automatically asks for a retransmission of the block of data. Compare with forward error control.

B Channel - the Bearer channel in ISDN; it carries 64 kbps of digitized voice or data.

B-ISDN - Broadband ISDN, a high speed version of ISDN which provides services, like HDTV, requiring multiples of the 64 kbps B channel of ISDN; carried by ATM.

BABT - British Approvals Board for Telecommunications is the body that approves equipment as suitable for connection to the telecommunications network.

Backbone - top layer of a hierarchical distributed system. A high speed network which is used to link other networks.

Balanced transmission - a method of sending data requiring two wires per circuit and where the signal levels are symmetrical about zero volts. The signal level on one wire is 'balanced' by the opposite signal on the other wire, as in RS-422-A. Also known as differential transmission.

Balun - passive device for connecting a balanced line to an unbalanced (single ended) line.

Bandwidth - strictly, the difference between the upper and lower frequency limits of a signal or circuit, usually expressed in hertz (Hz). The telephone speech channel frequency range is from 300 Hz to 3400 Hz, i.e. the bandwidth is 3100 Hz. Loosely, the capacity of a communication link expressed in bits per second (bps).

Baseband - a mode of operation of a communication channel. Digital data is not modulated on to a carrier but is transmitted either using a line code or as 'raw' binary data (e.g. using NRZ binary). As opposed to broadband.

Baseband modems - limited distance modems for use within a site or building, sometimes called Line Drivers.

Basic Mode - 1960s international standard communication protocol on which IBM's Binary Synchronous Communication was based.

Baud rate - maximum rate at which the state of a signal changes, i.e. number of signalling events per second. With simple two-state signalling this is the same as the bit rate (ignoring redundancy); the advantage of multi-state signalling is that the baud rate is less than the bit rate.

BBS - Bulletin Board Service; on-line information services accessible via modems.

BCC - in bisync and Basic Mode, a Block Check Character used for error detection.

Bearer channel - see B channel.

Bell 103/113 - AT&T's 300 bps FSK modem for FDX operation over the PSTN; now widely accepted as an industry standard.

Bell 202 - AT&T's 1200 bps FSK modem for HDX operation over the PSTN.

Bell 212A - AT&T's 1200 bps QPSK modem for FDX operation over the PSTN.

Bell Operating Companies (BOC) - previously AT&T subsidiaries, independent after divestiture. Responsible for local services in the USA.

BER - Bit Error Rate, the ratio of the number of bits received in error to the total number of bits sent.

Billion - commonly a thousand million, although strictly this is the US definition and the British definition is a million million.

Binary - a form of digital signalling in which the signal can take one of two states.

Binary Synchronous Communications - IBM's proprietary communication protocol based on Basic Mode, also known as bisync or BSC.

Bipolar - a form of binary signalling where the 1 and 0 voltage levels are symmetrical about zero. As opposed to unipolar. Not to be confused with balanced transmission.

Bis - 'Second' in Latin, used as a suffix to denote a second alternative of an ITU standard, e.g. V.22 *bis*.

Bisync - see Binary Synchronous Communications.

Bit - a binary digit, either a 1 or a 0. The term is used for either a unit of information or a two-state signal.

Bit error - a transmission error in which a 1 is received as a 0, or vice versa.

Bit-oriented protocol - a protocol which does not use control characters for communicating control information and is not sensitive to any bit combinations in the data, i.e. it is transparent to data - as HDLC.

Bit rate - rate at which bits of data are transmitted.

Bit stripping - see bit stuffing.

Bit stuffing - the process in HDLC and SDLC which ensures that the delimiting 'flag' characters are not transmitted inside a 'frame' of data. An extra 0 is inserted after every five 1s in the data. Bit stripping is the reverse process.

Block - a group of characters or bytes transmitted by a synchronous protocol.

bps - bits per second. A measurement of data rate, it is the number of bits transmitted (or received) in a second. Thousands of bps are expressed as kbps, millions of bps as Mbps.

BRA - Basic Rate Access. ISDN access 2B + D, i.e. two Bearer channels at 64 kbps and one signalling (D) channel at 16 kbps.

Breakout - allows a private network to carry a call to an external party a long distance before connecting ('breaking out') to a public network.

Bridge - a device to link two LANs. It operates at the data link layer, transmitting packets from one LAN addressed to the other.

Broadband - a mode of operation of a communication channel where digital data modulates a carrier. As opposed to baseband.

Broadcast - where one station in a network transmits to *all* other stations. Compare with multicast.

Browser - a type of client software to allow users to navigate the WWW.

BSC - see Binary Synchronous Communications.

BT plc - major world-wide telecommunication operating agency.

Buffer - a storage device used to compensate for different rates of data flow, or to store frames of data.

Burst - as in error burst: a sequence of bits which have been corrupted by noise. The burst length is from the first to the last bit in error inclusive (intermediate bits may well be random - i.e. equally likely to be right or wrong).

BUS - Broadcast/Unknown Server, see LAN emulation.

Bus - a network topology where all nodes are directly attached to a cable, which is the bus. Messages reaching the end of the bus are not repeated.

Byte - a group of eight bits.

Byte-oriented protocol - another name for a character-oriented protocol.

Call-back device - data security equipment, used with dial-up modems, which calls back users to verify their location.

Capacitance - the property of an electrical component to store an electrical charge. See farad.

Carrier - or carrier wave, a signal, usually a sine wave, which is modulated to carry information.

Category 3, 4 or 5 - see structured cabling.

CATV - British Cable TV, American Community Antenna TV.

CCITT - see *Comité Consultatif Internationale de Télégraphique et Téléphonie.*

CCITT No. 7 - a common channel signalling system linking digital exchanges.

CCU - Cluster Control Unit. Device that allows several terminals and printers to share the same communication line to a mainframe.

CDDI - see Fibre Distributed Data Interface.

Ceefax - see teletext.

Cell - a fixed length block of data with control information, as in cell relay. As opposed to frame.

Cell relay - a data network where data is split into small fixed-length units (cells) and routed through the network, sharing capacity with other traffic. Faulty cells are discarded, as are cells if congestion occurs. Type of switching used by ATM. As opposed to circuit and packet switching.

Cellular radio - based on low power radio transmitters in cells, enabling multiple use of a frequency in different (non-adjacent) cells.

Centrex - PABX functions provided by the operating agency at the local exchange.

Centronix - industry standard for a parallel interface to a printer.

Channel - the connection between a data source and destination, or transmitter and receiver. A point to point path through a data network along which information flows, carried over one or more physical links.

Channel-associated signalling - a mode of operation where signalling information is carried either in the same channel as the data or in a signalling channel permanently associated with it. As opposed to common-channel signalling.

Channel capacity - maximum data rate of a channel.

Channel coding - aims to ensure reliable communication in the presence of noise. To achieve this it adds redundancy to the signal so that errors can be corrected at the receiver (either by Forward Error Control or ARQ). Compare with source coding which aims to reduce redundancy.

Character - a letter of the alphabet, a number, a punctuation mark, or a special symbol used by devices to inter-communicate.

Character codes - methods of representing characters, typically as bit combinations.

Character-oriented protocol - a protocol using characters to communicate control information. Needs special arrangements to be transparent to data.

Characteristic impedance - a means of characterizing the electrical properties of a cable which is independent of the cable length.

Checksum - an error checking method where message characters are added together and the least significant bytes of the result appended to the message before transmission. The receiver performs the same addition and checks the result to determine if any error in transmission has occurred.

Circuit switching - a mode of operation in a network where a dedicated channel is established to transmit signals over the network. The link exists for the duration of the call. As opposed to packet switching and cell relay.

Client-Server - network applications are divided into those providing a service (servers) and those wanting to use a service (clients). Generally, server programs must run continuously, as a client may request the service at any time.

CMI - Coded Mark Inversion, a two-state line code.

Coaxial cable - a transmission medium consisting of a single wire surrounded by a core of insulating material with an outer conductive braid or wrapping, the entire electrically active parts then covered by an insulating sheath.

CODEC - a coder-decoder unit.

Collision - the result of two devices transmitting at the same time, usually causing data to be lost.

Comité Consultatif Internationale de Télégraphique et Téléphonie (CCITT) - the International Telegraph and Telephone Consultative Committee, now replaced by the ITU-T.

Common carrier - organizations that provide public, long distance communications.

Common-channel signalling - a mode of operation where the signalling channel is used as a data link to carry control and management packets and is not dedicated to particular bearer channels in a fixed pattern. As opposed to channel-associated signalling.

Common return - a single wire serving as a shared path to complete the circuit for electrical signals.

Communication processor - see FEP.

Concentrator - for Token Ring or FDDI, also called a MAU or hub, can be active or passive.

Concurrent processing - sometimes a synonym for parallel processing but, strictly, processes are concurrent if one starts before another has finished. Note that the tasks need not be done simultaneously. Multitasking supports concurrent processing.

Conductance - a property of an electrical component, the inverse of resistance, units siemens (S).

Connection oriented - see virtual circuit.

Connectionless - see datagram.

Contention - where data sources compete to gain access to a communication path.

Continuous ARQ - an automatic repeat request method in which the transmitter continues sending data blocks without waiting for acknowledgement messages, until a set number of unacknowledged blocks have been sent or a negative acknowledgement received, e.g. HDLC uses either go-back-N or selective reject, both types of continuous ARQ. As opposed to stop-and-wait ARQ.

Control character - character (of a character code) used to perform special control functions. Such a character is not normally printed.

Control information - in a protocol, the data sent to perform e.g. polling, selecting, ARQ, etc., as well as to convey status information to devices.

Control signals - in RS-232, RS-449, Centronics, etc., the pins indicating the status of a given connection.

Counter-rotating - two signal paths, one in each direction, in a dual ring topology.

CPU - Central Processing Unit. The part of a computer which performs the processing, usually containing an Arithmetic Logic Unit (ALU) and a control unit. Does not contain the main memory or input/output functions.

CPE - Customer's Premises Equipment.

CRC - Cyclic Redundancy Check. A sophisticated replacement of a checksum; it uses a complex mathematical formula (involving modulo-2 division) to detect errors.

CRO - see oscilloscope.

Crosstalk - a form of noise in which a signal on one channel causes distortion in another.

CSMA/CD - Carrier Sense Multiple Access with Collision Detection, a LAN access method (MAC protocol) used with physical (e.g. 10Base5, 10Base2) or logical (e.g. 10BaseT) bus networks, as in the IEEE 802.3 standard.

CTS - Clear To Send. The RS-232 control signal generated by the DCE indicating that the DTE can transmit data.

CUG - Closed User Group, access to a network is restricted to certain people, often as a security measure. See intranet and VPN.

Cycle - a full repetition of a sine wave, including one peak and one trough.

D Channel - the signalling channel in ISDN, carrying 16 kbps in BRA and 64 kbps in PRA.

D-connector - see DB25.

DAC Digital to Analogue Converter.

Data - information in a form suitable for electronic processing.

Data communications - the exchange of digital information between two devices using an electronic transmission system.

Data compression - facility that allows more information to be transmitted per second by removing redundancy from the data. Standards are MNP5 and V.42 *bis*.

Data link - a physical, point to point link between two adjacent DCEs, forming part or all of a channel. Multiple channels may be multiplexed over the same link.

Data link layer - layer 2 of the seven layer RM, it is responsible for ensuring error-free, reliable transmission of data over a data link.

Data rate - the speed at which bits are transmitted and received, usually measured in bits per second, or bps.

Data throughput - see data rate.

Datagram - a mode of operation whereby packets are sent across a network over the best route as determined for each packet individually. Also known as connectionless, compare with virtual circuit.

DB25 - a 25-pin connector defined in ISO standard 2110, available in male and female versions and often used with the RS-232 interface.

DCD - Data Carrier Detect. The RS-232 control signal generated by the DCE indicating that the DTE should expect to receive data at any time.

DCE - Data Circuit-terminating Equipment. Communication interface device such as a Modem.

Deaf node - an Ethernet node which loses the ability to listen for activity on the bus.

Decibel (dB) - unit of relative signal power = 10 $\log_{10}(P1/P2)$. Often used to express signal-to-noise ratio. If the input and output impedances are the same, also = 20 $\log_{10}(V1/V2)$, where $V1/V2$ is the voltage ratio.

Decision threshold - a level (often a voltage level) set at the receiver to differentiate between different digital signal levels.

DECnet - Digital Equipment Corporation's proprietary network architecture, also called DNA.

Delay distortion - distortion occurring when the propagation delay over the transmission channel is not constant with frequency.

Demodulation - converting modulated signals back to their original form; e.g. in a modem converting the line signals back to binary data.

Demux - demultiplexer or receive multiplexer.

Deterministic - a worst-case time for a process can be precisely calculated, or an upper bound set.

Dial-up - a telephone circuit connection that requires the user to place a new call each time, allowing destination flexibility.

Dibit coding - a technique for modulating two bits for every baud. Four-state signalling.

Differential Manchester - a 1B2B line code, as used in Token Ring. Ensures a bit transition in the middle of every bit period. Differs from Manchester code in that information is carried by the change between signals rather than individual signal values.

Differential transmission - see balanced transmission.

Digital - loosely, a way of representing information using 1s and 0s, see binary. Strictly, a digital signal is one selected from a discrete set of possible signals. Thus binary is only one form of a digital signal.

Digital PBX - computer that treats telephones as specialized input and output devices; voice is either digitized in the phone or at the PBX, and voice as well as data communications can be switched.

Digital phone - a device that digitizes voice, and is attached to either a digital PBX or the ISDN.

Digital transmission - loosely, where data is transmitted as an unmodulated digital signal. Strictly, the transmission part of data communications.

Digital waveform - a representation of a digital signal, showing the variation of signal amplitude with time.

Digitization - the process of coding information, normally into binary form, so that the information can be transmitted as data.

Distortion - an unwanted change in the shape of a waveform caused by: (a) phase shift not proportional to frequency; (b) non-uniform attenuation with frequency; (c) noise.

DNA - see DECnet.

DOVE - Data Over Voice Equipment, wideband modem used to send data in a frequency band above speech, allowing simultaneous speech and data transmission.

DPNSS - Digital Private Network Signalling System, a common-channel signalling system for linking private digital exchanges (enabling PABX facilities such as call forwarding to work over the entire network).

DPSK - either Dibit Phase Shift Keying (i.e. four state PSK) or Differential Phase Shift Keying (where information is contained in the difference between the current and previous phase).

DQDB - Distributed Queue Dual Bus, the IEEE 802.6 standard for a MAN.

Drop and insert - the ability to access a lower order (lower data rate) signal directly when it is carried in a higher order, multiplexed signal.

DSR - Data Set Ready. The RS-232 control signal generated by the DCE to indicate that it is powered on and is ready to begin communications. Data Set is an obsolete term for a Modem.

DTE - Data Terminal Equipment. End of the line digital equipment such as a terminal, host computer or printer.

DTR - Data Terminal Ready. The RS-232 control signal generated by the DTE to indicate that it is powered on and ready to begin communications.

E-1 Carrier - European standard for 2.048 Mbps digital transmission over two twisted pairs carrying 30 digitized telephone channels.

E-mail - a system whereby computer files containing messages can be exchanged, via a central computer, between many users.

EBCDIC - Extended Binary Coded Decimal Interchange Code. An 8-bit character code developed by IBM.

Echoplexing - system for manually detecting errors in asynchronous communications between terminal and computer. When a character is typed at the terminal it only appears on the VDU when echoed back by the computer.

EDFA - Erbium Doped Fibre Amplifier, a means of introducing optical gain for 1.5 μm systems.

EDI - Electronic Data Interchange, a means of automatically generating invoices, orders, etc. involving customers and suppliers internetworking.

EIA - see Electronic Industries Association.

EIA-232-D, EIA/TIA-232-E - see RS-232.

EIRP - Effective Isotropic Radiated Power, the transmitter power needed with an isotropic antenna (instead of a directional antenna) to give the same power at the receiver.

ELAN - Extended LAN. A 'stretched' LAN, i.e. faster and longer, but not with all the functionality of a MAN. Also Emulated LAN, see LAN emulation.

Electromagnetic compatibility - see EMC.

Electronic conferencing - an application of E-mail whereby users ask and answer questions on a particular topic, using a text file set up for the purpose, enabling them to exchange information even though they may be widely separated. Also called on-line conferencing.

Electronic Industries Association (EIA) - a standards organization representing many manufacturers in the US electronics industry.

Electronic mail - see E-mail

EMC - electromagnetic compatibility. The European EMC directive is mandatory from 1st January 1996. The installer of any system has a legal responsibility to ensure that it does not cause any radiated or conducted emission or interference problem.

EMI - electromagnetic interference, see EMC.

Encapsulation - 'surrounding' user data with protocol control information to make up a PDU.

Encryption - scrambling or coding of data before transmission to increase security.

Enquiry - in a protocol, when a device asks permission to send data.

Equalizer - a filter, fitted at a receiver, to compensate for distortion of a signal resulting from a non-linear frequency characteristic of a communication channel.

Error - a mistake in a regenerated digital signal caused by noise.

Error burst - see burst.

Error correction - see FEC and ARQ.

Error detection - determining whether any bits have changed value in transmission.

Error rate - see BER.

Ethernet - a common LAN standard (IEEE 802.3). Originally with a bus topology but now also likely to be met as a star topology (10BaseT). Or the original LAN developed by Xerox on which the 802.3 standard is based.

Even parity - an error detection method requiring an even number of ones in each byte, or word, transmitted (including the parity bit).

Exclusive OR - see XOR.

F - see farad.

Farad (F) - unit of capacitance.

Fast packet switching - packet or cell based protocol providing bandwidth on demand at high data rates.

Fax - facsimile, a method of sending still images, like a printed page, over telephone lines. An optical reading head scans the image in horizontal lines of dots which are encoded according to the darkness of the image.

FCS - Frame Check Sequence, two bytes at the end of an HDLC frame which are used to check that the contents of the frame have not been corrupted. Uses a CRC.

FDDI - Fibre Distributed Data Interface, a 100 Mbps LAN based on fibre optic links. The same protocol run over twisted pairs is TPDDI.

FDDI2 - based on FDDI with improved facilities for isochronous signals.

FDM - Frequency Division Multiplexing, a means of multiplexing signals using different carrier frequencies to carry signals over different parts of the channel frequency spectrum. Each channel has access to a restricted frequency range of the link bandwidth for all the time, as opposed to Time Division Multiplexing (TDM).

FDX - see full duplex.

FEC - Forward Error Control, the transmitted message contains enough redundant information to enable some errors to be corrected immediately. Compare with ARQ.

FEP - Front End Processor, device attached to a mainframe by a high speed parallel interface which handles communication lines on behalf of the mainframe. Also known as a communication processor.

Fiber - American spelling of 'fibre'.

Fibre optic cable - a high-bandwidth transmission medium allowing data to be sent by transmitting light through a special glass rod so thin and long that it is called a fibre.

File server - a shared storage device, e.g. a PC.

Flag - in HDLC, the pattern of eight bits (01111110) beginning and ending each frame.

Flow control - that operation of a network to limit the amount of data being sent over it.

FM - see Frequency Modulation.

FOIRL - Fibre Optic Inter-Repeater Link.

Four-wire - two (two-wire) telephone connections, one for the transmit and one for the receive direction.

Frame - a block of data, not necessarily of fixed length, with control information, as in a HDLC frame; or a repetitive sequence of time slots, as in a 30 channel PCM frame. See also cell and packet.

Frame relay - a network access protocol (as is X.25). A form of fast packet switching. Frames are discarded if faulty or if congestion occurs, as with ATM.

Frequency - the pitch of a tone, or the number of cycles per second of a sine wave. Units hertz (Hz).

Frequency Modulation (FM) - transmission of information by varying the frequency of a sine wave.

Frequency range - the lower and upper frequencies of a signal determine which part of the spectrum it occupies.

Frequency Shift Keying (FSK) - another name for frequency modulation with a digital signal as the information source.

FTAM - File Transfer, Access and Manipulation, international standard defining file transfer and record access between systems in an OSI environment.

FTP - File Transfer Protocol, a TCP/IP application layer service for transferring files.

Full Duplex (FDX) - communication mode which supports transmission in both directions simultaneously, see HDX and simplex.

Functional profile - a subset of OSI standards used to ensure correct interworking of computers performing particular applications, also called a functional stack; e.g. GOSIP, MAP, TOP.

Functional stack - see functional profile.

G - Giga, used in units to denote thousand millions (10^9); American billions.

G.703 - 2.048 Mbps digital service.

G.Series - series of recommendations specified by the ITU for digital multiplexers and line systems.

Gateway - a device used to connect two networks that use different communication methods. It operates at any or all layers of the seven layer RM as required. In TCP/IP terminology a gateway is actually a router.

Geostationary - see geosynchronous satellite.

Geosynchronous satellite - a satellite in orbit round the equator with period of one day, resulting in the satellite staying in the same position in the sky as seen from the ground.

GND - Ground, see Protective Ground.

Go-back-N - a type of continuous ARQ where transmission continues until a negative acknowledgement is received; the frame in error and all succeeding frames must then be retransmitted. Used in HDLC.

GOSIP - Government OSI Profile, a set of OSI standards for use by government departments.

GSM - Global System for Mobile Communication, a digital standard.

H - see henry.

H Channel - high capacity channel in ISDN, formed by bonding lower bit rate channels together.

Half Duplex (HDX) - communication mode which supports two-way transmission but in only one direction at a time, see FDX and simplex.

Handshaking - the interaction of control signals between devices.

HDB3 - a pseudo-ternary line code, as used in 30 channel PCM.

HDLC High-level Data Link Control - international standard data link layer communication protocol.

HDTV - High Definition TV.

HDX - see Half Duplex.

Header - control information sent at the front of the information field in a data frame or packet. See also trailer and PDU.

Henry (H) - unit of inductance.

Hertz (Hz) - unit of frequency, equivalent to cycles per second.

Higher layers - layers 4 through 7 of the seven layer RM (Transport, Session, Presentation and Application Layers).

Host computer - provides services for other computers on a network; it can perform numerical calculations, store and retrieve data, etc. It is more than a server as it provides processing.

HTML - HyperText Markup Language, for writing pages on the WWW.

HTTP - HyperText Transport Protocol, for moving hypertext files across the WWW.

Hub - a non-switching unit at the centre of a star cabling system. See also concentrator.

Hypermedia - as hypertext but mixed media.

Hypertext - an electronic text file that has links to other electronic documents. These documents are automatically retrieved when the user activates a hotspot on the page.

Hz - see hertz.

I-Frame - see Information Frame.

I.Series - series of recommendations specified by the ITU for transmission of data over the ISDN.

IBM - International Business Machines Corporation.

IC - Integrated Circuit, an electrical circuit manufactured on a single piece of semiconducting material, usually silicon.

Idle ARQ - see stop-and-wait ARQ.

IDN - Integrated Digital Network, the UK telecommunications network which supports the PSTN and ISDN.

IEC - International Electrotechnical Commission.

IEEE - Institute of Electrical and Electronics Engineers, an American professional organization.

IEEE 802.1 - a standard providing an overview of local area networks, including methods for connecting networks and systems management.

IEEE 802.2 - a Logical Link Control (LLC) standard for local area networks. Provides ARQ facilities for LANs, e.g. for LAN standards IEEE 802.3 ... 802.4.

IEEE 802.3 - CSMA/CD (Ethernet) set of standards for local area networks, e.g. 10Base5 where 10 refers to the maximum transmission rate in Mbps, Base refers to baseband or broadband transmission, and 5 refers to the cable segment length to the nearest 100 m

IEEE 802.4 - token bus standard for local area networks.

IEEE 802.5 - token ring standard for local area networks.

IEEE 802.6 - DQDB standard for a Metropolitan Area Network (MAN).

Impulse noise - a short duration burst of noise.

Inductance - property of an electrical component characterized by the formation of a magnetic field, units henrys (H).

Information field - in HDLC, the part of the information frame containing user data.

Information frame (I-frame) - in HDLC, the type of frame used to send user data.

Information services - large commercial data exchange services, e.g. Compuserve, Prestel.

Typically providing E-mail, and access to databases and the Internet.

Integrated Services Digital Exchange (ISDX) - private digital exchange.

Integrated Services Digital Network (ISDN) - an evolving set of standards for a digital network carrying both voice and data communications, based on digital access at 64 kbps by the user. ISDN alone now usually refers specifically to narrowband ISDN, as opposed to B-ISDN.

Intelligent modem - see smart modem.

Intelligent network - a network which is able to recognize and deal appropriately with different classes of traffic.

Interface - the point at which a device connects to a cable.

Intermodulation noise - noise due to the mixing of two or more signal frequencies creating terms at other frequencies (hence it is a non-linear effect).

International Alphabet No. 5 - ITU standard (V.3); a version of ASCII with minor variations.

International Telecommunication Union (ITU) - a UN telecommunication standards organization whose members include international organizations and governments. Parent body of the ITU-T and ITU-R.

Internet - the Internet refers to the public global system comprising many LANs and packet switched networks connected together by gateways or routers to allow internetworking using TCP/IP. An internet (no capital) is two or more interconnected networks.

Internetworking - connecting two or more separate networks.

Intranet - an internet restricted to a CUG.

Invert on zero - see NRZI.

IP - Internet Protocol, non-OSI datagram protocol standard used for LANs. Part of the TCP/IP set of protocols.

Irregular network - a network topology where devices are not connected according to the strict rules of e.g. a tree, ring, bus or star network.

ISDN - see Integrated Services Digital Network.

ISDN 2 - BT's ISDN BRA, see 2B + D.

ISDN 30 - BT's ISDN PRA, see 30B + D.

ISDX - see Integrated Services Digital Exchange.

ISO - International Organization for Standardization, in which each member country is represented by its own national standards organization. The body responsible for OSI standards in data communications.

ISO 8802.x - see IEEE 802.x.

Isochronous - data, from a source such as a speech or video signal, which must arrive at regular time intervals at the destination. Generally means that time-slots must be reserved and there is no time for ARQ. As opposed to anisochronous.

ISP - Internet Service Provider, an information service which provides access to the Internet.

ITU-R - Radio communication organization. Consists of those parts of old CCIR not in ITU-T plus the International Frequency Registration Board.

ITU-T - International Telecommunication Union - Telecommunication standardization sector. Consists of old CCITT and standards part of CCIR.

Jabber - to chatter or, in the case of an Ethernet, to transmit faulty data, e.g. a frame greater than the maximum size allowed or with a bad CRC value.

Justification - a process changing the rate of a digital signal in a controlled manner so that it conforms with another rate.

k - kilo, used in units to denote thousands (10^3), except in kilobyte.

kbit/s - see kbps.

kbps - kilo bits per second, or thousands of bits per second.

KERMIT - a file transfer protocol often used to send files from a PC to a mini/mainframe computer.

kilobyte - 2^{10} = 1024 bytes (see k).

KiloStream - BT's leased line digital transmission service operating up to 64 kbps.

LAN - see Local Area Network.

LAN emulation - ability to transport the datagram packets of LANs across the virtual circuit provided by an ATM network.

LAP - Link Access Procedure, various protocols based on HDLC. LAP-B stands for Balanced, as used in X.25. LAP-D stands for D-channel, as used for signalling in ISDN. LAP-F is used for frame relay. LAP-M is used in synchronous modems.

Latency - time taken for processing in a network. Or time taken for a response to appear after a request is made; which is first definition + twice the end-to-end propagation delay.

Layer - division according to function as found in the seven layer RM; see also application layer, presentation layer, session layer, transport layer, network layer, data link layer and physical layer.

Leased line - permanent 2- or 4-wire point-to-point connection rented from a telephone company. Not charged per call or second, so should be fully loaded. Compare with dial-up.

LEC, LECS - LAN Emulation Client, LAN Emulation Configuration Server.

LES - LAN Emulation Server.

Line - see link.

Line code - a means of coding a binary data stream to: (a) shape the frequency spectrum of the signal and (b) enable clock recovery at the other end of the link. As a subsidiary use it is also possible to (c) detect some transmission errors.

Line-drivers - see base-band modems.

Line of sight - the requirement that for microwave transmission there are no obstructions between two antennas.

Link - a physical communication circuit or transmission path. Channels may be multiplexed over a link.

Link layer protocol - a set of rules precisely defining methods for communicating over a communication circuit, or link.

LLC - Logical Link Control, the IEEE 802.2 standard relating to local area network functions like ARQ. The common LLC standard runs on different MAC standards.

Loading coil - device used in some analogue telephone circuits to improve voice quality over longer distances. It is an inductor which increases the overall inductance of the line resulting in a constant characteristic impedance over a restricted bandwidth.

Local analogue loopback test - a diagnostic technique that can be performed with a modem to test the local end of a modem link.

Local Area Network (LAN) - a communication system that provides reliable high-speed, point to point, connections for routing data packets between devices in a single building, campus, or complex.

Local loop - the part of the telecommunications network between a subscriber and their local exchange. Generally comprising a single twisted pair for private subscribers.

Longitudinal Redundancy Check (LRC) - has a parity bit for each character bit position, used in Basic Mode over a block of characters.

Loopback Testing - a diagnostic technique where transmitted data is returned to the sender for comparison with the original message.

lsb - least significant bit, the unit bit position in an integer binary word. See msb.

M - Mega, used in units to denote millions (10^6), except in megabyte.

m - milli, used to denote thousandths (10^{-3}).

M/F - see Mainframe

MAC - Medium Access Control, a group of IEEE standards relating to local area network access methods, describing how devices are to share a network, e.g. CSMA/CD, Token Ring.

Mainframe - host computer usually serving a large organization. Many users are normally active on a mainframe at the same time.

MAN - Metropolitan Area Network, a network spanning a city, or the Medium Access Control for such a network, e.g. the IEEE 802.6 standard DQDB.

Manchester - a 1B2B line code, as used in Ethernet. Ensures a transition in the middle of each bit period. Compare with differential Manchester.

MAP - Manufacturing Automation Protocol, an OSI functional profile providing interworking between manufacturing equipment in a factory environment. See also TOP.

MAU - see Medium Access Unit (Ethernet) or Multistation Access Unit (Token Ring).

Master/Slave - a possible way of organizing a communications network, e.g. with a host computer as the master and associated terminals as the slaves; uses polling and selecting procedures. As opposed to peer to peer.

Mbit/s - see Mbps.

Mbps - Millions of bits per second, or Mega bits per second.

Medium Access Unit (MAU) - an Ethernet transceiver, see NIC.

Megabyte - 2^{20} = 1 048 576 bytes (see M).

MegaStream - BT's leased line digital transmission service operating at 2 Mbps or higher.

Mercury - a UK telecommunication operator.

Message - one or more consecutive symbols.

Message switching - a form of switching intermediate between packet switching and circuit switching. A complete message is sent (using store-and-forward routing) rather like a packet, except in packet switching the message would be segmented.

Microwave - a way of transmitting data in the form of high frequency radio waves, using dish antennas with a clear line of sight between them.

MHS - see X.400.

MNP - Microcom Networking Protocol, a proprietary standard for Modems. MNP-3 allows synchronous transmission, MNP-4 covers error correction and is now part of V.42, MNP-5 covers data compression but is not compatible with V.42 *bis*.

Mobile phone - see cellular radio.

Modem - a device that performs modulation and demodulation, allowing data communication to occur over analogue telephone lines.

Modulation - methods of encoding information on to a tone, enabling the information to be carried over a link or transmission path.

Modulator - the part of a modem's circuitry that performs modulation.

MOTIS - Message Oriented Text Interchange Standard, international standard for sending messages in an OSI environment.

MPEG - Motion Picture Editors Group.

msb - most significant bit, the position which is raised to the highest power in a word. See lsb.

MSNF - Multi System Networking Facility, IBM SNA facility for interconnecting mainframes.

Multicast - where one station in a network transmits to a group of other stations. Compare with broadcast.

Multidrop - a configuration where several terminals are directly attached to, and share, a single communication line leading to a single front end or host computer port, contrast with point-to-point. Also known as multipoint.

Multiplexer (Mux) - a device used to allow a single communication circuit to take the place of several parallel ones. At the other end of the link a demultiplexer separates the channels.

Multiplexing - combining several channels over a single link.

Multipoint - see multidrop.

Multiprocessing - true parallel processing in which two or more connected CPUs execute processes simultaneously. This is one way to achieve a multitasking system but note that a multitasking system is not necessarily multiprocessing.

Multiprogramming - see multitasking.

Multistation Access Unit (MAU) - a Token Ring hub or concentrator.

Multitasking - a computer operating concurrently on more than one task. Time-sharing and multiprocessing are both techniques for achieving multitasking.

Mux - see multiplexer.

n - nano, used in units to denote 10^{-9}.

NAK - in bisync, the control character signifying a negative acknowledgement.

Network - a collection of communication facilities which together provide advantages in cost or capability over individual links.

Network Control Program (NCP) - SNA software running in a FEP.

Network layer - layer 3 of the seven layer RM, it is responsible for setting up the appropriate routing of messages through a network.

Network Termination - an interface enabling equipment to be connected to a digital network, especially the ISDN. NT1: for BRA this is a line box which connects the twisted pair of the local loop on one side (the U interface) to the S bus on the customer's side (the S interface); for PRA it connects the 2 Mbps line on one side (the U interface again) to the customer's PABX (the T interface). The PABX is a NT2 equipment, with a T interface on one side and an S bus (S interface) on the other.

NIC - Network Interface Card, an interface card allowing a node to be connected to a LAN. Contains a transceiver or has an interface to an external transceiver. Also called an adapter.

Node - equipment that physically accesses a network or a point where transmission paths are interconnected. Compare with station.

Noise - unwanted electrical interference that can produce errors in data; one cause of distortion in a signal.

NRZ - Non-Return to Zero, a way of encoding binary data on to an electrical signal where no change in state takes place in a bit period. The most common form of binary signal in a computer. As opposed to Return to Zero (RZ).

NRZI - Non-Return to Zero, Inverted, a way of encoding data on to an electrical signal where a change of state takes place every time a 0 is encountered (and no change occurs for a 1). Also known as invert on zero. With bit stuffing to ensure zeros, used as a line-code for HDLC.

NTx - see Network Termination.

NUA - Network User Address, user address on Packet Switch Stream.

NUI - Network User Identity, allows access to Packet Switch Stream.

OA - Office Automation, using computer networks to help with everyday office tasks such as sending memos, filing, arranging meetings.

Odd parity - an error detection method requiring an odd number of ones in each byte, or word, transmitted (including the parity bit).

Ohm (Ω) - unit of resistance.

On-line conferencing - see electronic conferencing.

On-line services - see information services.

ONU - Optical Network Unit.

Optical fibre - see fibre optic cable.

Oracle - see teletext.

Originate/answer modem - a type of modem that can place and answer calls.

Oscilloscope - electrical test equipment for showing the waveform of a signal. An electron beam is modulated by the signal, thus tracing out the same shape as the signal on an electro-luminescent screen. The principal component of the oscilloscope is the cathode ray tube (similar to the tube in a TV), hence the alternative name of Cathode Ray Oscilloscope (CRO).

OSI - Open Systems Interconnection, a set of international standards which aims to define how different computer systems can be connected together and do useful work. See also, seven layer RM.

ρ - pico, used in units to denote 10^{-12}.

p.r.f. - pulse repetition frequency. The fundamental frequency of a pulse train, reciprocal of the period.

P/F bit - the bit in the HDLC control frame that can be used for polling by the master station or to indicate the final frame of transmission by the slave station.

PABX - Private Automatic Branch Exchange, a telecommunication switching system owned by the customer, it acts as an in-house telephone exchange with advanced features and capabilities.

Packet - a block of data with control information, as in an X.25 packet The length is generally not defined. Also known as a frame, contrast with cell.

Packet switching - a data network where data is split into small units (packets) and routed through the network, sharing capacity with other traffic. As opposed to circuit switching, message switching and cell relay.

Packet Switching Exchange (PSE) - equipment, usually a minicomputer, which is a node of a packet switching network and performs the switching function.

Packet Switching Network (PSN) - network providing a routing service, where data is sent in packets through nodes over various routes and is recombined at its destination in the proper sequence.

Packet Switch Stream - BT's X.25 Public Data Network.

Packet terminal - terminal which includes packet formatting functions.

Packetization delay - time spent filling a packet with data, one cause of network latency.

PAD - Packet Assembler Disassembler, a device used to connect a packet switching network to equipment that does not perform packet formatting.

Parallel data - see parallel transmission.

Parallel processing - simultaneous processing of two or more tasks. Parallel processing implies concurrent processing, but the inverse is not necessarily true. Multiprocessing supports parallel processing.

Parallel transmission - data transmission where a whole character (typically 7 or 8 bits) is transmitted at once along parallel wires. Hence bit parallel, byte (or character) serial.

Parity bit - an extra bit added to a character for error checking. See even or odd parity.

Passive - see active.

Passive bus - see S bus.

PBX - see Private Automatic Branch Exchange.

PC - Personal Computer, a computer usually serving only a single user.

PCM - Pulse Code Modulation, a method of digitally encoding speech.

PDH - see Plesiochronous Digital Hierarchy.

PDN - Public Data Network.

PDU - see Protocol Data Unit.

Peer - of equal rank or status, e.g. peer to peer communication in LANs. As opposed to master/slave.

Period - time interval for one cycle of a repetitive waveform. Reciprocal of the fundamental frequency.

Phase - the position of a signal compared to a reference signal, measured in degrees or radians in terms of a complete cycle of the reference signal.

Phase Modulation (PM) - transmission of information by varying the phase of a sine wave.

Phase Shift Keying (PSK) - another name for phase modulation with a digital signal as the information source.

Physical layer - layer 1 (the lowest layer) of the seven layer RM, it is responsible for the transmission of bits and is implemented in hardware. Describes the equipment interface.

Physical layer protocol - describes the actual DTE to DCE interface.

Physical Unit (PU) - an IBM SNA term defining a set of services provided by a node in an SNA network to logical units within the network.

Piggybacking - the inclusion of acknowledgements on outgoing data, as in HDLC.

PIN - Personal Identification Number, the password used with an Automatic Teller Machine (ATM).

Plesiochronous Digital Hierarchy (PDH) - a TDM hierarchy where the signals are nominally at the same rate but can derive from different clocks. A process of justification is used to ensure that data bits are not double-clocked or missed. As opposed to the Synchronous Digital Hierarchy (SDH).

PM - see Phase Modulation.

Point-to-point - link between just two devices. Clearly does not require any addressing by the protocol (as opposed to a multidrop connection).

Polling - the method used by a host computer or front end processor to ask a terminal to send any data it has (as opposed to selecting). Often the terminals will be connected to the computer by a multidrop line.

PON - Passive Optical Network. Contains no electronic components and the full fibre bandwidth will be available for future services.

Port - an interface enabling a device or software to be attached to a computer.

POTS - Plain Old Telephone System; i.e. the traditional telephone network used for carrying speech, ignoring all recent technological advances.

PPP - Point-to-Point Protocol, a TCP/IP protocol to enable dissimilar devices to communicate.

PRA - Primary Rate Access, see 30B + D and 23B + D.

Presentation layer - layer 6 of the seven layer RM, it provides format and code conversion services.

PRESTEL - BT's videotex service.

Primary Station - in HDLC, the single device or station that communicates with all of the other (secondary) stations.

Private circuit - see leased line.

Propagation delay - transmission time across a network or link.

Protocol - a set of rules precisely defining the methods used to communicate.

Protocol Analyser - equipment to monitor, decode and display packets being sent across a network. Modern protocol analysers have many other functions built in, e.g. traffic generation, both general and targeted at a particular node, and cable testing.

Protocol Converter - device which allows one communication device to emulate another. Most commonly used to allow asynchronous terminals or personal computers to emulate IBM 3278 terminals.

Protocol Data Unit (PDU) - a packet, including information, header and/or trailer, exchanged between similar processes at either end of a channel. See encapsulation.

PSK - Phase Shift Keying. See Phase Modulation.

PSTN - Public Switched Telephone Network.

PTT - Posts, Telephones and Telegraphs. A government department responsible for these services. A type of operating agency, see also TeleCos.

PVC - Permanent Virtual Connection in ATM (contrast with SVC).

QAM - Quadrature Amplitude Modulation, a modulation method (used in many high-speed V. series modems) that combines changes in phase and amplitude to send multiple bits with each baud.

QPSK - Quadrature Phase Shift Keying, four state PSK (i.e. with 4 phases to implement dibit coding).

Quantization - the process of converting an analogue signal level to a discrete, i.e. digital, level.

Quantization noise - the error in signal level caused by the quantization process.

Queuing delay - time spent waiting for equipment to service a request.

R interface - see TA.

r.m.s. - root mean square. This is an amplitude derived from the power of a signal (mean square being power). For a sine wave the r.m.s. voltage is $(1/\sqrt{2}) \times$ the peak amplitude.

Rec mux - receive multiplexer or demultiplexer.

Receive Data (RXD) - the RS-232 data signal received by the DTE from the DCE.

Reference Model (RM) - see seven layer RM.

Regenerator - device used at stages in a long distance channel to recover a digital signal and retransmit it.

Reliable - a network is generally available for service.

Remote digital loopback test - a modem diagnostic technique that can test the phone line itself, as well as parts of the modem.

Repeater - device used at stages in a long distance channel to boost or amplify a signal and retransmit it. Also, an Ethernet repeater (actually a regenerator) used to connect two bus segments. It operates at the physical layer.

Residual error rate - error rate remaining after error correction.

Resistance - a property of an electrical component resisting the flow of current; units ohms (Ω).

Return to Zero (RZ) - a form of binary signalling where a one returns to the zero state level (usually 0 V) half way through the bit period.

RI - Ring Indicator, the RS-232 control signal generated by the DCE to alert the DTE that a remote device wants to initiate communications.

Ring network - a network topology where devices are connected in a continuous loop.

RM - see seven layer Reference Model.

Router - a device used to connect networks together. It operates at the network layer. See gateway.

RS-232 - one of the most common serial interface standards (RS - Recommended Standard) for data communications in use today, it is an EIA standard defining exactly how ones and zeros will be transmitted, including voltage levels, transmission method, pin numbers, etc. RS-232-C (1969) - third revision of RS-232). EIA-232-D (1987), EIA/TIA-232-E (1990) are later revisions.

RS-422-A and RS-423-A - EIA transmission standards. RS-422-A is a higher performance standard using balanced transmission whilst RS-423-A uses unbalanced transmission.

RS-449 - an EIA standard describing the mechanical and functional characteristics of a DTE/DCE interface using a 37 pin connector.

RS-485 - an EIA transmission standard. Same data rates as RS-422-A but bidirectional operation allowed.

RS-530 - an EIA standard describing the mechanical and functional characteristics of a DTE/DCE interface using a 25 pin connector.

RTS - Request To Send. The RS-232 control signal generated by the DTE to ask permission to transmit data.

RXD - see Receive Data.

RZ - see Return to Zero.

S Bus - a passive bus on the user's premises to connect ISDN compatible devices to the ISDN at BRA. Up to 8 devices can be connected, although obviously only 2 of them at a time can use the B channels. See TA and Network Termination.

Sampling - the process of measuring the instantaneous signal amplitude at regular time intervals.

Satellite transmission - use of an orbiting satellite to repeat signals to all antennas in view of the satellite.

SDH - see Synchronous Digital Hierarchy.

SDLC - Synchronous Data Link Control, IBM's proprietary data link layer communication protocol based on HDLC.

SEAL - Simple and Efficient Adaption Layer for ATM.

Secondary station - in HDLC, a device or station that communicates with the primary station; there may be several secondary stations.

Segment - a continuous length of cable used for the bus in an Ethernet LAN. Maximum length 500 m in 10Base5 and 185 m in 10Base2 (i.e. 200 m to the nearest 100 m). Or a message is segmented into packets or cells.

Selecting - method used by a host computer or front end processor to ask a terminal if it is ready to receive data (as opposed to polling).

Selective reject - a type of continuous ARQ where transmission continues until a negative acknowledgement is received, when only the frame with the error is repeated. Used in HDLC.

Selective repeat - see selective reject.

Serial transmission - data transmission where the individual bits in the character are transmitted one after another along a single channel.

Server - software or a computer that provides storage and access facilities for a remote client. See Client-Server, compare with host.

Session - layer 5 of the seven layer RM. Or the SNA term for the connection between two logical units across the SNA network.

Session layer - layer 5 of the seven layer RM. It requests that a logical connection be established or terminated, and handles logon and password procedures as well as fall-back procedure in the event of a fault.

Seven layer Reference Model (RM) - the OSI model which splits communication functions into seven layers: physical, data link, network, transport, session, presentation and application.

SG - see Signal Ground.

Shield - a screen or mesh designed to reduce the effects of external electric fields.

Siemens (S) - unit of conductance.

Signal - one or more signalling events. Same as a message.

Signalling event - transmission of a symbol over a line. Indicates possible transitions on the line. Units of baud.

Signal Ground (SG) - the RS-232 ground that acts as a zero volt reference for all other signals.

Signal-to-Noise Ratio (SN or SNR) - ratio of signal power to noise power, usually expressed in decibel.

Simplex - a communication mode allowing transmission in one-direction only, see FDX.

Sine wave - an electronic or mathematical representation of a pure tone.

Sliding window - a method of flow control whereby a data source can only send a certain number of frames before receiving an acknowledgement. This number is dependent on the size of the 'window' which, with a sliding window, can be dynamically altered.

Smart modem - a modem that can accept dialling instructions from the user and dial the call, as well as perform the necessary modulation and demodulation.

SMDS - Switched Multimegabit Data Services, a form of cell relay.

SNA - see Systems Network Architecture.

SONET - Synchronous Optical Network, defined by ANSI for use in the USA.

Source coding - aims to eliminate redundancy from the source information so that the average code word length approaches the minimum possible value (which is the entropy of the source). Generally produces a binary data stream. Compare with channel coding.

Space switching - every channel through the switch takes a dedicated, physically separate path (for each time slot). As opposed to time switching. Note that a space switch can be time division multiplexed between many channels, hence the reference to time slots.

Spectrum - the variation of the signal amplitude with frequency; from this the frequency range and bandwidth of the signal can be determined. As opposed to waveform.

SSCP (Systems Services Control Point) - the SNA entity residing in the mainframe which controls an SNA network (or part thereof).

STA - Spanning Tree Algorithm, a means of ensuring that an irregular network operates as a tree network. For linking Ethernet LANs by bridges to ensure that there are no loops in the network.

Stack - a set of protocols. Or a set of standards, see functional profile.

Standards organization - group or committee which devises specifications or standards for a particular industry or country.

Star network - a network topology where each device is connected to a centre point and all data is routed through that point.

Start bit - in asynchronous transmission, the bit sent before each character. The line is idle before this bit is sent so the transition signals the start of a new character.

Start-stop transmission - another name for asynchronous transmission.

Star-wired ring network - a network topology where data flows in a continuous loop through each device but the wiring returns to a central access point between each device.

Statistical multiplexer (stat mux) - a device that combines several slow channels into one fast channel where the capacity of the fast channel is only allocated to currently active tributary channels. The identity of any idle channel is signalled to the receiver which outputs an idle signal from the appropriate tributary.

Station - a DTE connected to a network. A node which has a MAC layer.

STM - Synchronous Transport Module, the organization of bytes as a frame in the Synchronous Digital Hierarchy. An STM carries Virtual Containers (VCs).

Stop bit - in asynchronous transmission, the bit or bits sent after each character to return the line to an idle state.

Stop-and-wait ARQ - a type of automatic repeat request in which transmission halts after each block until an acknowledgement is received, as used in bisync. Also called idle ARQ, as opposed to continuous ARQ.

STP - Shielded Twisted Pair.

Strowger - electromechanical telephone exchange or the name of the switches used in such an exchange. The technology is over a century old.

Structured cabling - to enable effective management of wiring, including changes. Typically requires a building to be 'flood' wired with twisted pair or fibre optic cables in a star topology, with horizontal and vertical wiring systems. For twisted pair, category 3 cable supports 10 Mbps, category 4 - 16 Mbps and category 5 - 100 Mbps.

STX - in bisync, the character indicating the start of user data.

Subscriber - a person who has rented access to the PSTN. Originally telephone exchanges were run as clubs, hence the name.

SVC - Switched Virtual Connection in ATM (contrast with PVC).

Switch - a device allowing a dedicated point-to-point channel to be set up to one of many destinations.

Symbol - a group of signalling events or a character.

SYN - in bisync, the sync characters transmitted before the start of actual data.

Synchronisation - the process whereby the receiver is kept in step with the transmitter, either in respect of bit or character reception.

Synchronous - communication where the unit of transfer is a block of characters and the receiver clock runs at the same rate as the transmitter clock. Or, in computer terminology at a higher functional layer, when processes are kept in step by having to wait for an acknowledgement to any inter-process message before they can proceed. As opposed to asynchronous.

Synchronous Digital Hierarchy (SDH) - a TDM hierarchy where all clocks are derived from the same source, i.e. the signals are synchronous. As opposed to the Plesiochronous Digital Hierarchy (PDH).

SYSTEM-X - BT's digital telephone exchanges of UK origin or BT's digital telephone system.

Systems Network Architecture (SNA) - IBM's proprietary standards for all aspects of data communications.

T - Tera, used in units to denote million millions (10^{12}); British billions.

T interface - see Network Termination 1, Network Termination 2.

T-1 Carrier - US and Japanese standard for 1.544 Mbps digital transmission over two twisted pairs, carrying 24 digitized telephone channels.

T-1 Multiplexer - a device that multiplexes 24 separate channels of digitized voice or data to the 1.544 Mbps T-1 carrier rate.

TA - Terminal Adaptor, a device to connect a non-ISDN terminal to the S bus. The interface between the terminal and the TA is the R interface.

TCP - Transmission Control Protocol, one standard in the TCP/IP set of standards. Used to provide a virtual circuit across a network.

TCP/IP - Transmission Control Protocol/Internet Protocol, non-OSI open standards used for LANs and internetworking LANs. TCP and IP are two protocols in the set. Originally developed for the US Department of Defense.

TDM - Time Division Multiplexing. A method of allowing lower-speed channels to share a high-speed communication circuit, by allocating separate time slots to each channel. Each channel has access to the entire bandwidth of the link for a restricted time, as opposed to Frequency Division Multiplexing.

TE1 and TE2 - Terminal Equipment of type 1 is compatible with the ISDN network, whilst type 2 equipment is not and needs a TA.

Telecommunications - the exchange of information, usually over a significant distance, and using electronic equipment for transmission.

Teleconferencing - using telephone speech channels to enable three or more people to engage in a discussion.

TeleCos - Telecommunication operating Companies; operating agencies, see also PTT.

Telematics - general name for user oriented communication services, e.g. teletex, fax, etc.

Teletypewriter (TTY) - electromechanical terminal device which combines a keyboard and printer.

Teletex - two-way, text communication between office systems.

Teletext - one-way, broadcast, text/graphics systems, e.g. Ceefax, provided by the BBC, and Oracle, provided by the ITV.

Telex - an old, text oriented (upper case only), international standard for a circuit switched network generally used for business. It required a separate network of telex exchanges which were essentially in parallel with the telephone exchanges of the PSTN. Hence the attraction of the ISDN.

Telnet - TCP/IP application layer service allowing remote login.

Ter - 'third' in Latin, used as a suffix to denote a third alternative of an ITU standard, e.g. V.26 *ter*.

Terminal - a device permitting users to communicate with a computer, typically it consists of a screen and keyboard; any device at the end of a communication circuit is sometimes considered a terminal.

Thermal noise - noise introduced by the random movement of electrons in circuit devices. Decreases as devices are cooled.

Thick Ethernet - see 10Base5.

Thin Ethernet - see 10Base2.

TIA - Telecommunications Industry Association, a US trade organization.

Time sharing - the means by which a single computer appears to be simultaneously available to many users for interactive tasks. Each user has access to the full computing power of the system for a short time slice before their request joins the queue for the next time slice. The computer deals with these requests so quickly that the user is not usually aware of any delay.

Time slice - see time sharing.

Time slot - the time reserved for a particular channel's communication in Time Division Multiplexing.

Time switching - a channel in one time slot is switched to another time slot. Often combined with space switching, e.g. in a T-S-T (time-space-time) switch.

Token - a special frame in token passing networks, typically used to control access to the networks.

Token Bus - a LAN using a bus topology and token passing (token ring MAC protocol), as in the IEEE 802.4 standard.

Token Ring - a MAC protocol for LANs, with stations connected topologically (e.g. token ring LAN, FDDI) or logically (e.g. token bus) in a ring. Or the IEEE 802.5 LAN standard.

TOP - Technical and Office Protocol. An OSI functional profile used in office environments. Looked after by the MAP/TOP users' group.

Topography - the physical layout of a network.

Topology - the relationship of the connections in a network.

TPDDI - see FDDI.

TPON - Telephony PON, installed between local exchange and customers.

Trailer - control information sent at the back of the information field in a data frame or packet. See also header and PDU.

Trans mux - transmit multiplexer.

Transceiver - transmitter-receiver pair.

Transmission medium - the physical path for carrying information, such as a twisted pair, coaxial cable, fibre optic cable, or free space.

Transparency - ability to pass any data, i.e. all bit combinations not just printable characters.

Transport layer - layer 4 of the seven layer RM; it is responsible for isolating the function of the lower layers from the higher layers.

Tree network - a network topology where devices are connected via branches (which may branch from intermediate nodes) to the root node.

Trellis coded modulation - a modulation technique as used in high speed modems, usually at 9600 bps and above, relying on a special error correction process.

Triple X - PAD protocol standards consisting of the three standards: X.3, X.28 and X.29.

TTL voltage levels - Transistor-Transistor Logic unipolar voltage levels, used in many computer systems.

Twisted pair - typically used in a local loop, it consists of two wires twisted together throughout their entire length.

Two-wire - a single telephone line connection, typically carried in the local loop by a twisted pair.

TXD -Transmit Data. The RS-232 data signal sent by the DTE to the DCE.

U interface - see Network Termination.

UART - Universal Asynchronous Receiver Transmitter, a device which performs asynchronous transmission functions. Also known as an ACIA - Asynchronous Communications Interface Adaptor.

Unbalanced transmission - a method of sending data requiring one wire for data and a common return (or reference) wire that can be shared with other signals, as in RS-232. As opposed to balanced or differential transmission.

Unipolar - a form of binary signalling where one state is at 0 V. As opposed to bipolar.

URL - Uniform Resource Locator, on the WWW identifies a file's location and how it should be handled.

UTP - Unshielded Twisted Pair.

V.21 - modem standard: 300 bps over the PSTN, FDX, using FSK.

V.22 - modem standard: 1200 bps over the PSTN, FDX, using QPSK.

V.22 *bis* - modem standard: 2400 bps over the PSTN, FDX, using QAM.

V.23 - modem standard: 1200 bps over the PSTN, HDX, using FSK.

V.24 - standard defining the interface between a modem and a DTE. V.24 defines the signals, pin numbering and handshaking. See V.28.

V.28 - standard defining the interface between a modem and a DTE. V.28 defines the electrical characteristics (transmission rate and mode of operation). Commonly assumed to be part of V.24.

V.29 - modem standard: 9,600 bps over a leased line, FDX, using QAM.

V.32 - modem standard: 9,600 bps over the PSTN, FDX, using QAM.

V.32 *bis* - modem standard: 14,400 bps over the PSTN, FDX, using QAM.

V.34 - modem standard: 28,800 bps over the PSTN, FDX, using trellis coded modulation.

V.42 - error correction standard.

V.42 *bis* - error compression standard.

V.Fast - new modem standard, now confirmed as V.34.

V.Series - series of recommendations specified by the ITU for transmission of data over the analogue telephone network.

Value Added Network (VAN) - a network which provides more than just the basic bearer service of transporting information; e.g. access to other networks, protocol conversion, EDI.

VC - Virtual Container. An arrangement of bytes to transport data from particular sources. VCs are carried by an STM in the Synchronous Digital Hierarchy.

VCI - Virtual Channel Identifier.

VDU - Visual Display Unit, another name for a monitor or screen.

Video conferencing - speech and video channels are used together to allow a semblance of a meeting to be held between remote parties.

Videotex - an interactive information retrieval service, with a database (usually with graphics) accessed by the subscriber (using text only), also known as Viewdata; e.g. Prestel in the UK, Minitel in France. Differs from the text and graphics, one-way system of Teletext, and from the peer to peer, text exchange of Teletex.

Viewdata - see Videotex.

Virtual circuit - a circuit that appears to the user like a permanent connection but uses the network's resources only when data is transmitted. Also known as connection-oriented, contrast with datagram.

Voice grade circuit - a standard telecommunication circuit.

Voice mail - voice messages stored and retrieved using centralized equipment.

VPN - Virtual Private Network, where a public switched network has the facility to segregate users into Closed User Groups so that it appears to the users as though they are attached to a private network.

VTAM - Virtual Telecommunications Access Method. SNA software which runs on a mainframe.

VTP - Virtual Terminal Protocol, international standards to allow terminals on one system to access applications on another system within an OSI environment.

WACK - in bisync, the control character indicating that the device is temporarily busy but will be available soon.

WAN - Wide Area Network, a network covering a large geographical area.

Wireless LAN - a LAN using free space as the transmission medium. Needs a similar MAC protocol to that used by a passive bus.

Wiring concentrator - a passive hub, as in a MAU for Token Ring.

WWW - World-Wide Web, the links of hypertext pages form a web. A browser is needed to navigate across the web and display the pages, which are written in HTML.

X.3 - the ITU standard for the functions and parameters of an internal PAD.

X.20 - ITU recommendation governing the interface to a digital data service for asynchronous operation. X.20 *bis* is an alternative for terminals designed to operate via their RS-232 interface.

X.21 - ITU recommendation governing the interface to a digital data service for synchronous operation. X.21 *bis* is an alternative for terminals designed to operate via their RS-232 interface.

X.25 - an ITU recommendation for a standard access protocol to packet switching networks; a network layer protocol in the seven layer RM. Or the set of protocols for a packet switching network, including X.25 (layer 3), LAP-B (layer 2), X.21 / X.20 (layer 1), triple X, etc.

X.28 - the ITU standard for connecting an asynchronous terminal to the local PAD in a packet switching network.

X.29 - the ITU standard for communication between a local PAD and the remote PAD or packet terminal.

X.400 - a set of ITU recommendations covering public messaging systems. Also known as MHS (Message Handling System).

X.Series - series of recommendations specified by the ITU for transmission of data over public data networks.

Xmodem - a file transfer protocol used to provide error free communication on asynchronous links.

Ymodem - a variant of Xmodem.

XOR - the exclusive OR operation, as in an XOR logic gate: Ips 00/11 $\rightarrow$Op 0; Ips 01/10 $\rightarrow$Op 1.

Zero deletion - see bit stripping.

Zero insertion - see bit stuffing.

Zmodem - a variant of Xmodem.

Index